# Praise for *A Time Fo*

M000031897

I have been Joe Steinfield's friend for nearly sixty years, as well as his professional colleague and fellow Red Sox fanatic. Joe has really hit this one out of the ballpark—lots of homespun common sense combined with trenchant analysis of some of the key constitutional issues now facing us. It should be required reading for every member of Congress—Democrats and Republicans alike.

> —**MICHAEL S. DUKAKIS**, Governor of Massachusetts (1975–79, 1983–91), 1988 presidential nominee, Distinguished Professor Emeritus of Political Science, Northeastern University

The only fault I'd find with Joe Steinfield's collection of columns is his title: The adjective he chose for his life was "curious." A more apt one, I think, is "captivating," or perhaps "instructive." His writings are both—just the right telling details to grab readers with each bite-sized nugget, along with nuanced and illuminating epistles on everything from constitutional crises in the Era of the Virus to how to be a better friend and father, grandson and grandpa.

> —**LARRY TYE**, author of *Demagogue: The Life and Long Shadow of Senator Joe McCarthy*

Joe Steinfield's marvelous book combines touching, humorous ruminations on friends, family, and life generally, reminiscent of E. B. White's iconic *One Man's Meat*, with penetrating insights into our legal system. His observations on emerging Supreme Court decisions are especially impressive—the best I have ever seen at providing clarity without over-simplification. Time For Everything is at once a deliciously pleasurable read, a generous meditation on our human dilemma, and a compelling tutorial on this moment in our constitutional history.

> —**MICHAEL A. PONSOR**, author of *The New York Times* bestseller, *The Hanging Judge*

This is a love story and a life story. It's a story of priorities and passions—from baseball to the law—with advice and encouragement if we want to see it. Joe makes complex legal issues understandable, offers nugget-sized history lessons, and encourages us to examine more closely, with new curiosity, decisions that impact our lives. He shows us that it is possible to make time for everything that's important. His incredible memory and storytelling gifts provide rich texture, and it's in the details that we learn how he values his relationships with his family, friends, and passions, all intricately connected. I laughed and learned.

> —**HEATHER MCKERNAN**, publisher, *Monadnock Ledger-Transcript*

*Time for Everything: My Curious Life* is a delight. Joe Steinfield's columns reflecting on family, love, friendship, and life growing up in Claremont, New Hampshire, reveal a man with an enormous heart, a deep interest in and compassion for others, and a commitment to building community. And his columns analyzing developments in constitutional law and the Supreme Court—with a particular focus on the First Amendment, Joe's area of special expertise—advance a compelling understanding of the Constitution that emphasizes the responsibility of government to act for the common good and to protect the rights and dignity of all.

—**JOHN M. GREABE**, professor of law and director, Warren B. Rudman Center for Justice, Leadership & Public Service, University of New Hampshire Franklin Pierce School of Law

Joe Steinfield is curious about a lot of things, not least people he's encountered in his eighty-three years, including taxi drivers, clothiers, firefighters, judges, politicians, old friends and new. When he writes about these people—for example, the visitor from Alabama who gets escorted out of Fenway for shouting something into the visiting Yankees dugout—Steinfield transports you to the scene; you don't just read about what happens, you directly witness it as he did.

The second part of this collection is a clear-headed primer on the law for the lay reader. Steinfield makes sense of what's in the news, whether about subpoenas, torts, the pardon powers of the president, the right of assembly, or tensions between conflicting constitutional rights.

The success of all these columns owes not merely to the author's understanding of the law and interest in the human condition, but also his considerable skills as a writer. Steinfield is quite simply a joy to read.

—**JIM ROUSMANIERE**, author, *Water Connections—What Fresh Water Means to Us, What We Mean to Water*; retired editor, *The Keene Sentinel*

Why anyone would choose Charlie Dole over Joe Steinfield [see page 34] is a question for the ages. Joe is a delight both on and off the page; I find his curious life captivating.

—**JUDY ROGERS**, Owner, Prime Roast, Keene, New Hampshire

# Time for Everything

JOSEPH D. STEINFIELD

# Time for Everything

## My Curious Life

Bauhan Publishing

Peterborough · New Hampshire

2022

ISBN 978-0-87233-362-8
Library of Congress Control Number 2022017547
Cataloging information available at the Library of Congress


Cover photograph by Frank Steinfield
(Complete photo credits on page 283)

Typeset by Sarah Bauhan in Robert Slimbach's Arno Pro
with Michael Harvey's Ellington Pro titles
Cover designed by Henry James

To contact Joe, email him at joe@joesteinfield.com

PO BOX 117 PETERBOROUGH NEW HAMPSHIRE 03458
603-567-4430
WWW.BAUHANPUBLISHING.COM


Printed in the United Kingdom

*Earth's the right place for love. . . .*
—Robert Frost, "Birches"


*This book is for my children, Frank, Ken, and Liz,*
*and for my grandchildren, Jacob, Susie, and Solomon.*

*It is also for my wife, Virginia Eskin (the "Pianist" in*
*many of my essays), my stepson Alex ("Sacha") Eskin,*
*and his children, my grandchildren, Iris, Kodai, and Shota.*

*This book is also dedicated to the memory of my cousin from*
*the Old Country, Martin Feldman, who died in 2020.*
*He was our family's last remaining Holocaust survivor.*

# Contents

## ARTS AND TECHNOLOGY

## SPORTS AND HUMOR

## HEALTH

## LIFE AND POLITICS

# Part 2—Thinking About The Law

## THE RULE OF LAW

## EXECUTIVE POWER

## THE FIRST AMENDMENT

# THE INTERNET

# THE FOURTEENTH AMENDMENT

# CONSTITUTIONAL ISSUES IN THE TIME OF CORONAVIRUS

# ELECTIONS

# THE SUPREME COURT

# Foreword

For as long as I can remember, I have been drawn to the Old Testament's book of Ecclesiastes, according to which "there is a time for everything, and a season for every activity under the heavens." Ecclesiastes meant that our lives are made up of chapters, as he makes clear in the verses that follow, beginning with the words "a time to be born and a time to die."

I know perfectly well that no one has "time for everything." We all make choices in how we allocate our waking hours, and our lives are a constant struggle to find the right balance among the things we care about—family, friends, work—and still leave time for self.

I started writing articles early in my legal career. Since then, like most trial lawyers, I have spent a large portion of my working hours writing memoranda and briefs. Fortunately, I learned in college that, in the words of the poet Robert Graves, "There is no such thing as good writing, only good rewriting."

In the spring of 2006, I submitted an article to the *Monadnock Ledger-Transcript*, published in Peterborough, New Hampshire, which became the start of a monthly column under the title "Looking Back" that continues to this day. With close to two hundred articles so far, I still worry that I won't be able to come up with anything to say next month. Those essays deal mostly with family, friends, and experiences, and some with self, a memoir of sorts written two pages at a time. I compiled the first several years' worth of those essays into a book called *Claremont Boy: My New Hampshire Roots and the Gift of Memory*, published in 2014.

Part One of this book picks up where *Claremont Boy* left off, while Part Two adds articles about the law. When I started writing about the Constitution and the Supreme Court in 2015, I tried to stay neutral and simply inform readers about important decisions and other legal matters. My articles were now appearing in *The Keene Sentinel,* and my editor told me I should put more of myself into them. I soon began doing so, which has been liberating and has produced some interesting e-mails from readers, not always complimentary. The problem is that there is too much to write about.

As I was rereading pieces and deciding which ones to include in this collection, I realized that many of them needed some updating or freshening. Following Graves's maxim about rewriting, I have made many revisions and corrected earlier mistakes. I have also added footnotes in an attempt to bring some of the articles up to date, or to express an opinion I didn't think of at the time.

# Part I

# Looking Back

# FRIENDS AND HEROES

## My Antonio and the Stitch that Binds

In the fall of 1973, I needed a suit. We were on our way to Russia, and I heard you dressed up for the Bolshoi Ballet.

I had seen a sign near my office, "J&T Tailors, One Flight Up," and I decided to climb the stairs to the shop. The proprietors, Joe and Tony, greeted me, and I saw that they had quite a selection of men's clothing. I told them I was going to Russia and needed a nice suit. Tony helped me picked one out and, with chalk in hand and pins between his teeth, he took the measurements.

I returned a week later to pick up the altered suit. While I tried it on, I asked Tony where he grew up, and he told me he was from a village in Italy called San Sossio Baronia. His English wasn't great, but his personal warmth more than made up for his lack of fluency. I looked at a certificate on the wall, written in Italian, and learned that his full name was Antonio Natola.

From that first walkup visit until July 3, 2016, a span of forty-three years, Tony was "my tailor," the only one I will ever have. I bought suits, jackets, slacks, and coats from him, and when my sons were old enough, I took them to the shop. Joe and Tony moved a few times, but somehow, they were always close to where I worked.

Tony was more than my tailor; he became my friend. Sometimes I would drop in just to chat. If too long went by, I would get a call. "Giuseppe, it's Tony, Tony the Tailor. How come I no see you?"

Over the years we shared quite a bit. We both had two sons and a daughter, and we both became widowers in the 1980s. Our friendship got stronger.

Joe decided to retire, and a few years later Tony followed suit, so to speak, but not for long. He missed his customers, he told me, so he took a corner in a shop owned by a Dominican woman named Theresa and continued as

Tony the Tailor (R) with his partner Gaetano Cataldi (L)

before, though now mostly from catalogues. When my grandson graduated from high school in 2015, I took him to see Tony, who knew just what jacket and slacks were right for him to take to college. As we left, Tony told Jacob to pick out a tie, "my gift to you."

My lawyer son turned fifty in the spring of 2016, and I made a date to take him in to see Tony. When we got there, Tony gave me a hug, as always, and they then went through the catalogue and picked out a beautiful blue suit. Tony said he would call when the suit arrived.

Several days later, I got a message, not from Tony but from Theresa, telling me that the suit was ready. When my son and I went to the shop the next week, she told us, "Tony's in the hospital, he's very sick." With tears in her eyes, she made sure the suit was just right.

I then spoke with Tony's daughter, Anna, who was not optimistic. A few weeks later she called, and I knew what I needed to do. I hung up, went to my car, and drove from downtown Boston to the Lahey Clinic in Burlington, Massachusetts. Anna was there and so was Lena, Tony's daughter-in law.

Despite the oxygen tube and other hospital room paraphernalia, Tony gave me a big smile and extended his hand, which I held throughout the visit. We had a wonderful conversation, reflecting on our long friendship.

Anna and Lena looked on, taking it all in. He told me he loved me, and I told him I loved him.

As I was getting ready to leave, knowing this would likely be our last time together, I asked a question. "Tony, what color was the suit you sold me before I went to Russia in 1973?"

His eyes twinkled. "Beige," he said.[1]

---

1    Tony died on July 3, 2016.

## My Friend Bob and a Meaningful Life

Bob Abernethy died on May 2, 2021, at the age of ninety-three. He was a remarkable man who enriched many lives.

My path crossed his before his crossed mine. Like millions of others, I watched him on NBC News, where he appeared almost nightly to deliver news from Washington, London, and, beginning in 1989, from Moscow. He was NBC's chief Russian correspondent when Gorbachev became the Russian leader, when the Berlin Wall came down, and when the Soviet Union came to an end.

During his five years in Moscow, Bob witnessed some of the most momentous changes of modern times. He then "retired" from NBC, but only to begin a new stage in an extraordinary career.

Bob was a man of faith. His grandfather was the pastor of Calvary Baptist Church in Washington, DC, which Bob attended as a boy. In 1984, more than thirty years after graduating from Princeton, he left NBC to attend Yale Divinity School. I don't know whether Bob was thinking of becoming a minister—we never discussed it—but a year later, he went back to broadcasting, first in Washington and later to take up his post in Moscow.

Bob's path first crossed mine around 1990, when he bought a house near

Bob Abernethy

us on Gilmore Pond in Jaffrey. I remember that first meeting, down by the water; and I remember our many hours together with gratitude and pleasure.

At first, he would arrive from Moscow during the summer, and we would sit and talk. Soon we developed a regular routine that continued for nearly thirty years. One of us would provide doughnuts or muffins, and we had what can best be called a single, open-ended conversation about whatever was on our minds. We talked about life on the pond, local goings-on, the state of the world, and sometime about feelings. At various times, we wondered aloud what we could do to help make the world a better place.

One day, Bob told me he had an idea for a television show that would deal with religion and ethics. This "second career" would not be on the pulpit in the usual sense, but a ministry of a different kind. All Bob needed was a sponsor, and when the Eli Lilly Endowment agreed to fill that role, the PBS program called *Religion & Ethics NewsWeekly* was born, with Bob at the helm as executive editor and host.

From 1997 to 2017, Bob and his formidable team covered faith and religion in all its forms—"a news program, not preaching"—as Bob put it, producing 1017 shows on 250 Public Broadcasting stations. They traveled the world, from war-torn Cambodia to crime-ridden Camden, New Jersey, always finding reasons for hope in the midst of despair. Among those interviewed were Jimmy Carter, the Dalai Lama, Billy Graham, Archbishop Desmond Tutu, and Milford, Michigan's poet-undertaker Thomas Lynch.

The programs are timeless, and in case you missed them, they are preserved on the Internet. You can also pick up Bob's 2007 book, *The Life of Meaning: Reflections on Faith, Doubt, and Repairing the World.*

Three years ago, the Pianist and I attended Bob's ninetieth birthday party at his daughter Jane's home in Brunswick, Maine. It was a wonderful event, complete with a cappella music provided by the Bowdoin College "Meddiebempsters"[2] and a video tribute from Bob's NBC colleague, Tom Brokaw.

Bob was a man of the world, and of Jaffrey. When our Gilmore Pond neighbor and lifelong Jaffrey resident, Bill Royce, died in 2016, Bob mourned the loss of a personal friend. "He knew so much about this area," Bob told me. "How will we ever replace him?"

And now Bob, who knew so much about the world and about what matters in life, is gone. He made the world a better place, and we will never replace him.

---

2   In the late 1940s and early 1950s, Bob was a member of one of the country's oldest a cappella singing groups, the Princeton Nassoons.

# My Neighbor Kahlil and the Stolen Urn

Kahlil Gibran was born in 1883 in Bsharri, Lebanon. He lived for many of his forty-three years in Boston's South End, home at that time to a large Lebanese American community. His 1923 book, *The Prophet*, is one of the most translated books in the history of literature and has never been out of print.

I read the book when I was in high school and can still quote parts of it from memory. One of his essays, "On Children," describes parents as "the bows from which your children as living arrows are set forth" and says that our children "are with you yet they belong not to you. . . . You may strive to be like them but seek not to make them like you." When I became a parent, I understood the wisdom of those words.

About marriage, he said, "Let there be spaces in your togetherness." And about friendship, "In the sweetness of friendship let there be laughter and sharing of pleasures."

I especially like what he wrote about knowledge. "Say not, 'I have found the truth,' but rather, 'I have found a truth.'"

In middle age, I came to know his cousin, Kahlil Gibran, who, like his namesake, lived much of his life in the South End. He and his wife, Jean, resided down the street from the Pianist and me, but that neighborhood was more than a collection of connected brownstone houses. It really was the street itself, where we engaged in front stoop conversations and did "night patrol." In a sense we all lived together.

Kahlil, who died in 2008, was more than just a neighbor. According to Wikipedia, he was a sculptor, but the man I knew was a force of nature. He could create or restore or fix just about anything. One of my favorites was an elegant hand-carved pool cue that housed a secret weapon. Another was a violin that he made from scratch. A person needs a lot of self-confidence to undertake such a project, and to produce a beautiful, varnished instrument and hear a professional violinist bring it to life.[3]

But to me, Kahlil's best work is his gift to his South End neighborhood—a sculpture of a young girl with a jump rope. You can see it in Hayes Park at the corner of Warren Avenue and West Canton Street.

---

3  Arnold Steinhardt, first violinist of the Guarneri String Quartet and author of Violin Dreams, has performed many times and made recordings with the Pianist. One time, when the Quartet was in Boston and he stayed with us, we took him to the Gibrans', and Arnold played Kahlil's violin.

Kahlil Gibran with his sculpture of a young girl

We no longer live in the South End, but we keep in touch with our friends there. Recently, Jean e-mailed that she had opened her front door that morning and "spotted something missing," the wrought iron urn that held "a bright red mandevilla [a flowering vine] and trailing sweet potato vine." Gone overnight, after guarding the house for more than fifty years. This was a special urn, in Jean's words their "personal symbol of life and love."

According to *The Prophet*, "the righteous is not innocent of the deeds of the wicked . . ." and "the robbed is not blameless in being robbed." As I read those words now, I remember that nearly fifty years ago I went into our garage in Needham and "spotted something missing," my father's fishing kit. Such a theft can take away an object but not the memory of what it represents.

As for the stolen urn, if Kahlil were here, he would simply make a replica so exact that you would never know the difference. But he is gone, so Jean's e-mail took what can only be described as a "Gibranian" way of looking at things. "Hope whoever ends up with it, waters it often."

## My Birthday and the Gift of Friendship

In February of 2019 I became old, meaning that I turned eighty. It is an odd sensation, since I don't feel much different. A bit creaky, perhaps, somewhat shorter, and undeniably grayer. But otherwise, just about the same.

When I was in high school, we had to write an essay entitled "What Is the Best Stage of Life?" I don't have the paper I wrote, but I remember the answer I gave. "Old age." And I remember my reason—because then you can look back at your life and see what you have accomplished.

Whether I would make the same choice today is an open question, but all in all I have no complaints about reaching the four-score stage, except one: I'm losing dear friends. It is part of surviving, I know, but I don't like it.

This is not something that just began. By the time I finished Stevens High School in 1957, I had attended the funerals of two friends, gone before they even had a chance. One of them helped get me through sophomore Latin. The other had been a regular part of our after-school pickup games. I have never forgotten Wayne Gray or Billy Stringer.

This past year was marked with continuing losses, including three men who made a difference in many lives, including mine.

Carl Sapers was my law firm supervisor when I started work in 1965. He soon

Carl Sapers

went from "Mr." to "Carl," and over time from supervisor to colleague to friend. He was a man of principle who served as a mentor to a generation of Hill & Barlow lawyers and to his students at Harvard's School of Design. Carl believed in public service and in our law firm which, for at least most of its 106 years of existence, served both its clients and the community. Carl grew orchids, loved music and sailing, and cared about the public good.

Camille Sarrouf had such impeccable judgment and integrity that just being with him was an honor. He exemplified what it means to care about others. One time, on a bus in London, the guide was telling us about the Duke of Westminster, landlord of much of the City. Camille had one question: "Is the Duke charitable?" (The answer was yes.)

Of Camille's service on public and charitable boards, one deserves mention—his thirty-one years on the board of St. Jude's Hospital in Memphis, which treats children with cancer free of charge. After everyone was seated at his funeral in the fall of 2018, St. Jude's board members from

Camille Sarouf

all over the country, including Marlo Thomas, whose father Danny founded the hospital, entered the cathedral in West Roxbury and sat in pews up front, reserved for them.

Lewis Eigen was, in some ways, the most remarkable of those I lost in 2018 or, for that matter, of anyone I have ever known. He could seemingly master any subject, from higher mathematics (he had a PhD at age twenty), to quantum physics (which he once offered to explain to me), to public health and education, and on and on.

The day after we met in 1957, as counselors at a camp on Lake George in upstate New York,

Lewis Eigen

Lewis asked me to help him blaze a trail. When we came to a gully, he said, "We'll build a bridge."

I asked, "Do you know how to do that?" "No," he said, "but I will read a book tonight and know how tomorrow."

If ever there was someone who had time for everything, it was Lewis. He designed President Johnson's Job Corps program and was its deputy director, wrote nineteen books, created websites, and engaged in countless humanitarian activities. Even while dealing with years of health problems that would have undone most people, he managed to find time for everything, including friendship.

During the decades between my early losses of Wayne and Billy, and last year's losses of Carl, Camille, and Lewis, other friends departed this earth. Some lived to be as old as I have recently become, others did not. They gave me the gift of friendship, and I miss them all.

## My Chance Encounter and the Gifts that Last

I grew up thinking the word "friend" was a noun, something you have if you're lucky. In today's world, it has become a verb. People go online and "friend" each other. If only it were that easy.

Not only can you "friend" people on Facebook, but you can also "unfriend" them. There is even an app you can download to end a romantic relationship and get rid of anything that might remind you of what once was—photos, past posts, expressions of love. I suppose it makes sense. Lots of relationships begin online, so why not end them there?

My father told me a long time ago that it is a lot easier to lose a friend than it is to make one. He understood the gift of friendship and taught me to hold my friends close. He often said that you can count your friends on one hand.

I did not understand what he meant back then, but I do now. He was talking about those few people who accept you as you are, and who would do just about anything for you, and towards whom you feel the same way. I am fortunate to have a full handful of such people in my life, and the older I get the more important they are to me.

Hon. David J. Fischer

I was recently at a conference in London and met a woman who knew my college and law school friend, Ted Boehm. She told me that since retiring from the Indiana Supreme Court, he had returned to the practice of law.

A few days later, she sent me Ted's e-mail address. I wrote to him, shared a few updates, and mentioned that I have only one wedding gift from my first marriage—a tray he gave us. I asked whether he had remained in contact with our mutual college friend, Dave Fischer, whom I last saw more than fifty years ago.

Ted wrote back and said he had not been in touch with Dave until recently, when they caught up in San Francisco, where Dave now lives after a long career in the Foreign Service. Ted provided me with Dave's e-mail address.

I sent an e-mail to Dave and told him I was coming to San Francisco after Thanksgiving. Would he like to get together?

Dave replied yes, and we made a date to meet at his house. Neither of us would have recognized the other, but after a while he started to look more like the person I used to know.

We talked for a few minutes and then spent two hours over lunch at a nearby restaurant. I asked whether my e-mail had taken him by surprise, and he said that it had. I explained that I decided a while ago to try and reconnect with people who have been important to me at some point in my life. He was such a person.

I recalled a conversation we had when he was a senior and I was a junior. I was halfway through the retelling when he finished it for me, reciting the rest of the conversation exactly as I remembered it.

Then I brought up the time he came home with me for Thanksgiving, in November of 1960. Dave says it never happened; he had never been in Claremont. One of us is wrong, of course, but I have no way of knowing whether it's him or me. I guess I will just live with that uncertainty.

Then Dave told me that he only has one present left from his long-ago wedding, silver nut dishes from Firestone and Parson, my uncle's store in Boston. "You gave them to us," he said.

I do not remember giving that gift, but on this point, I defer to my friend Dave. Thanks to a chance encounter with a woman in London, we rekindled our friendship. Yes, he is still my friend, still an important person in my life, someone I want to keep close.[4]

---

4   Dave Fischer's illustrious career in the Foreign Service included participation in the Strategic Arms Limitation Treaty with the Soviet Union, assisting with the reunification of Germany, and serving as ambassador to the Seychelles. After a long battle with cancer, which he told me about during our lunch, Dave died on November 22, 2016, a year after our reunion.

# My Love of Tennis and a Valentine for Bud

My parents bought our house in Claremont in 1943, when I was four. The last thing we needed was a tennis court, but apparently the previous owners, the Fry family, played tennis, so we inherited the court along with an arrangement with a group of local businessmen. The deal was that they would maintain the court and, in exchange, get to play there on Wednesday afternoons, when Claremont stores were closed, and Sunday mornings.

Growing up with a backyard tennis court instilled in me a love of the sport, so when I ended up in Boston it was only natural that I started going to the annual US Pro and the National Doubles tournaments at Longwood Cricket Club in Brookline. During the 1960s and 1970s, I watched such great players as Rod Laver, Ken Rosewall, Roy Emerson, Jimmy Connors, Arthur Ashe, Billie Jean King, Martina Navratilova, and Björn Borg.

And I remember seeing Bud Collins, whose articles I regularly read in the *Boston Globe* sports pages. He was plainly visible in the television booth, broadcasting the matches on WGBH-TV, Channel 2. You could hardly miss him, given his flamboyant outfits.

In the mid-1970s, Bud needed a lawyer, and he picked me. The result was a friendship that has endured ever since. Every year until the late 1990s, when Longwood stopped holding national tournaments, Bud would host us and others for dinner on the Longwood grass among women in flowery dresses and men in striped pants, followed by the tennis matches.

Bud didn't just write about tennis. He covered all sports and, for twenty-five years, wrote a *Globe* travel column called "Bud Collins Anywhere." He was more than a journalist; he was a man of the world. Whatever he was writing about, he was lucid, erudite, and funny. He had nicknames for just about everyone.[5]

In 1994, Bud was inducted into the International Tennis Hall of Fame in Newport, Rhode Island, and for many years thereafter he continued as a tennis commentator on NBC Television and the Tennis Channel. In recent

---

5   In his travel columns, Bud's name for his wife, Anita Klaussen, was "Aurelio," which is what gave me the idea of referring to my wife as the "Pianist" in my columns. Bud had a different name for her—"Fingers." Bud died on March 4, 2016, at the age of eighty-six. His given name was Arthur.

times, however, Bud has had some health problems that have kept him away from center court, and pretty much at home when he hasn't been in the hospital.

In September of 2015, Anita drove Bud to the Billie Jean King National Tennis Center in Flushing, New York, for the US Open. Surrounded by the world's greatest players and 23,000 spectators in Arthur Ashe Stadium, Bud was honored by the renaming of the US Open's media center in his honor. The words inscribed on the commemorative plaque are simple and accurate: "Journalist, Commentator, Historian, Mentor, Friend."

Bud Collins

# My Father's Words and the Hand of Friendship

*Judge not, lest you be judged.*

Matthew 7:1

My first wife, Susan Ross Steinfield, died in November of 1983, meaning that the holiday season that year was a difficult time. Looking for a way to cheer ourselves up, my children and I decided to take a trip to Antigua.

We were delayed for several hours in the Philadelphia airport, where we met a man and his family. Unlike me, his wife had thought to bring snacks, and their three children matched up with my three, almost to the day. Over the next week, on that beautiful Caribbean island, the two families were together almost full time.

During the years that followed, our Antigua beginnings developed into a real friendship. Then one day, about twenty years ago, I called my friend, and he made it clear that he did not want to hear from me. It was as if we had never met, much less shared important times together. All contact between us ended, and I had no idea why he had blown me off.

I never mentioned this to anyone, but I thought about it quite a bit. As my father often told me, making a friend isn't easy, and losing one is painful. Especially when you don't know why.

Not long ago, he sent me a letter. Our last conversation had apparently been on his mind, and he wanted to make amends. "I have apologized to you many times," he wrote, "but only in my head."

I wrote back and told him I had always been grateful for that Christmas trip in 1983, when he and his family "rescued" my children and me at the airport, and for the friendship we had shared for many years. We made a date to get together.

When we did so, neither of us raised the subject of that long-ago phone call or the break in our friendship. Sometimes it is just as well to leave the past in the past.

After two hours together, we parted on the sidewalk and agreed that being in touch once again was a good thing for us both. The friendship may not be the same as it was, and I do not know where it will go from here. I do know that we still enjoy each other's company, and that is a good start to a new chapter.

My friend and I are both Jewish, but telling this story during the Christmas season feels just right. His letter brought me good tidings, and I give him great credit for doing what must have been difficult, and what I could not have been the one to do.

My father would often remind me that you can count the number of real friends on one hand. When the time came, of course I had room for my old friend on my hand of friendship.

# My Old Friend and the Time It Is

*Time it was*
*And what a time it was*
Simon & Garfunkel, "Old Friends"

I will always remember the day, midway through first grade, when a new kid moved to Claremont and entered Miss Dyer's classroom at the Way School. Her name was Linda, and she sat across the aisle from me. I was hooked from the first look.

Together, we went through that year and the next eleven, attending the same schools, sitting in the same classrooms, learning the same subjects. She was a "straight A" student, and hardly a week went by that I didn't call her up or drop over to her house, looking for help with my homework. She was not only my friend but, in a sense, my tutor as well.

I have only one unhappy memory connected to Linda. We were both members of the Claremont Skating Club on Maple Avenue, and when it came time for the annual Carnival, I asked her to be my skating partner. So did Charlie Dole, and she picked him. He was older, and a better skater, but it still stings.

In fifth and sixth grades, we were in the same square dance group. For some unknown reason, Mrs. Rollins, the school principal, thought that everyone should become proficient in square dancing.

And we both played in the band, she the French horn and I the clarinet. I can picture us wearing our Stevens High Band uniforms, marching down Pleasant Street in Claremont and, in January of 1957, Pennsylvania Avenue in Washington.

We never became boyfriend and girlfriend, just close friends. She was smart, funny, wholesome, and idealistic. I used to wonder whether she even had bad thoughts.

By the time we graduated, she was spelling her name "Lynda," but other than that she was the same person who sat across from me in first grade. She went off to Smith College in Massachusetts and then Stanford Law School in California, where she met a Canadian graduate student. They married, she took on a new last name, and they moved to Vancouver, where she has lived ever since.

The years went by and, for reasons I cannot explain, we did not stay in touch. Out of sight, but never out of mind. Then, about twenty years ago, the Pianist and I decided to visit relatives in Vancouver. I called Lynda, and she invited us for dinner at her house.

When we arrived and entered the living room, there were childhood pictures of us on display. It had been over forty years, but of course we hadn't changed a bit. Later that evening, two of Lynda's children came to the house, and one of them said, "I've been hearing about you all my life."

The same is true of my children, who have been hearing about Lynda as long as they can remember. She was the girl who sat across from me in first grade, the one who did not pick me as her skating partner, the one who helped me get through senior math.

Last month, two of my children, their spouses, and two of my grandchildren met Lynda on our way back from a trip to Alaska. The word "memorable" is inadequate to describe the afternoon we spent with her.

There is something about friendship that cannot be put into words, but you know it when you feel it. A shared history often keeps a friendship alive, but there is more to it than that. In the case of Lynda and me, there is a kind of kinship, a sense that we will always be important to each other, even if we are not in the same place. Our recent visit was not just about Paul Simon's "what a time it *was*" but also about what a time it still *is*.

Linda (Lynda) and Me - then and now

## My Truthful Response and an Apology Overdue

I don't know whether our first president, George Washington, really said "I cannot tell a lie." I do know that if someone tells you they never told a lie, they're lying.

Telling the truth feels good, but it can get you into trouble. When I was in my twenties, my wife and I became friendly with a couple from Alabama. When they came to New England to attend law school, they brought their southern accents and good manners with them. They invited us to their apartment for dinner, and Elaine went to a lot of trouble preparing an excellent meal.

Then came dessert, some kind of cooked banana. I ate a couple of bites and put down my fork.

"Do you like it?" Elaine asked.

"It's interesting," I said.

"But do you like it?" she asked again.

I don't remember my exact words, but I made a mistake and said something like, " It's not my favorite." One look told me I had hurt her feelings, and that look has stayed with me for nearly sixty years. I wish I had come up with a better, kinder answer. Even a "lie" would have been preferable.

A long time ago, I decided not to use the word "lie," or accuse someone of lying, in any legal document with my name on it. I would say, instead, that the lawyer on the other side of the case was "mistaken" or "misunderstood" what had happened or, perhaps, was "confused" or had "overlooked" a critical piece of evidence." I figured the judge would get the point.

Then I started to see younger lawyers sprinkle the word "lie" in their briefs, and even use the L word in the courtroom. It always makes me bristle, and I have held my ground. To this day, I will not do it.

My reason is that a "lie" is not just a factual mistake; it is saying something false *knowing* it is false. If a person says, "Climate change is not man-made," that may be incorrect, but it is not a lie. The same can be said for racist or bigoted remarks, hateful though they may be, because the narrow-minded speaker probably believes what he or she is saying.

For a long time, mainstream journalists shied away from using the word "lie," but the public landscape has changed dramatically. You cannot pick up the newspaper or turn on the news these days without seeing or hearing that so-and-so is "lying." You see it not just on editorial pages, but on front pages as well. Unlike my decision not to use the word in my professional writings, much of the mainstream media has decided to do so.

Lying has infected our public life. According to *The Washington Post*, Donald Trump told over 30,000 lies during his four years as president. He is hardly the first president to say things that are not so, but as we have recently seen, using untruths as a political strategy has created uncertainty, confusion, and, ultimately, mayhem. According to the former president's lawyer, there is no truth. Claiming it is raining on a cloudless day is no longer false; it is an "alternative fact."

In her book *Surviving Autocracy*, Masha Gessen writes that some lies are "surmountable," such as when a guest tells the host (as I should have done), "I like the fish overcooked." Then there are the far more serious "power" lies, the grandaddy of all being when a recounted, certified vote tally comes out one way and the person with fewer votes says, "I won."

Elaine, my old friend, I know it has been a long time, but I'm very sorry I told the truth and hurt your feelings, and I apologize.

# My Maestro and the Gift of Music

The Pianist and I became part-time Jaffrey, New Hampshire, residents in 1986. One day that summer, we saw there was an orchestra concert in nearby Peterborough, so we went and discovered an organization called Monadnock Music. The conductor was a man named James Bolle.

"I know him," the Pianist told me. "He conducts the New Hampshire Symphony, and I played a concerto with the orchestra a few years ago."

After the concert, Jim and Jocelyn Bolle invited us to a reception at the "Cheese Shop" across the street, and thus began a long and meaningful relationship that has continued over the years, in good times and bad.[6]

We soon became part of Monadnock Music, I mostly as a listener, the Pianist as a soloist and chamber player. I began calling Jim "Maestro," and he called me "Counselor," which always made me think of my years trying to corral campers at various summer camps, including one in Hillsborough Upper Village.

In the mid-1960s, Chicago-born Jim and Keene-born Jocelyn saw an opportunity, or perhaps a need or just an empty space waiting to be filled. There may have been concerts back then, but Monadnock Music brought the gift of music in a whole new way to a part of the state best known for its much-climbed mountain. Beginning in Nelson in 1966, and quickly spreading to cities and towns throughout Cheshire County and beyond, and to the public schools as well, Monadnock Music became an important part of the cultural landscape. Village concerts were free of charge, and world-class musicians from all over the country, and from far-off places such as Norway and New Zealand, came back year after year.

After a period of failing health, Jim died on April 14, 2019. And on Sunday, August 25, a concert was held in his memory, fittingly in Nelson.[7] Many of the Monadnock Music musicians from the 1980s and 1990s, including the Pianist, performed works by Jim's favorite composers. While listening, I

---

6  The Bolles's son Christopher, known as Kit (and to his friends at St. John's College in Annapolis as "Group Captain Biggies"), died too young in 1990. I had met him only once, but Jim and Jocelyn asked me to give the eulogy at his memorial service. "He did not live a complete life," I said, "but he lived life completely."

7  Nelson, New Hampshire, with a population of less than 1,000, is not only the birthplace of Monadnock Music but also of Alfred B. Kittredge, who grew up in Jaffrey, practiced law in Keene with the firm now known as Bradley & Faulkner (Jocelyn Bolle was born a Faulkner), moved to South Dakota, and became a United States senator in 1901. It was also the home of the novelist-poet May Sarton, who is buried there.

The Maestro – Jim Bolle

read Jocelyn's written recollection entitled "Opening Night at Monadnock Music," which describes that long-ago beginning more than fifty years ago. She relates how two bikers showed up on Harleys, stayed to the end, and became front-row attendees for many years to come. I didn't see any Harleys outside the Nelson Meeting House on the day of the service, but the bikers may well have been there in spirit.

Jim lived a life of the mind. Music and books were his constant companions. But it would be incomplete to leave it there. He was a cultural activist, a rebel with a cause.

Some of what he programmed was challenging to our ears, but Maestro Bolle had a purpose, and nothing was going to deter him. Yes, he was willing to include Beethoven and Brahms and other composers whose music we recognize, but he wanted us to know that contemporary music was important and worth our attention as well. So Monadnock Music programs included works by such twentieth-century composers as Virgil Thompson and Elliott Carter, and by the Maestro himself. If the "new" wasn't to everyone's taste, that didn't bother Jim. A concert, as he saw it, was not a popularity contest. It was about testing boundaries and forcing people out of their musical comfort zone.

Jim retired a decade or more ago, and the Bolles moved from Francestown to Harrisville, which is where I last saw him. He was struggling with Parkinson's Disease, barely able to get around, having difficulty speaking. "Maestro," I asked, "Are you still having fun?"

"Yes," he answered, "I listen to music."

# My Incurable Addictions and America's Lost Heroes

*Where have you gone, Joe DiMaggio?*
*Our nation turns its lonely eyes to you.*

Simon & Garfunkel

If we are lucky growing up, we have heroes. I'm not talking about Superman or Wonder Woman but about real people whom we admire and would like to emulate.

I had such heroes in Claremont, including the Leahy brothers, Albie and Chuck. They were athletes, musicians, scholars, and leaders. I looked up to them, literally, and wanted to be like them.

And I had Normand Paquette, my senior year English teacher. He was small of stature but one of the giants in my life, the person who not only taught me how to write but how to think.

And there were other heroes of my youth whom I never met. Dwight ("Ike") Eisenhower was one of them. He saved the world, with some help from the "British Bulldog," Winston Churchill. I was thirteen when Ike defeated the Democratic nominee, Adlai Stevenson, and became president. In retrospect, maybe Stevenson, who seems to have had no nickname, should have been part of my group of heroes. But I lived in a Republican household, and the subject never came up.

Another hero was heavyweight champion Joe Louis. I named my junior league basketball team the "Brown Bombers" after him. Our team didn't pack much of a punch, but I have always been proud of having chosen his nickname as our emblem.

I have two incurable addictions. One is baseball, the other is politics. Both have provided me with equal parts of pleasure and frustration, and with quite a few heroes.

"Teddy Ballgame" has been one of them ever since my baseball-addicted grandfather taught me about baseball. Ted Williams joined the Red Sox in 1939, the year I was born, and retired in 1960. That career span was twice interrupted by service to our country, first in World War II and then again in the Korean War, where he flew as a wingman for "Old Magnet Ass," John Glenn.

I saw play him several times at Fenway Park. My Uncle Eddie, who became a flight instructor after flying combat missions in the Pacific, taught Williams how to fly and, after the War, gave my grandfather one of his lifetime's most unforgettable moments—a visit at Ted's Boston apartment. Ted would have been one hundred years old on August 30, 2018, but for those of us who saw him swing a bat with effortless grace, he will always be known by yet another of his nicknames, "The Kid."

If we are doubly lucky, we will continue to have heroes beyond childhood. For millions of Americans, both Franklin and Eleanor Roosevelt played such a role, and so did John F. Kennedy and Martin Luther King Jr. a generation later. In the world of sports, Lou Gehrig (the "luckiest man alive" despite the disease named after him), Mildred "Babe" Didrikson Zaharias, Jackie Robinson, Althea Gibson, Billie Jean King, and others were pioneers who became role models for those who followed.

And then there is John McCain. Even those of us who did not vote for him in 2008 or agree with his politics have long recognized that he belongs in that special pantheon. He was heroic in life, first as a prisoner of war, and in some ways even more so during the months before his death on August 25, 2018, standing up for principle and fighting an incurable disease at the same time.

John McCain had a lot in common with Ted Williams. They were both fighter pilots, they were both Republicans, they both had strong tempers, and they both swore a lot. McCain also had a lot of nicknames, including "White Tornado," "The Sheriff," and "America's Maverick." To those we can add "America's Hero."

# My Recent Workout and First Responders

April 15, 2014, marked the one-year anniversary of the Marathon Day bombing, an event that took three lives, and then a fourth, and injured 260 people. It is a day that scarred the City of Boston for the rest of time and gave new meaning to the words "first responders."

Late in the afternoon on that recent anniversary date, I walked down the stairs at my office to a room where we have workout equipment. After about fifty minutes on the treadmill, I showered and headed back to my office. At the top of the stairs were three firefighters in full firefighting regalia.

"What are you doing here?" one of them asked.

"Working out," I replied. I paused for a moment and could smell the smoke.

"Didn't you hear the fire alarm?" he asked.

I confessed I had not, leaving out the fact that I remove my hearing aids before exercising. He looked at me with doubt on his face. Thinking of nothing better to say, I added, "I work here."

"Where's your office?" he asked. I wondered why he wanted to know. Did I look like an arsonist? I told him it was at the end of the hallway, and I would get my stuff and leave.

"The elevators are shut down," he said, "and it's a lot of stairs for someone who just worked out. I suggest you wait until we get the all-clear signal."

I decided to take his advice, so I sat down, and we continued the conversation. He explained that this was a one-alarm fire, meaning that three units responded. I think he said forty firefighters plus three chiefs. "We've had a lot of fires lately," he told me.

"I know," I said, thinking of the recent fire in Back Bay that claimed two firefighters' lives. "Are you married?" I asked.

"Yes," he answered, "and I have nine kids, the youngest is thirteen."

"Does your wife worry?"

"Yes, she does," he answered, "but I always let her know where I am. I've been a fireman for thirty years. I'm retiring this year."

I looked at the next firefighter, a middle-aged man with a handlebar mustache. "I've been with the department twenty-nine years, at three different stations," he volunteered. "Right now, I'm stationed in the North End, and you wouldn't believe how friendly everyone there is."

"As a matter of fact, I would believe it," I told him. "I sold Fuller Brushes in the North End when I was a law student. It was a very friendly neighborhood."

"You're a lawyer?" he replied, with a raised eyebrow. "Can I have your card?"

The youngest of the three firefighters turned to me and, apparently reading my mind, said, "Two years."

"Do you like it?" I asked.

"It's a great job," he answered. "I used to be in sales, but this is a lot better."

Then the one with the mustache, said, "You should drop in at the station. We like company."

I thanked him for the invitation and told him that my father used to drop in at the fire station and sometimes took me with him. He and a Claremont fireman named George Plante were great friends and owned an old, wooden fishing boat together until it sank in a storm in Newburyport harbor.

At that point, the senior member of the trio told me I could hitch a ride on an elevator that two other firefighters were about to unlock and take down. By then another lawyer had shown up from downstairs. He and I joined the two firefighters, who were wearing fifty-five pounds of equipment and carrying hoses and other equipment with them.

I stepped outside and the building was ringed with fire engines. I thought to myself, *I'll never complain about waiting when a firetruck holds up traffic while pulling back into the station.* I felt safe coming down in that elevator and grateful for first responders.

# My Vaccine and Thank You for Coming

A writer named Jane Brody appears every Tuesday in the "ScienceTimes" section of *The New York Times.* I like reading her columns, maybe because I like it when a fellow senior citizen writes about subjects that matter to me, but even more so because she is a realistic optimist.

Don't sugar-coat the inevitable shortcomings of advancing years but suck it up and do what you can to enjoy each day.

So, I was immediately drawn to her March 2, 2021, column entitled "Why I Overcame My Vaccine Hesitancy." She writes about how her initial skepticism went away as numerous reputable experts gave assurances that the vaccine was safe and effective. She registered and went to the round-the-clock vaccination site in Brooklyn at the appointed time.

Except when she signed up to get her shot (or "jab" as it is now called), she mistook AM for PM, something I do all the time when setting my alarm clock, and arrived mid-afternoon, twelve hours too late.

Anyone who has dealt with the government might have expected a curt greeting, "Sorry, too late, come back another time," but that is not what happed to Ms. Brody. Instead, the check-in woman said, "Don't worry, you'll get the vaccine," and she did.

Just a week earlier, I had a somewhat similar, though less dramatic, experience. My appointment that day was in the afternoon, but when I woke up it was snowing, and I feared the weather would shut down the outdoor vaccination site in Keene. The Pianist, who was a week ahead of me, said "Let's go now," and off we went several hours ahead of time.

I gave my name to the check-in officer and said, "I'm early." Just like the woman in Brooklyn, he said, "Don't worry" and told me where to go. At that point words heard a lot during this pandemic occurred to me: We really are all in this together.

What followed was a pleasurable experience, the last thing I would have expected when getting a shot in the arm. There we were, safe and warm in the car, while several bundled up vaccine workers scurried around taking care of senior citizens. They had handwritten nametags, and Dawn came over to my driver's side window. Her first words were, "Thank you for coming." She then explained everything and introduced me to

Michael, the shot giver. Another woman was carrying a basket containing the vaccine vials, protected from the snow by a mini-umbrella. No way were these people letting the snow interfere with carrying out their mission.

The shot was painless. And before I could thank Michael and the woman with the basket, *he* thanked *me* for coming. Dawn then gave me the card showing that I was one down and one to go in a few weeks. She asked me to turn on my car blinkers and wait fifteen minutes, just to be on the safe side. "If you have any reaction," she told me, "just honk and we will be right over."

We waited. No reaction so no need to honk the horn, and off we went to carry on with the day. What a remarkable experience, very much like Ms. Brody's in Brooklyn.

The members of the vaccine brigade are lifesavers, volunteers helping restore the planet to something resembling normalcy. They are heroes, the most recent generation of first responders whom we should all be thanking. And to think they thanked me for coming so they could help me!

# FAMILY

## My Cousin from the Old Country and Bob Dylan

*The answer, my friend, is blowin' in the wind.*

Bob Dylan (1963)

On February 22, 2020, I went to New York City to see my grandson, Jacob, who works for an advertising agency, and my granddaughter Susie, who is a student at Barnard College. We met that afternoon at the Museum of Modern Art, ate dinner at an excellent restaurant, and saw a Broadway play called *Girl from the North Country*. It features more than twenty Bob Dylan songs and is set in Duluth, Minnesota, where Dylan was born in 1941. Other than our time just being together, the play was the highlight of the weekend.

In 1947, what was left of the large Feldman family arrived in Claremont, New Hampshire, where I was born eight years earlier. Chaim and Lisa, with their sons Martin and Stephen, came to New Hampshire from a displaced persons camp in Germany and, before that, from the forest where they had eluded the Nazis for two years.

My grandmother, Lillian Firestone, and Chaim Feldman were cousins, both originally from a Russian village named Dereczyn.[8] In the late 1930s, my grandmother's Uncle Bernstein, who had become a successful businessman in Lowell, Massachusetts, went back to Dereczyn to see the relatives he had left behind decades earlier. When he returned, he brought Chaim's teenage sister, Ruchel, with him. Her English name should have been Rachel, but my mother suggested an alternative, and Ruchel became my Cousin Romaine.

While Chaim and Lisa got settled in New York, the boys remained with my grandparents in Claremont and attended the nearby Bluff School. There had been no time for sports in the Polish forest, but they did know how to skate, and that winter my father flooded a rink next to our house.

By the end of the school year, they were fluent English speakers. They left

---

8   Dereczyn today would be in Belarus.

Martin Feldman

Claremont, attended New York public schools, graduated from City College of New York, and became CPAs. Martin went to work for an accountant named Marshall Gelfand who, by sheer coincidence, grew up in Claremont. In 1967, the firm became Gelfand, Rennert & Feldman, with offices in New York, and later in Nashville, Los Angeles, and London as well. They specialized in representing entertainers.[9]

As time passed, I mostly lost touch with Stevie, but not with Martin. And not with his Aunt Romaine, whom he cherished. Following his grandson's bar mitzvah in Armonk, New York, I had my last conversation with Chaim, who was sitting next to his sister Romaine outside Martin's house in Armonk. "Joey, if you think you understand how bad it was, imagine something a thousand times worse than the Holocaust," he told me, "and you still wouldn't know how terrible it was."

At Chaim's funeral, I looked a few rows ahead and saw Martin and Stephen side by side, Martin's arm around his brother's shoulders. It wasn't hard to answer the question I remember asking myself. "What are they thinking right now?"

Martin retired many years ago after a long and successful career. Part of his

9  They still do. Marshall Gelfand, who ran the firm from its Los Angeles office for many years died on April 1, 2021, at age ninety-three. He not only represented Peter, Paul & Mary, Neil Diamond, and many other "A-list performers," but he became a well-recognized philanthropist. His son Todd is now the firm's CEO.

professional life was to accompany his clients on tour and keep watch over the box office. I saw him do so when his client, Bob Dylan, performed in Boston in 1974, and again in 1975 with the Rolling Thunder Revue. Yes, my Cousin Martin was the accountant and financial manager for the winner of the 2016 Nobel Prize in Literature.

When I spoke with Martin a few days after my February trip to New York, I told him how much we had enjoyed seeing *Girl from the North Country* and hearing the iconic Dylan songs. He told me he planned to get tickets but had just received disturbing news from his doctor —advanced cancer.

On March 12, 2020, Broadway shut down. And on April 10, Martin Feldman died. He was more than my cousin. He was a righteous person, a dear friend, and my last direct family connection to the Holocaust.

*May your song always be sung*
*And may you stay forever young.*

Bob Dylan (1974)

# My Bitter Herbs and Songs of Hope

*Though April Showers may come your way*
*They bring the flowers that bloom in May.*
"April Showers" (1921)
by Louis Silvers and B. G. De Sylva

April brings showers and, usually, the holiday of Passover, which commemorates the Exodus, the liberation of the Jews from slavery in ancient Egypt. It is a joyful holiday, a time when Jewish families, often with non-Jewish friends, gather for the seder ("arrangement"), a combination religious service and dinner that includes symbolic foods, readings, songs, and several cups of wine.

Passover is closely linked to Easter both by its symbolism and its date. They are holidays of hope, "moveable feasts" in the sense that they have no fixed date on the Gregorian calendar.

When I was young my mother was doubtful that I could sit through an entire seder. I wanted to attend and promised to be good. A family member saw me grimace when we ate bitter herbs dipped in salt water (a reminder of the bitterness of slavery) and asked me how I liked it. Fearing maternal disapproval, I answered, "Delicious."

At the end of our family's seder, my father would launch into singing "Chad Gadya"— "One little goat, one little goat"—and we would all chime in with the chorus, "which my father bought for two zuzim." The song is a mix of Hebrew and Aramaic and is said to represent an historical allegory of the Jewish people, with "two zuzim" referring to the tax on every adult Israelite male.

The second verse repeats the first and adds two more lines, followed by the chorus. My father, just warming up, would then sing the third verse. By now you get the idea. Like "There Was an Old Lady Who Swallowed a Fly," it keeps repeating itself, for a total of eleven verses. My father would always sing it to the end, while the rest of us dropped out along the way.

My father's favorite singer was Al Jolson, who was born Asa Yoelson, a cantor's son who sang his first songs in the synagogue. I think that was part of his appeal. He was the star of the first full-length talking picture, *The Jazz Singer*.

In 1946, a movie named *The Jolson Story* came out, and my father took me to see it. An actor named Larry Parks played Jolson, but all he had to do was move his lips, and the sound was that of Jolson's voice.

Like father like son, I wanted my children to see *The Jolson Story*, so I bought it on videocassette when they were young and told them they had to watch it with me. They gave me one of those "Why is he making us do this?" looks. It is the only movie I ever forced them to watch, and they liked it.[10]

Al Jolson recorded Israel's national anthem, "Hatikvah" ("The Hope"), which expresses the 2,000-year-old longing of the Jewish people to return to Israel. Passover this year begins on April 14, and I'm thinking "Hatikvah" would be a good song to include. It fits nicely with the traditional last words of the seder ("Next year in Jerusalem"), and it's a lot shorter than "Chad Gadya," which Jolson never recorded.

We could also include his trademark song, "April Showers," which is also a song of hope.

*So if it's raining, have no regrets,*
*Because it isn't raining rain, you know, it's raining violets.*

---

10   I would think twice before doing so today but would probably do it again. Jolson sang "Mammy" and other songs in blackface, which was accepted in his time. But now, I would use the movie as an opportunity to discuss racism, and I would couple it with former New Orleans Mayor Mitch Landrieu's 2017 speech on the removal of confederate monuments.

# My Father the Elk and Breaking Even

My father was a member of Elks Lodge No. 0879 on Summer Street in Claremont. The lodge is housed in an old brick building on the corner, with an elk statue on the lawn protecting the building. My father used to play poker there, and I grew up believing that the principal activity of the BPOE (Benevolent and Protective Order of Elks) was to hold poker games. But the Elks actually have a somewhat broader mission, which is to support Veterans Administration hospitals and disabled veterans, fund youth programs and scholarships, and promote Americanism.

Founded in 1868, and with over a million members in more than 2,100 lodges, the Elks is one of the largest and most active such organizations in the United States. Its lengthy motto is, "The faults of our brothers and sisters we write upon the sand, Their virtues upon the tablets of love and memory."

Not too long ago I represented someone in a case involving an Elks lodge. That made me think about my father, of course, and I learned quite a bit about the organization, including the good works. I should have known there was more to it than five-card stud. My father was a charitable person.

Back in his day the admission rules were different, but the BPOE has moved with the times and eliminated most of its restrictive rules. Now, to qualify to become a member, you need to be at least twenty-one, an American citizen, and believe in God.

As an Elk, my father was in good company. President Harding, for whom my father voted in 1920, was a member, and so were Presidents Roosevelt, Eisenhower, Kennedy, and Ford. Other well-known members include Babe Ruth, Harry Houdini, Lawrence Welk, and Clint Eastwood, not to mention George Babbitt, the fictional character created by Sinclair Lewis.

In one of Robert Heinlein's novels, the principal character goes to the Elks Club to play pinochle. I think he got the wrong card game. And in an episode of *The West Wing*, a character says, "My dad's an Elk." So, I'm not alone.

I've never considered applying for membership in the Elks, or the Eagles or the Moose for that matter, but I recently came across a reference to the Elks that made me smile. A man named Ethan Zuckerman invented that bane of the Internet, the pop-up ad, and now regrets it. To make amends, he has become the director of a new research center at the University of

Massachusetts called The Initiative for Digital Public Infrastructure. Its mission is to turn the Internet from a private profit marketplace into a digital place for public good.

And he cites the Elks as a model. According to Zuckerman, "Elks Club meetings were what gave us experience in democracy. We learned how to . . . handle disagreement [and] how to be civilized people who don't storm out of an argument."

I never thought of the Elks that way, but those words aptly describe my father the Elk. He rarely got into arguments, and I doubt he ever stormed out of one. It would not have been in his nature since he was always the calmest person in the room.

Of course, I wasn't there during those late-night poker games, but he never had any reason to storm out of the room. As I recall, he usually won. And when he didn't, he always reported, "I broke even."

In the tradition of Elkdom, his virtues are inscribed upon the tablets of my love and memory.

# My Family's Business and Rooting for Arthur T.

I know something about dysfunctional family businesses. I grew up in one, owned by my father, Frank, and his brothers, Sam and Bill. My father and Sam, who each owned 40 percent, stopped speaking to each other before I was born. I never found out why.

I thought about my father and Sam as I, like most New Englanders, watched the recent Market Basket shootout. But unlike the dysfunctional management at the shoddy mill in Claremont, the Demoulas cousins, Arthur S. and Arthur T., waged their battle in the public arena for many years and, this year, 2014, in the newspapers.

When Arthur S. fired Arthur T. last June, we witnessed an amazing phenomenon. Thousands of employees stopped showing up for work, and hundreds of thousands of customers "voted with their feet" and did their grocery shopping elsewhere. The timing was convenient for those of us who usually focus on baseball during the summer months. The Red Sox were eight and a half games out of first place, and as the "strike" by these non-union men and women gained steam, the air went completely out of the Red Sox. By August 15, the team was comfortably mired in last place, and no one was shopping at Market Basket. I went into the Rindge, New Hampshire, store just to see what it was like to be the only customer. It was creepy, and I made a quick escape, empty-handed.

On August 28, with the Red Sox eighteen and a half games out, the two Arthurs agreed to a buyout, which New Englanders celebrated as if the Red Sox had won the pennant.

A few days later, I went back to the Rindge store, where my friend Vernon greeted me. He and the other "Associates," as Market Basket employees are called, were busy restocking shelves, and they were smiling. I took my time and bought a few items. It felt good.

Like Market Basket, my father's mill was non-union, and that is how he wanted it. (When I was a boy, I thought "union" was a swear word.) And, also like Market Basket, employees usually stayed for a long time. I remember a Scandinavian man named "Andy." He had been with my father from the beginning, sometime around 1912.

The parallels between the Steinfield and DeMoulas family businesses are far from exact. It was widely known in Claremont that Frank and Sam didn't get along, and it seemed likely that sooner or later one brother would buy out the other. I suspect many of the employees wanted Frank to buy Sam's interest, but when the showdown came in 1955, my father's poor health prevented him from being the buyer. Our side of the family went on to other things, and my cousin eventually took over the company.

My father had no middle initial, but even so I think he and Arthur T. had a lot in common. When I was young, he would often tell me, "The most important thing in life is your good name."

# My Tall Grandson and the Question of Stature

My Uncle Bill was five two, my father was five four, and I used to claim I was five eight. That was not true. Maybe five seven and a half if I stretched, but I wanted to make the basketball team and five eight sounded better. Now, the shrinking that comes with age has brought me somewhat closer to the ground, and it feels like I'm in free fall.

No member of my family ever made it even close to six feet until a few years ago when my grandson, Jacob, crossed that mark on his way to his current six feet three inches. I wish my mother had lived to see this. For her, being tall was a virtue.

I recently read that out of the thousands of players who have made it to the National Basketball Association, only twenty-three were five nine or shorter, and many of those didn't last long. My favorite is Muggsy Bogues who, at five three is the shortest of them all, and the only one named "Muggsy." He played in the NBA for fifteen years, mostly for the Charlotte Hornets, and could have fit perfectly between my Uncle Bill and my father. In his rookie year he had a teammate named Manute Bol who, at seven feet seven inches, was the tallest player in NBA history, and the only one named "Manute."

I won't mention Eddie Gaedel who, in 1951, played for about a minute in one major league baseball game for the Cleveland Indians. He was a three-foot seven-inch dwarf, and he made one appearance at the plate. To no one's surprise, he walked on four straight pitches. The reason I won't mention him is that Indians owner Bill Veeck used him as a publicity stunt, thereby creating a footnote in baseball history but doing no service to short people. One of my purposes here is to praise short people whose success was due to pluck and skill and determination, not because of their size but despite it.

I recently asked a very tall person whether there was any disadvantage to height. "Yes," he told me, "when you're on an airplane." Other than that, he couldn't think of anything. Since even I feel squeezed in coach these days, imagine how it must be for him.

At six two, George Washington was usually the tallest person in the room, including the convention hall, unless Thomas Jefferson was there, in which case it was a tie. But you did not have to be tall to be a Founding Father. Alexander Hamilton was five seven, and my personal favorite, James

Madison, was five four, just like Napoleon and my own father.

We can all learn from the Bogueses, the Madisons, and the Frank Steinfields of this world. They accomplished a lot. Bogues had a distinguished basketball career and wrote a book about his life called *In the Land of Giants*. Madison wrote the United States Constitution and became our fourth president. Napoleon? They named an era after him.

Frank Steinfield never played basketball or achieved high office or led any military campaigns. But in my eyes, he was a great success. He created a manufacturing business in Claremont, built a reputation for honesty and integrity, and at age forty-eight became my father. I wish I had expressed my appreciation for him back then when he could have heard me. And I wish he had been younger when I was born so I could have had him longer. He was a man of stature.

Henry David Thoreau, 1856

## My Grandson's Visit and Catching Two Fish on One Hook

*Many go fishing all their lives without*
*knowing that it is not fish they are after.*

Henry David Thoreau

I don't have a lot in common with Henry David Thoreau. He "went to the woods" in order to live "deliberately." I, on the other hand, have spent most of my adult life in the city, and have lived somewhat "fortuitously."

We do share one thing, however. He enjoyed fishing, often going out on Walden Pond late in the day to fish under the moonlight and meditate about the universe. He cast his line "upward into the air, as well as downward." When a fish gave a "faint jerk" on his line, he would return from the spiritual to the natural. As he writes, "I caught two fishes as it were with one hook."

My father taught me to fish on Lake Sunapee when I was young. Long before I read *Walden*, he took me fishing in New Brunswick. I did catch some bass, but the time with my father, already in declining health, was meaningful beyond anything the lake could produce. It was my "second fish," even if I didn't know it at the time.

I haven't had very good luck fishing in Jaffrey's Gilmore Pond, but now that I have reached a certain age, the fishing license is free and good for life. So, getting skunked costs less, and I plan to get my money's worth.

In the summer of 2015, my grandson Solomon came to visit from California, and I outfitted him with a child's fishing rod. He caught a few small fish, and we had a good time. I promised him that the next time he came, we would go fishing again. When he arrived the following summer, the first thing he asked was, "When are we going fishing?"

"Tomorrow," I told him. "We'll buy some bait and then go out for the big ones."

The next morning, we went off to Pelletier's, the fish and game store in Jaffrey. I introduced Solomon, now almost seven, to Bruce the owner, and we talked about fishing. "We're going out for the big ones," my grandson told him. Two fishermen, standing nearby, asked where we planned to fish. We said Gilmore Pond, and they told us to fish early in the day or at dusk.

We left with our nightcrawlers. By now it was mid-morning, but neither of us was about to wait for dusk. When the first spot we tried didn't produce any bites, we agreed to raise the anchor and move closer to shore.

Soli was doing a pretty good job casting and waiting for Thoreau's "faint jerk" on his line when, suddenly, his rod bent over, and he started reeling. "I think you're stuck on the bottom," I said. The minute I took the rod I realized this was no bottom and handed the rod back. Several minutes later, Soli said, "Grandpa, I think I need some help." So, together, we managed to land a three-and-a-half-pound bass, eighteen inches long. "It's unbelievable," he said. As we made our way across the pond to show off the fish, Solomon said, "Grandpa, fishing is a great sport. Do they have it in the Olympics?"

My grandson's great catch is one of those rare events in life that feels each day like it just happened. I understand what Thoreau was talking about, although in my case I experienced the wonder of catching two fish on my grandson's hook.

# My Christmastime Reflections and Guardian Angels

My father died on Christmas Day, 1957. The holiday has never been the same.

This Christmas column is about reflections, not only on my father, who was drafted in World War I but never made it overseas, but on those who stood guard that we might live in a free country.

Francis Emond, now 103, was stationed on the USS Pennsylvania on Pearl Harbor Day, December 7, 1941. In a Boston Globe interview, he put it understatedly: "A lot of different things were going on." I have never met him, and the same is true of Si Spiegel, a ninety-seven-year old Jewish New Yorker recently written up in The New York Times. He was a heroic bomber pilot over Germany in World War II. After the war he became wealthy selling artificial Christmas trees.

I did know Stephen Bower Young, who was also at Pearl Harbor on "the date that will live in infamy." Like Mr. Emond, he was assigned to a battleship, the USS Oklahoma. The ship capsized after being hit by torpedoes, leaving Steve and at least a dozen others trapped in the lower compartment of turret No. 4.

Water rose around them, there was no way out, and all they could do was tap on the ceiling (formerly the floor) and pray. The next day, civilians from Ford's Island heard the tapping, cut through the exposed hull, and rescued Steve and the others. In 1991, Steve wrote a book about his experience, Trapped at Pearl Harbor: Escape from Battleship Oklahoma.

In the mid-1990s, Steve and I went to Houston along with three others and visited the Oklahoma's sister ship, the USS Texas, which is now a museum. We got permission to see the turret in the stern, where the lower handling room is identical to the Oklahoma's. For me and the others, it was an extraordinary experience. We revisited history with Steve as our guide.

Bob Dole also served our country, in his case on the ground in Italy as the leader of a platoon of mountain troops. After his recent death, I read about his heroic war service and the horrific battlefield injuries he sustained. I think of him, as I do of his fellow senator John McCain, as an exemplar of bravery, sacrifice, and patriotism. They, like Francis Emond, Si Spiegel, and Steve Young were our country's guardians.

The same is true of this year's Medal of Honor recipients, Alwyn Cashe, Christopher Celiz, and Earl Plumlee, only one of whom, Army Master Sergeant Plumlee, survived his feats of battleground bravery and lived to receive the award. I rarely use the word "awesome," but that is an appropriate word to describe what these men did, in Iraq and Afghanistan.

As we look around our country today, we see men and women serving as guardians of our freedom, and we see others who would deny us the democracy for which so many fought in wartime. Like the men I have named, the former are heroes, the latter are not.

Heroism comes in different forms. George Bailey, the fictional character played by Jimmy Stewart in the movie It's a Wonderful Life, was ineligible to serve in World War II but he was a hero. He stayed home where he led a life of sacrifice and saved a community. Every year, I watch the movie on Christmas Eve.

In a time of despair, luck shone on George Bailey in the form of a guardian angel. Of course, there is no such thing—the mind plays tricks on us—but in these troubled times we could all use one. My father, who let us have a Christmas tree when we were young—not from our coreligionist Mr. Spiegel but from the woods out back—wakes me up every Christmas morning at 6:15 a.m., the time the hospital called. He is my guardian angel.

# TRAVEL

## My Trip to Japan and Words That Have Meaning

In June of 2015 we went to Japan. Before we left, I knew the Japanese word "sayonara" ("goodbye") from a 1957 movie of that name starring Marlon Brando. During the trip I picked up a couple of expressions, *ohayo gozaimas* ("good morning") and *arigatou* ("thank you"). I've never been good with languages, and my time in Japan simply confirmed that particular deficiency.

While getting ready for our trip, I looked up the "Jews of Japan" and learned about a diplomat named Chiune Sugihara, the "Japanese Shindler." While stationed in Lithuania at the beginning of World War II, he saved thousands of Jews by issuing hand-written travel visas so that they could escape. In 1995, the government of Israel designated Mr. Sugihara as one of the "Righteous Among the Nations," the only Japanese person ever given that honor.

Many of those lucky enough to receive Sugihara's visas made their escape by way of Russia to the port of Kobe, which became a "safe haven" for thousands of Eastern European Jews. The city, which now has more than a million

Chiune Sugihara

inhabitants, is our daughter-in-law's hometown. We ended our trip there and met her parents, Tetsuo and Masako. I had planned to teach them the Yiddish word for the parents of your child's spouse—*machatunim*—but I forgot.

In 1940 and 1941, over four thousand Jews made their way to safety in Kobe. Today, there are only a handful of Jewish families but enough, it seems, to maintain a synagogue. Together with our daughter-in-law and twin grandsons, we visited Congregation Ohel Shelomoh, which is beautiful and seemingly still open for services and social activities.

That evening at dinner, I told our *machatunim* about the visit and asked if they knew any of Kobe's Jews. They did not, but when I asked about Mr. Sugihara, their eyes lit up. Tetsuo told me they venerate his memory.

I'll probably forget the few Japanese words I learned during the trip, but I will not forget Mr. Sugihara. And I won't forget the Japanese word he knew so well, "biza."[11]

---

11  Years after writing this piece, I mentioned to a friend of mine that a Japanese man saved Jews and was one of the "Righteous." No," she corrected me, "he was Chinese." I held my ground, she held hers, and it turns out we were both right. A Chinese diplomat named Ho Feng-Shan, who served as consul-general in Vienna during World War II, is credited with saving thousands of Jews and, like Mr. Sugihara, is recognized by Yad Vashem, the World Holocaust Remembrance Center in Jerusalem, as "Righteous Among the Nations." Both of these heroic Asian diplomats are mentioned in Jonathan Kaufman's excellent book, The Last Kings of Shanghai, which tells the fascinating story of two Jewish families from Baghdad, the Sassoons and the Kadoories, who arrived in Shanghai in the nineteenth century and became incredibly wealthy, not to mention influential, both there and in Hong Kong.

# My Ancestral Homelands and a Hill of Crosses

I regret that I did not ask more questions when I was young and still had grandparents with direct links to the Pale of Settlement.[12] And never more so than on our recent trip to the countries of my grandparents, Lithuania and Poland, where I was reminded of how little I know about my own heritage. Somewhere, maybe just miles from where we traveled, my grandparents on both sides were born and raised. "We're Litvaks," my father used to say.

Back then, my grandfather Steinfield's family name was "Pollack." None of his three living grandchildren, of which I am one, knows the name of their town. How embarrassing.

My Firestone grandparents were from shtetls called Dereczyn and Bobrovich, which today would be in Belarus. When I was young, I tried without success to locate them on a map. As an adult, I finally located them on a display at the Holocaust Museum in Washington. They are among the many towns destroyed by the Nazis.

My grandparents grew up in those no-longer existing towns, speaking both Russian and Yiddish, and some Polish, I believe. They had good reason to pack up and leave. Their childhood and teenage years were a time of anti-Jewish "pogroms" (rioting against Jews), so it was not a safe place. Besides, my grandfather told me he wanted to avoid serving in the Tsar's army.

I am eternally grateful that my Pollack and Firestone grandparents decided to leave. How different, and how much shorter, my life would otherwise have been. This recent trip deepened my understanding of what happened to those who lacked the wisdom, the means, or perhaps the strength, to do as they did. As my grandmother Firestone put it, "All gone."

Walking through Auschwitz-Birkenau, the Pianist and I saw thousands of shoes, eyeglasses, and other personal possessions. Most unforgettable were the large bins filled with human hair. Did some of the relatives I never knew spend their last days here? Did I see something that once belonged

---

12   Between the late eighteenth century, during the reign of Catherine the Great, and 1917, this was the area of Eastern Europe where Jews were allowed to reside, mostly in shtetls (Yiddish for "little towns"). Anatevka is the fictional shtetl in Fiddler on the Roof. The expression "beyond the pale," contrary to what I believed until writing this footnote, did not originate with the Pale of Settlement but rather is derived from the counties in Ireland over which England took control in the Middle Ages.

Auschwitz

to or was part of one of them? Probably not, and it doesn't matter. All these victims, over one million human beings killed at Auschwitz, were members of someone's family.

World War II ended a long time ago, but the German and Russian occupations have left scars that will never go away. In these Baltic countries, we met people who are determined to make future generations aware of what happened in those dark days. One such person is a ninety-two-year-old woman named Dorota, whom we met at an outdoor museum in Rumsiskes, Lithuania. When she was a teenager, the Soviet government deported her entire family to Siberia, where she lived for seventeen years before returning to her home country. She picked up her life, married a "wonderful man" (her words), and set out to create a living history of what she had experienced.

Her "museum" includes a train car like the one that took them away, and a replica of the hut in which they had been forced to live. We went inside, and she patiently explained what it was like to live in such conditions. She was one of the lucky ones. Many, including her parents, never came back.

We met others whose parents or grandparents lived under the Nazis and who themselves lived under Soviet occupation. I asked whether they

The Hill of Crosses in Lithuania

dreamed back then about becoming free. One of them said, "It never occurred to me. We thought that is how things were."

Trips are full of surprises, as I was reminded at the "Hill of Crosses" in northern Lithuania, our last stop before entering Latvia. The Soviet government repeatedly bulldozed the hill, but the crosses kept coming back. At the top of the hill, amidst over half a million crosses, I discovered a combined cross and Star of David with an inscribed apology "from Germany to the Jewish people," written in German.

# My Friend's Road Trip Idea and the Moving Needle

The other day a friend of mine called with an idea. He and his wife would like to go on a road trip with the Pianist and me. "Let's take a walking tour of Claremont," he said.

It seems they have read my reminiscences in these pages about growing up in Claremont, and "would like you to take us around so we could see the place through your eyes." It took me some time to be sure I heard that right.

My reaction, typical as the Pianist will confirm, was negative. "You want to do what?" I asked.

My friend repeated the idea and mentioned something about seeing my father's factory, the "shoddy mill" in Lower Village. I said it was an old building even when I was young and today, while it still stands, has not improved with age. It's not much to look at.

As for Claremont, I added, "It's not really a walking place," thinking but not saying "unless you want to walk past a bunch of boarded-up storefronts."

Later the same day, another friend sent me an e-mail with a link to a lecture by a retired University of New Hampshire professor named John C. Porter. So, I watched "The History of Agriculture as Told by Barns," which includes photos of barns from all over New Hampshire. Towards the end of the documentary appears a barn in Claremont, no address provided. I took a screen shot, so we can go looking for it if we ever get around to taking this road trip.

We have a friend in Keene who owns a hydroelectric power plant in Claremont located near what was my father's mill, alongside the Sugar River. If we schedule this trip on a date when he will be in town, we can ask him to show us the plant and explain how it works. When that thought came to mind, my negativity needle started moving towards positive.

What else? I suppose we could visit my boyhood home. Its address used to be "Edgewood," but now it's on Foster Place. I haven't lived there since I went off to college, but I remember my mother's words—"five bedrooms, five bathrooms, and five fireplaces." I stopped by several years ago, and the owner asked whether I would like to buy it.

I'm running out of ideas, but here's one more—the Temple Meyer-David Cemetery, on the road to West Claremont. I was there in May 2021 on my way to the West Claremont Burial Ground for the graveside funeral service of Albie Leahy, who, like his father, served for many years as the local judge. That cemetery is located next to Old St. Mary's Church, built in 1823. I didn't even know it existed when I was young, but it is an impressive two-story brick building that happens to be the oldest Roman Catholic Church in New Hampshire.

Hmm. The needle just moved again.

From there we could drive over to Claremont Junction, which is the only station in New Hampshire (platform only, no building) where you can board (or get off) the Amtrak *Vermonter*. My friend is a train buff.

The Pianist says we should show our friends the Opera House, which is connected to City Hall. I like that idea, and not just because she has given several concerts there. It was in that very space that I entered a pie-eating contest when I was nine, went home with my clothes covered with blueberry stains, and had to explain to my mother that I didn't win.

You can walk a short distance from the Opera House to the Civil War monument on Broad Street. They held Friday night concerts at the bandstand, and my Uncle Billy played the trumpet.

# My Rosebud Visit and Keeping a Promise

Like most kids growing up in the 1940s and 1950s, I played cowboys and Indians after school, listened to *The Lone Ranger* on the radio, and paid twelve cents for a Saturday afternoon movie ticket to watch him and his sidekick, Tonto. To this day, I can hear the opening cry "Hi-Yo Silver, Away!" and the words "kemo sabe" (faithful friend), which is how Tonto addressed the masked man.

I vaguely knew that New Hampshire had Indians, and that the name of the lake where we had a cottage, Sunapee, comes from an Algonquin word.[13] I did not know much about our country's broken promises—they were not part of the school curriculum.

My boyhood introduction to the language of sports also had an Indian connection. In 1948, when my lifelong addiction to baseball (now being tested)[14] began, "my team" was the Boston Braves. They lost the World Series to the Cleveland Indians, a defeat that still stings.

I never questioned the use of Native American names by professional sports teams. The Boston (now "New England") Patriots did not exist, but the Washington's Redskins, quarterbacked by Sammy Baugh, did. Like many Jewish kids, I believed that Chicago Bears quarterback Sid Luckman was as good as "Slingin' Sammy."

My first real connection to American Indians came in 2003. As part of a lawyers' group, I traveled to South Dakota, where I spent an afternoon at the Crazy Horse Memorial in the Black Hills. That monument remains unfinished to this day, more than eighty years after Lakota Chief Henry Standing Bear invited a Boston sculptor named Korczak Ziolkowski to come out there with a hammer and chisel.[15] His widow, Ruth, gave us a guided tour.

---

13   When the Pianist and I bought a house in Jaffrey, New Hampshire, in 1986, I looked up the word "Monadnock," the name of the mountain that overlooks our pond and learned that it comes from the Abenaki language.

14   The 2020 baseball season tested my loyalty not only because the Red Sox traded Mookie Betts, and not only because they were a terrible team, but also because somehow, in that pandemic-shortened and fan-less season, the game no longer seemed important. I assume I will get over it.

15   Ziolkowski was a graduate of Rindge Technical School, now called Cambridge Rindge and Latin School, whose alumni also include basketball star Patrick Ewing and actors Ben Affleck and Matt Damon. He had worked on Mount Rushmore during the 1930s, and his sculpture of Paderewski won first prize at the 1939 New York World's Fair.

The next day we took a long bus ride from Rapid City to the Rosebud Reservation in Mission, South Dakota, stopping off on the way at Pine Ridge. Rosebud takes up much of Todd County which, both then and now, is one of the poorest counties in the United States. The Reservation had an unemployment rate of around 75 percent and was afflicted by practically every social problem you can think of, domestic abuse and alcoholism to name just two. Even so, our hosts, one of whom told me that they call themselves "Indians" not "Native Americans," gave no indication that they despaired for the future. But they didn't smile a lot.[16]

A welcoming committee took us around to meet people and visit homes, the school, the tribal court, and Sinte Gleska University, a tribal land grant university founded in 1971. And they treated us to a lunch of Native American food. It was not the tastiest meal we had in South Dakota, but it was heartfelt and hearty, and the after-lunch Lakota songs touched our

---

16  The purpose of our mission to Rosebud was to present a grant from the American College of Trial Lawyers to an organization named "Dakota Plains Legal Services."

The Crazy Horse memorial

hearts, even if we did not understand the words.

These and other memories of that trip came to mind last month when Indians won two victories, one symbolic and the other substantive.

The symbolic one was sports related: The Washington Redskins are no more.[17] Not earth-shattering, perhaps, but despite Shakespeare ("What's in a name?"), a sensitive decision.

The win of substance came from the Supreme Court. The Court ruled that much of Eastern Oklahoma belongs to the Creek Nation. That was the deal Congress made nearly two hundred years ago when it forced more than 100,000 Indians from their ancestral land in Georgia and Alabama. According to Justice Neil Gorsuch's majority opinion, "On the far end of the Trail of Tears was a promise."[18]

---

17    And neither, as of late 2020, are the Cleveland Indians.

18    Late 2020 brought a significant political appointment. President-Elect Biden announced that he would appoint Congresswoman Deb Haaland of New Mexico as Secretary of the Interior. She is a member of the Laguna Pueblo people (population around 7700) and previously served as Chair of the New Mexico Democratic Party and as a tribal leader on the issue of economic development for the Laguna. The Senate confirmed her appointment on March 15, 2021, by a vote of 51 to 40. Four Republican senators—Collins (Maine), Graham (South Carolina), Murkowski (Alaska), and Sullivan (Alaska) voted to Confirm. Senator Romney (Utah) voted "nay."

# My Wandering Trip Mate and the Special Cream Cakes

On our trip to Croatia, I became friendly with a man who makes his own fishing rods. Along with our wives and eleven other members of the tour group, we spent two weeks exploring part of what used to be Yugoslavia.

One evening in Zagreb, a few of us met with the trip leader to talk about the trip and offer constructive suggestions. My fisherman friend complained that the travel company had not told him to bring a compass or provided better maps of the cities. He said something about getting lost earlier in the day. I heard what he said but, as it turned out, I had not listened closely enough.

The next day, on our way to Split, we visited a small town called Samobor. Upon arrival, the local guide told us we could go on a hike with her and then enjoy the cream cake (a "Samoborska kremšnita") for which the town is known.

"If anyone prefers not to take the hike," she said, "we will meet here, at the fountain in the central square, at four o'clock," which was about an hour later. Then she said, "It's a very small town. It's impossible to get lost." Then, little did she know, she added, "Famous last words."

We embarked on our uphill hike, my friend and I bringing up the rear and

Samoborska kremšnita

talking about fishing. Within a few minutes, he became somewhat red-faced and said, "I don't think I'll do the hike. I'm going back."

"Good idea," I said, not thinking about the conversation of the day before with our trip leader . I continued with the group on what turned out to be a pretty steep incline and thought to myself, maybe I should have gone with him.

We completed the hike, returned to the main street, and walked a few meters beyond the fountain. There we installed ourselves at tables outside the restaurant, where we ordered the special cream cakes and caught our breaths. It was a few minutes after four.

My friend was nowhere to be seen. Others, including his wife, noticed his absence, and for the next forty-five minutes our collective emotions turned from concern to worry to dread. The trip leader and the local guide went looking, and the local police were alerted.

A waiter brought us the cream cakes—a puff pastry with custard cream filling and powdered sugar on top. Despite the hike, no one seemed to have much of an appetite.

I joined the search and came back to the fountain around 4:45 p.m. Our trip leader was waving at me with a smile on her face. A local woman had found our missing member wandering outside the town, and she gave him a ride.

Our relief was palpable, as was my friend's embarrassment. "I must have walked five miles," he told me. "Now I've ruined everyone's trip."

"No, you haven't," I told him. "I should have paid more attention to what you said yesterday about maps and a compass."

"I guess I have a problem," he said, tears forming in his eyes.

"Maybe so," I said, "but now it's time to enjoy your special cream cake. You've earned it."

## My Drop-In Visit and the Unlikely Professor

When we take a trip to another country, we enjoy seeing the sights and eating the local food, but we especially like meeting the people who live there. It gives you a better sense of the place than the guidebooks. We may not speak their language, but fortunately many of them speak ours.

Before this year, our most recent trips were to Russia, where I taught law and the Pianist performed. In May of 2014, we spent two weeks as tourists in Croatia, Montenegro, Bosnia and Herzegovina, and Slovenia, all parts of the former Yugoslavia. The sights were spectacular, and the food was very good.

And we did get to meet local people, including a middle-aged widow and her daughter who welcomed us to her home in Sarajevo for dinner. It was a memorable evening, filled with conversation about what happened in the 1990s in that war-stricken country, and what it was like to live through the Siege of Sarajevo. In Croatia we spent a morning at our trip leader's family's farm, complete with home-cooked food and an impromptu flute concert.

We ended our trip in Ljubljana, Slovenia. I knew I liked the city as soon as I saw that much of it is car-free, and its principal square is named after a poet.

Lubljana Old Town

I decided to look for the local law school, thinking that perhaps we could find out about teaching there at some future time. With the help of two young musicians whom the Pianist spotted, we found our way and entered the building. The dean's office was dark, and the door was locked.

We walked down a hallway and saw an office with the light on behind a closed door. I knocked,

Danilo Türk

and a tall, handsome man opened the door. We introduced ourselves, and he did the same. "I am Professor Danilo Türk."

"Happy to meet you, Danilo," I said.

He invited us to sit down, and we had a good conversation. He specializes in international law, he told us, but he was somewhat vague about just what he did and what programs the law school offered. I asked whether visiting American lawyers came to the school, and he wasn't sure. "I don't spend too much time here," he offered.

*Odd*, I thought, especially for someone whose office is the nicest professor's office I have ever seen. "Let's see if we can find the dean," he suggested.

We walked back down the hallway, and Danilo took out a key and opened the dean's door. We stepped inside and found an assistant in an inner office. Danilo spoke to her, in Slovenian I assume, and she printed out a piece of paper providing the dean's contact information. Then the Pianist and I returned to Danilo's office, where we continued the conversation.

By now we had spent nearly a half hour with this very gracious Slovenian law professor, and I apologized for taking up so much of his time. As we stood up to leave, I thanked him and added, "Danilo, I think there is more to you than you have told us."

He smiled and replied, "I'm on the Internet."

We returned to our hotel thinking how nice it is to meet local people, and I went directly to Wikipedia. My suspicions were correct. In 1992, Danilo Türk became Slovenia's first representative to the United Nations, where he went on to become president of the Security Council. Then he returned to Slovenia and served as its president from 2007 to 2012.[19]

---

19   I spent two weeks teaching at the University of Ljubljana in 2016, but Danilo Türk was out of the country at the time. That year, he was an unsuccessful candidate for the position of United Nations Secretary-General. He later became a visiting professor at Columbia Law School in New York. He founded the Danilo Türk Foundation, which is devoted to the rehabilitation of child victims of armed conflict, and he is chairman of the Global Fairness Initiative, a Washington organization that helps developing nations. In 2019 he became president of the Club de Madrid, a forum of former presidents and prime ministers who seek to promote democracy around the world.

# My Iceland Trip and Touching Her Leg

Jessica Kensky grew up in California, got a nursing degree, and went on to become an oncology nurse at Massachusetts General Hospital. Patrick Downes grew up in Cambridge, attended Boston College High and then Boston College, making him a "Double Eagle." When he was a boy in Cambridge, one of his Little League teammates was the son of a Boston lawyer named Rob Barber.

On April 15, 2013, the day of the Boston Marathon bombing, Jessie and Patrick were newlyweds.

Rob Barber became our ambassador to Iceland in 2014, and in 2016 he invited the Pianist to give a recital at his official residence. We flew from Boston to the Keflavik airport, where our American-Icelandic granddaughter picked us up.

One day, I got a tour of the Reykjavik courthouse with Judge Skúli Magnússon as our guide. It was Ambassador Barber who got the tour invitation, and he invited me to tag along. Skúli (everyone in Iceland uses first names) introduced us to the chief justice, and the four of us had coffee and an Icelandic delicacy that looks like a pancake. I have been in a lot of American courthouses, but no judge ever served me treats.

From the courthouse we went to an open house at a building called "Ocean Cluster" which houses several companies that turn fish byproducts into something good for you, instead of throwing them away. The developer, Thor Sigfusson, looks like a movie star and is tall, even for Iceland. Thor has created a clone of his innovative project, called the "New England Ocean Cluster," in Portland, Maine.

Meeting such people as Skúli and Thor shows how useful it is to know an ambassador. But not even those tall, hospitable people with interesting Icelandic names compare to Patrick and Jessica, the young couple mentioned at the beginning of this article. They were visiting Iceland as Ambassador Barber's guests, and we met them at the Pianist's recital, along with various ambassadors and other dignitaries and friends.

Rob invited us, along with Jessica, Patrick, and a man named Greipur to stay for dinner after the concert. The six of us sat around the dining room table set with beautiful china and silver, attended by the chef and his

Rob, Jesse, and Patrick

assistant. What a meal—two kinds of soup, lamb, mushrooms foraged by the chef, and reindeer!

The people we met in Iceland were interesting, but the time we spent with Patrick and Jessica was *memorable*. They each lost a leg on April 15, 2013, Marathon Day, and eventually Jessica lost her other leg. They were in Iceland to visit Össur, the company that manufactured their prosthetic legs.

Before dinner we had drinks and hors d'oeuvres in the ambassador's living room. Much of the conversation was about what Patrick and Jessica have been through—two years of surgeries, rehab, and learning how to walk, even dance.[20]

---

20  Jessie had many setbacks after our evening at the ambassador's residence, including nearly three years at Walter Reed Hospital in Maryland. She was eventually able to return to her job as a nurse at Massachusetts General Hospital and is pursuing a doctorate in nursing practice. On April 18, 2016, Patrick became the first marathon bombing amputee to finish the Boston

At some point I turned to Jessica: "May I touch it?" I asked.

"Sure," she said.

So, I reached over and touched her leg.

"Would you like to hold it?" she asked me.

Who could resist such an offer? "Yes," I said.

Before I could blink an eye, Jessica took off a leg and handed it to me. While I held it, two thoughts came to my mind. One was that that modern prosthesis technology is quite remarkable. The other was that this cheerful young couple is unbelievably brave and resilient.

With Jessica's permission, I handed the leg around the room. When it reached the Pianist, she looked at the shoe and said "Blahniks?" referring to a maker of expensive women's shoes.[21]

"No," Jessica replied. "Knock-offs."

---

Marathon. He finished in a time of 5:56:46, and Jessica greeted him at the finish line. They have written a children's book, Rescue and Jessica: A Life-Changing Friendship. The "Rescue" in the title of the book is a black Labrador service dog.

In 2018, Senator Elizabeth Warren (D-MA) sponsored the "Jessica Kensky and Patrick Downes Act," a federal law that provides treatment at military facilities for survivors of domestic terrorism.

21   Just out of curiosity I checked out the prices. Blahnik shoes start at over $500, and a pair of alligator boots sells for $14,000.

# My Portugal Trip and the Cab I Took Twice

Last month, the Pianist and I went to Portugal. Her job was to give a recital at the American ambassador's residence. My job was to keep track of our passports.

We arrived on a Monday and left on Friday, but thanks to a local guide we crammed a lot of sightseeing into our short stay. After lunch on Thursday, the Pianist went off to prepare for the recital, and I decided to wander around on my own. I left our B & B and walked up the hill and down the other side, where I found myself in front of the Basilica Estrela. After a look inside, I decided to return to Camões Square, where we had been the day before.

I hopped into a cab and told the driver where I was going. The driver nodded and asked me if I liked Edvard Grieg, the Norwegian composer. I said I thought I did, and he pointed to the car's CD player and informed me that we were listening to Grieg's *Piano Concerto*. I knew right away that this was not just any driver, and I told him my wife was giving a piano recital that evening.

The music changed, and the driver said, "That's Massenet. Do you like him?" I told him the name sounded familiar, but he didn't seem convinced.

Luís Vaz de Camões, Lisbon (1524-1580)

As we neared the Houses of Parliament, the driver pointed to his left and told me that António Salazar, the dictator of Portugal for over thirty years, had lived there. I asked what he thought of Salazar, and he said, "The same as I think about Hitler and Mussolini."

As we approached the square, he asked if I knew who Camões was. Thanks to the guide from the day before, I knew the answer. "A poet," I said.

The driver nodded. "I always ask that question, and you're only the second or third American who has known." Fortunately, he did not ask me when I learned about Camões, whether I liked his poetry, or what century he lived in.[22]

That evening, I told the Pianist about my music-loving driver and said that I wished she had been with me. "Grieg only wrote one piano concerto," she informed me. "It's in A minor."

Friday morning, I made sure the passports were where I had left them, we packed up, and the lady at the B & B called a taxi to take us to the airport. "I gave them your name," she said.

We walked outside, and a cab pulled up right away. The driver loaded our bags, we got into the car, and just then another cab came along going the other way. The driver motioned to our driver, they rolled down their windows, and the second driver said, "Mr. Steinfield?"

We were in the wrong cab.

So, we removed our luggage and told the first driver, who was not happy about this lost fare, that we were sorry. We managed to hold up several cars while we put our luggage and ourselves into the right cab.

I told the driver where we were going. He looked in his rear-view mirror and asked, "How was the concert?" It took me a minute to realize that it was my music-loving driver from the day before. I introduced him to the Pianist.

She told him she had heard about his love of music. For the next half hour, they talked about classical music, while I listened to replays of Grieg and Massenet.

As we passed where Salazar had lived, I interrupted and mentioned what he had said the day before about Salazar, Hitler, and Mussolini. He then added Francisco Franco's name to the list, thereby converting the trio of dictators into a quartet.

---

22  Luís Vaz de Camões (1524–1580) is considered Portugal's greatest poet.

# My Connecting Flight and Making a Claim

The year 2016 has been a busy one for travel. When we checked in Friday night at Logan Airport, I told the ticket agent we were connecting the next day from Paris to Ljubljana, Slovenia. She studied her computer for quite a while and then told us that there is no such thing as an Air France connection to Ljubljana on Saturday. "You're on the Sunday flight," she told me.

"That's not right," I said. "We're on tomorrow's connecting flight. I booked it through Citibank Travel Service." She repeated herself: "There is no such flight."

While waiting to board the plane, I showed off my smartphone skills by reserving a room at the Airport Marriott in Paris. That was the easy part. Have you ever tried to find the hotel shuttle at Charles de Gaulle Airport? Apparently, there is a French rule against signs, so we wandered from one person to the next, asking "Où est shuttle?" and getting a French shrug in return.

We eventually made our way to the town of Roissy, which is where the airport hotels are located. We checked in, ate at the hotel restaurant, and agreed that the cost of this unexpected layover was not going to be on us.

Two weeks later, the return flight from Slovenia left late, due to unexplained "technical difficulties." We made our connection in Paris, barely, and ended up at Heathrow Airport in London, the world's busiest airport. By that point we were traveling light since our checked bags (containing a fresh loaf of Slovenian bread) didn't make the connection. It was just as well since we had to go through customs, and Heathrow has the world's longest passport lines. Once again there were no airport shuttle signs, this time because there is no hotel shuttle service at Heathrow.

The next day we made it to Boston, and eventually our luggage showed up after a stopover in Detroit. Customs left a note that they had opened my bag, but they did not confiscate the bread.

A few days later, I called Citi Travel to see about reimbursement for our unscheduled hotel stay. The "concierge" was very cordial and asked me to send a copy of the hotel bill, which I did. A few days later, she informed me that it was up to Air France to notify us when they terminated Saturday service from Paris to Ljubljana.

I then entered the bottomless pit that is Air France "Customer Care." It turns out you cannot complain to a person, you have no choice but to go online and fill out a form. I became "Case number 19539057."

Weeks passed, and then an e-mail arrived telling me that just because the airline issues a ticket doesn't mean that they make any promises. Funny, I thought it did. Besides, the e-mail went on, the schedule change took place before departure (when else could it take place?), so the travel agency should have let me know. The Air France e-mail concluded, "I know that's not the answer you were hoping for."

By that point I should have known better, but I called the travel agency again and went straight to the supervisor. When I told her what Air France had said, she had a simple response: "They're wrong." And of course, I knew she was right.

I then wrote to Air France "Customer Care" and suggested that they change their name to "Do Not Care About Customer." I never heard back.

# My Iceland Students and the Answers They Gave

I just got back from Reykjavik, where I spent a week in March 2019 teaching the American legal system and American Constitutional Law at the University of Iceland. My thirty-three students were mostly Icelandic, but several were from other countries, including Switzerland, Poland, Belgium, Norway, and France. Fortunately for me, they were all interested in American law and they all spoke English.

The first case I taught was *Dred Scott v. Sandford*, the 1857 decision in which the Supreme Court ruled that Scott could not seek his freedom in federal court because neither he nor any other slave or descendants of slaves qualified as a "citizen."[23] Abraham Lincoln called the decision an "astonisher," and it is widely regarded as the worst decision in the history of the Supreme Court.

My course was for credit, meaning that after sitting through twelve lectures, the students had to take an exam. One of the exam questions asked the students to identify the Supreme Court case they considered most interesting and to explain why.

Several students wrote about Dred Scott, whom they saw not just as a party in a lawsuit but as a human being. One wrote that she could not "imagine that the right of being a citizen could be doubted because of his skin color." "It's strange," she continued, "that before I took this class I had never heard of this case before! And now, for four whole days, I can't think of anything

Dred Scott

23   Article II, Section 2, of the Constitution allows federal courts to hear "controversies" between citizens of different states.

else." Another student was puzzled by "how vitriolic the mindset of the legal system must have been at the time." Yet, noted another, the case shows that "leaving aside the notion of one being able to own another person, through the bad or wrong decisions the rule of law can progress." A student said she was "glad to hear that it is 'the worst case' in America."

*Brown v. Board of Education*, the 1954 school desegregation case, was also a popular choice. "I love that case," a student wrote. "I found it really interesting that the same body that created the Fourteenth Amendment, overruling *Dred Scott*, then also made law to separate people by color [in schools]." Another student was struck by "how legal 'facts' are in essence sensitive to the moral and social practices of the times," and by the "vivid contrast between originalist interpretation in constitutional law and the 'living document' approach."

Several students picked the Court's free speech cases. A French student was "very surprised, in a good way, by the decision to consider burning a flag being a form of speech." Another student thought it was "really smart" of the Court in *New York Times v. Sullivan* to create "a dichotomy between public figures and private ones" in defamation cases. The *Citizens United* decision did not come off so well. "I think there should be a 'cap' on donations," wrote an Icelandic student. "I look forward to watching if it will be overruled in the future." A student majoring in both political science and law" was "shocked, amazed, angry, sad and more to see how much money rules politics."

Our class spent considerable time discussing human rights decisions. "The right to marry whomever you love has always hit home," one of my Icelandic students wrote, adding that she "never in a million years expected the outcome of the *Obergefell* case." "I don't think I will ever forget the day your fine country finally put everyone on an equal footing with regards to marriage." Although one student was impressed by Chief Justice John Roberts's view that the gay marriage issue should be decided by the people, not by the Court, he "couldn't help but be mesmerized with Justice Anthony Kennedy's words on the importance of marriage in society."

My hours in the classroom and reading the students' exam answers were pure pleasure. As usual, I learned more than I taught.

# BEING JEWISH

## My Boyhood Shul and the Sadness We Share

I loved the 2018 Red Sox. With the team leading the World Series against the Dodgers, two games to one, I was looking forward to the fourth and fifth games on Saturday and Sunday, October 27 and 28. Then, that Saturday morning, a man killed eleven men and women in a synagogue in Pittsburgh. Suddenly, baseball did not seem important.

I thought back to my childhood days in Claremont. Until I was nine, we had no rabbi, but we did have a shul, the Yiddish word that many Jews use instead of "synagogue" or "temple." The word has a homelike sound to it, and in postwar Claremont it really was *hamish* (the Yiddish word for homelike) because the shul was a room in Mr. Blumberg's house on Central Avenue. He was a *shochet* (kosher butcher), and he was also a *hakham* (learned man) who conducted the services.[24]

In 1948, the Jews of Claremont purchased an old building on Putnam Street and turned it into "Temple Meyer-David," named for Second Lieutenant Meyer Satzow and Private First-Class David Blumberg, Mr. Blumberg's son, the two Jewish boys from Claremont who died in Europe during World War II.

At the same time the Jews of Claremont acquired a building, they hired their first rabbi, a Holocaust survivor from Hungary named Michael Szenes. He was tall, handsome, soft-spoken, learned, and kind. Being in his presence was and remains one of the privileges of my life.

Until it became a Sabbath unlike any other, October 27, 2018, was a typical Sabbath at Pittsburgh's *L'Simcha* ("Tree of Life") synagogue. Then a gunman shouting anti-Semitic threats entered that house of worship and violated the Sixth Commandment when he opened fire on innocent men

---

24  Although ordinarily the rabbi leads Jewish services, the religion doesn't require it. All you need is a minyan, meaning that nine rabbis won't suffice but ten adult cobblers will.

and women who had gathered to observe the Fourth Commandment to honor and observe the Sabbath.

My first thought when I heard the news on the radio was, "Not again." My second thought was to recall what a Japanese woman told me a few years ago when we visited Japan and I asked her whether she would like to live in the United States. "No," she said, "It isn't safe there."

It is ironic that that these murders happened in a synagogue during a bris, the traditional Jewish ceremony of circumcision and naming, held on the eighth day of a baby boy's life. It is a joyous occasion when parents, grandparents, family members, and close friends celebrate the gift of life.

According to Scripture, whoever destroys a single life is considered to have destroyed the whole world. But Scripture also tells us that to save a life, as did first responders in Pittsburgh, is like saving the entire world.

The Red Sox won those two games, but I didn't watch very much, and I was not as joyful as I would have wished. A person has only so much room for emotions, and my feelings of sorrow over what happened in Pittsburgh took up most of my space.

On November 9, 1938, Nazis throughout Germany burned synagogues, killed Jews, and wreaked havoc. Broken glass littered the streets, which is why it is called Kristallnacht, the Night of Broken Glass. That night is considered by some as the beginning of the Holocaust, the darkest time in human history.

Last Thursday, I attended the annual commemoration of Kristallnacht at the Colonial Theatre in Keene. This gathering of over a thousand people occurred just days after two mass killings in our country. The theatre was full, as people of all races, ethnicities, and religions gathered to remember and to mourn.

# My Coming of Age and the Importance of Ten

My grandson, Solomon, was born in 2009. In 2022, at age thirteen, he will stand in front of family and friends and celebrate his bar mitzvah. Those Aramaic words mean "Son of the Commandment," and they mark the passage from childhood to adulthood—if not in society in general, at least within the Jewish community. It is an important milestone, and with it comes both responsibility and status. Thereafter, my grandson will qualify to be part of a minyan, the quota of ten Jewish adults necessary to hold a prayer service.[25]

This is no small matter. I remember how proud my father was when I reached that stage in life. Every year he would say prayers on the anniversaries of his parents' deaths (called yahrzeit, a Yiddish word meaning "anniversary"), and he would take me to Temple Meyer-David to be part of the minyan. I'm sure I didn't want to interrupt my more important activities to stand around while old men said Hebrew prayers. The foolishness of youth did not pass me by, apparently, despite my "adult" status.

I now look back on the time between my bar mitzvah and my father's death just a few years later with a mixture of longing and regret. I wish I had known enough to say, "Dad, it is a privilege to be part of this minyan." Instead, I must be content with knowing he was proud of me, that my being there was meaningful to him.

Today, in Claremont, I'm not sure it is possible to raise a minyan, as the saying goes. I was in Claremont last fall on a Saturday, the Jewish Sabbath. The front door of Temple Meyer-David was locked.[26]

These thoughts came to me recently while reading the paper on my way to see my grandson in California. The article described a Holocaust survivor's funeral in Israel, where there is no shortage of Jews. Even so, the family of Nate Remer was worried that they wouldn't have a minyan, so they

---

25  During the 2020 coronavirus pandemic, several governors restricted the number of people who could gather in a church or synagogue. On November 25, 2020, the Supreme Court ruled that limits imposed by New York governor Andrew Cuomo were overly broad and therefore infringed on religious freedom. In his opinion, Justice Gorsuch reflected on the impact of limiting houses of worship to only ten people: "In the Orthodox Jewish community that limit might operate to exclude all women, considering ten men are necessary to establish a minyan, or a quorum."

26  It did not occur to me during that visit that a few years later the situation would go from bad to worse.

posted a notice on Facebook. Old ways have a way of merging with modern technology.

Over 150 people saw the notice and came to the Mount of Rest, the largest cemetery in Jerusalem, to mourn the death of someone they had never met. The New York Times reported that one mourner, a young American woman from Memphis spending a year in Israel before entering college, was part of the minyan. "I just want to be here," she said, adding that her own grandfather was a Holocaust survivor. Another woman who answered the Facebook call said, "It's a Jewish thing, you know."

I'm looking forward to Solomon's bar mitzvah. I will be there, part of his minyan. And when my day of rest comes (mind you I am in no great hurry), he will be part of mine.

# A New Year Arrives and a Temple Dies

Starting at sunset on September 18, 2020, Jews around the world and in New Hampshire welcomed the Jewish New Year 5781. Services were held that evening, and they were real even though they were virtual. Then came the news that Ruth Bader Ginsburg, our esteemed Supreme Court Justice and fellow Jew, had died. A light had been extinguished.

Every year at this time, I think back to my days growing up Jewish in Claremont. My grandfather, Maurice Firestone, and my father, Frank Steinfield, were two of many who spearheaded the purchase and conversion of an old school on Putnam Street into Temple Meyer-David.

Having a real synagogue in Claremont represented a milestone for at least two reasons. It was a living statement that the Jewish population was large enough to support its own religious home. And it served as a symbolic message that, in the shadow of the Holocaust, this small, overwhelmingly Christian, New Hampshire community was a place where Jews could live, worship, and be safe.

Several years after the temple on Putnam Street was established, my grandfather decided that we should have our own cemetery. Members of the congregation put up the funds to purchase land on North Street, and Temple Meyer-David Cemetery, where all gravestones are the same size, was born. My father chose the plot nearest the entrance.

Rabbi Michael Szenes was with us only a few years. By the time of my bar mitzvah in 1952, he had moved on to Temple Beth Jacob in Concord, and he later became the rabbi at Temple Gates of Heaven in Schenectady, New York, where he served for twenty-five years.[27] He was long retired, and in well into his eighties, when I called him in 1998 and asked him to officiate at my mother's funeral. The next morning, he came from Schenectady to Boston for the funeral, and then continued to Claremont for her burial. That is the last time I saw Rabbi Szenes, who died in 2010 at ninety-three.

Over the years, the Jewish population of Claremont kept shrinking, to

---

27  Rabbi Szenes's successor was a man named Moshe Maggal, also a Hungarian refugee. He chastised me for looking at my new watch while he was giving my bar mitzvah benediction. Rabbi Maggal married Rachel Diamond from Claremont and went on to considerable success, which included serving as an advisor to Cecil B. DeMille during the filming of The Ten Commandments. His last congregation was in Las Vegas, where he died in 1994.

Rabbi Michael Szenes

the point where only a few families remained. Even so, the Temple survived, albeit on a much-reduced scale, with no rabbi. Arnie Cover, married to Donna Diamond from Claremont (Rabbi Maggal's niece) and, like Mr. Blumberg, a learned layman, came from Massachusetts to officiate at monthly Friday night services.

Mr. Cover died earlier this year, and then, on September 13, 2020, the small Temple Meyer-David congregation made the fateful decision to bring my boyhood temple, tangible evidence of a Jewish presence in Claremont, to an end.

What is there to say when a synagogue dies? What will become of the Memorial Scrolls, which include the names of my family members and many others who, like my grandparents, were immigrants from Eastern Europe? And what of the cemetery where they are buried? Who will maintain it? I don't have the answers, and I can't think of words to comfort myself.

This is a time of national mourning. Justice Ginsburg is dead; and so are George Floyd and Breonna Taylor. Covid-19 has taken over 200,000 lives. I do not compare the closing, I hesitate to use the word liquidation, of Temple Meyer-David to these losses, but for the Jews of Claremont, past and present, the loss of that eternal light on Putnam Street is an occasion of incalculable sadness.

# My Jewish Holidays and the Survival of Faith

The Jewish High Holidays are based on the Hebrew calendar. What this means is that you never know from one year to the next when the Jewish New Year (Rosh Hashanah) and the Day of Atonement (Yom Kippur) will arrive. This year, the Hebrew New Year 5780 began at sundown on September 29, 2019. Ten days later, beginning at sundown on October 8, Jews observed Yom Kippur and atoned for their transgressions during the past year.

Starting in 1948, when I was nine, I attended Hebrew School in Claremont at Temple Meyer-David, which—like the State of Israel—was born that year. I didn't like being cooped up in a basement classroom learning how to pronounce Hebrew words and read from right to left, but it wasn't optional. I had to get ready for my bar mitzvah, a Jewish boy's coming of age, four years later. My ten-year-old grandson is now in the same situation, but unlike me he actually likes it, at least so long as it doesn't interfere with playing soccer.

My family was not Orthodox, and we were not weekly temple-goers. But on the High Holidays we always went to shul, which means "school" in Yiddish. [28]

One of my clear memories from those days is hearing the shofar, which is the Hebrew word for a ram's horn used as a musical instrument, a trumpet of sorts. It is an important Jewish symbol, calling up the Biblical story of how Abraham found a ram stuck in a bush, which he sacrificed in place of his son, Jacob.

I tried my luck at blowing the shofar when I was a boy, with limited success. When the Pianist and I were in Safed, Israel in 1986, we came upon a street vendor selling shofars—small, medium, and large. When I declined his offer to "try it," the Pianist immediately accepted, picked up the small one, and out came a full blast, which became even fuller when she picked up the larger ones. "She's a musician," the vendor said.

I read an article recently about a man named Chaskel Tydor, who was a prisoner at Auschwitz during the Holocaust. The Nazis assigned him to dispatch work details, and on Rosh Hashanah 1944 he devised a plan to

---

28  Disclosure: My grandparents and my father spoke Yiddish, and I managed to pick up a few words. Thanks to my grandson, I have learned quite a few more in recent years (you will learn how this came about in a few pages).

A shofar

send fellow prisoners far enough away from the camp so they could observe
the holiday and pray. What he did not know was that one of them took a
hidden shofar with him. Imagine the risk of having such a possession in
a concentration camp, not to mention blowing it. If you have ever heard
someone blow the shofar, you know that it cannot be done softly.

Mr. Tydor survived, and when the camps were liberated in 1945, he was
given the shofar for safekeeping. He carried it with him as he made his way
first to a displaced persons' camp, and then to Montana, South Dakota,
Manhattan, and finally Israel. It remains intact to this day, and this year,
seventy-five years (by both calendars) after that work detail, his daughter
added it to a traveling exhibition at the Museum of Jewish Heritage in
Manhattan, which looks out directly at the Statue of Liberty. The president
of that museum says, "If there's an artifact that symbolizes the Jewish soul,
you'd be hard-pressed to find something more indicative than a shofar."

Other faiths have their own important symbols, not to mention stories of
survival in difficult times. The story of this surviving shofar should encourage
all of us, whether Jewish or not. It is about more than a ceremonial ten-inch
horn. It is a testament to the survival of a people and, more broadly, to the
survival of faith itself.

# My Bedside Radio and "Good Like Nedicks"

According to Jewish legend, the Maccabees defeated the wicked Syrian King Antiochus IV and recaptured the Second Temple in Jerusalem. Hanukkah, the "Festival of Lights," is the holiday that commemorates that victory more than two thousand years ago. Today, the "Jewish Olympics," are called the Maccabiah Games.

When I was young I would listen to a New York radio station, WMGM, which somehow reached Claremont loud and clear and carried the Knicks basketball games. This childhood memory came back to me last summer when I read an article entitled "In Berlin, Remembering Jewish Feats Well Beyond the Track." The article related that the 2015 European Maccabiah Games were being held in Berlin, Germany. What makes this an especially meaningful milestone is that when the Olympic Games were held in Berlin in 1936, Hitler used the occasion to show the world that Aryans were the dominant race.

Marty Glickman and Sam Stoller were the only two Jewish members of the 1936 United States Olympic track team. They marched in the opening day ceremonies but were then dropped from the team. Just why this happened has long been a matter of dispute. One explanation is that two faster runners replaced them, which leaves open the question of why they were selected in the first place. A likelier reason is that United States officials did not want to offend the Führer. At least they did not drop an African American runner named Jesse Owens. He foiled Hitler's Aryan-superiority propaganda by winning four track and field medals.

Why, you may be wondering, did the article I read last summer remind me of listening to basketball games a long time ago? The answer is that Marty Glickman, who was denied the opportunity to compete in Berlin in 1936, became the radio voice of the New York Knicks, and whenever the Knicks scored, I would hear him exclaim, "Good like Nedicks!" on my bedside Motorola radio.[29] Nedicks, which sponsored the broadcast, was the name of a fast-food chain known for its orange drink.[30]

---

29  The Knicks star player was Carl Braun, like Glickman a Brooklyn-born Jew. Braun came up with the word "swish," and Glickman popularized it when a Knick scored.

30  The company, which once had 135 locations in the Northeast, went out of business in the 1980s. Efforts in 2003 to revive the brand name in New York were unsuccessful.

Glickman's daughter, Nancy, went to Berlin and lit the torch to mark the commencement of the 2015 games. Officials explained that they wanted to honor her late father, and, at the same time, send a message about the survival of Jewish life.

The story is filled with irony—how two Jewish athletes were denied the opportunity to compete; how, while the 1936 Olympics were underway, the Sachsenhausen concentration camp was opened just north of Berlin; and how, some seventy-nine years later, two thousand Jewish athletes from around the world, went to Germany to compete.

Jews around the world will light the Hanukkah candles starting next Sunday evening, December 6.

# My Grandson and Yiddish Words

One of the things I have in common with my grandson, Solomon, is a love of words. During my recent visit to San Francisco, we did our customary spelling bee, and it was tough to stump him, but I managed with "enthusiasm." Then he noticed that I was reading a book called *Outwitting History*, and he asked me what it was about.

I told him that it is about a man named Aaron Lansky who, with the help of some friends, started searching for Yiddish-language books when he was a student at Hampshire College and has continued doing so for more than twenty years. So far, he has saved over 1.5 million volumes from destruction—scholarly works, poetry, novels, short stories, memoirs, you name it—and he was awarded a MacArthur Fellowship for his work.

I asked Soli whether he knew what "Yiddish" means. He did not, so I told him it means "Jewish." "It's a language," I told him.

"Does anyone speak it?" he asked.

"Yes," I said, "It's a language that doesn't want to die."

I told him that when my grandparents were growing up in Russia, they spoke Yiddish at home. And, like thousands of others who emigrated from Eastern Europe at the turn of the twentieth century, they brought it with them to this country. They learned English but never stopped speaking Yiddish, the *mamaloshen* (mother tongue).

I grew up on the fringes of their conversations, hearing but not paying close enough attention. I told Soli that I regret not learning the language but do know some words. "Would you like to hear a few?" I asked.

"Sure," he answered.

The first word I came up with was "shul." Then I asked if he could pronounce "*kh*," a sound that doesn't exist in English, which has been compared to a backward snore. He could, so I gave him *chedar*, which literally means "room" but is commonly used to refer to religious (Hebrew) school. I heard those words a lot between 1948, when Temple Meyer-David was born, and 1952, when my bar mitzvah took place there.

Soli remained interested. "Let me get a paper and pencil," he said.

He loved the next word, *meshuganah*, which means "crazy," and the one after that, *chochem* (two "*kh*" sounds in one word), which means "wise man" but, when said with a certain intonation, means the opposite, someone who thinks he knows everything, a jerk.

He wanted more, so I came up with *tsores* (troubles), schmooze (chat), and kibbitz (gossip). "I like the way these words sound, Grandpa," Soli told me.

How wonderful it is to share something with your grandchild, even if it happens accidentally. On the last day of my visit, we drove Soli to school, and I told him that my grandmother used to say, "Oy, vey iz mir" (oh, woe is me). As he got out of the car and walked towards the school entrance, he turned his head towards us, laughing, and said, "Oy, vey iz mir."

At that moment, I decided not to let this be a one-time event. Later that day, I bought him a book, *The New Joys of Yiddish* by Leo Rosten. "What should I look up?" he asked me.

I suggested *naches*, the Yiddish word for the pleasure and pride a parent or grandparent derives from a child's accomplishments. "That's what you're giving me."

In other words, I kvelled.[31]

---

31  According to Rosten, the word "kvel" means "to beam with immense pride and pleasure, most commonly over the achievement of a child or grandchild." He adds a typically Jewish second meaning, which is to kvel over the mistake of someone you dislike.

# My Jewishness and Our Distressing Times

I was born Jewish on February 19, 1939, at Claremont General Hospital. My Stevens High School classmates included seven Jewish kids out of a class numbering just over a hundred. Our numbers were more than double the percentage of Jews in the United States at that time, which was about 3 percent, and more than nine times the state's Jewish population of about .75 percent. Since then, the numbers have diminished in Claremont but grown nationally, from about four million to 7.6 million, while the national percentage has dropped to about 2.4 percent and New Hampshire's percentage has remained about the same.

Was there antisemitism in Claremont back then? I have no doubt that the answer is yes. Prejudice exists everywhere. Did it affect us as children and teenagers in our small New Hampshire city? Not that I recall. I do not remember feeling that I lived in a hostile environment or that I was treated differently on account of being Jewish.

Jewishness can come about in two ways, by birth, as in my case, or by choice. Judaism does not seek converts, but whoever converts to Judaism is considered fully Jewish, with no asterisk next to his or her name.

As with other faiths, some Jews are observant while others are not. I fall somewhere in the middle. Whatever the case, it's not easy for a Jew to become un-Jewish. When I was a high school senior, I worked part-time as a chauffeur for an elderly widow named Mrs. Newell. On Sunday mornings, I would transport her and her friend, Miss Baum, to the Episcopal Church on Broad Street. One fall afternoon, driving between Newport and Goshen to view the foliage, Mrs. Newell and I got to talking about religion, and she said, "Joe, I haven't known many Jews in my life." Then, after a pause, she added, "Except Miss Baum, of course. She's Jewish."

Like all forms of bigotry, antisemitism is a way of thinking that demonizes a group, whether by reason of religion, race, ethnicity, gender, sexual orientation, or nationality. Antisemitism can cross international borders, as in the case of the man who recently traveled from England to a synagogue in Texas, where he held the rabbi and members of the congregation hostage for eleven hours. Or it can be home grown, as in the case of the Pennsylvania man who murdered eleven Jews in a Pittsburgh synagogue in October 2018.

Jew hatred can also show up in the form of constitutionally protected hate speech, such as when the Proud Boys marched in Charlottesville chanting "Jews will not replace us," or when people deny that the Holocaust happened. But truth is truth, despite the disturbing belief among some nowadays that it isn't.

Antisemitism may or may not be motivating public school officials when they adopt measures to "protect" students. As an example, one of the most compelling books dealing with the Holocaust is a Pulitzer Prize-winning graphic novel titled *Maus*, written by the son of Auschwitz survivors and published more than thirty years ago. Last month, a Tennessee county school board voted unanimously to ban the book from its classrooms on account of its "inappropriate" content.

Inappropriate? What's inappropriate is not teaching about the Holocaust and racism and antisemitism and bigotry of all kinds. In 2020, under a law sponsored by State Senator Jay Kahn of Keene, New Hampshire became the fourteenth state to require genocide education in public schools. (In fairness, Tennessee does teach fifth graders about the Holocaust.) But the 2021 "Freedom from Discrimination in Education" law, despite its innocuous name, represents a step backwards by imposing constraints on what New Hampshire's public school teachers may say. (The law is currently being challenged in New Hampshire federal court).

I grew up in safe times. I still feel safe, but times in America today are not what they were. In a recent column, New York Times columnist Bret Stephens, a Jew, wrote chillingly that "our luck in America may have run out." On a more positive note, combatting antisemitism is high on the Biden administration's policy agenda. The president's nomination of Deborah Lipstadt to serve in a new position as the State Department Envoy to Monitor and Combat Antisemitism is finally on track for bipartisan confirmation. (Her courtroom victory over British writer David Irving over whether he was a Holocaust denier is the subject of the 2016 movie *Denial* starring Rachel Weisz.)

In 1790, President Washington wrote these words in a letter to the Hebrew Congregation of Newport, Rhode Island: "May the children of the Stock of Abraham . . . enjoy the good will of the other Inhabitants, while every one shall sit in safety under his own vine and fig tree, and there shall be none to make him afraid."

It's not just about Jews, however, or any other group that encounters prejudice in today's America. As Washington understood, it's about the principles on which the United States was founded.

I don't believe that our luck has run out, but I do agree with what Inaugural poet Amanda Gorman wrote on the same page as Bret Stephens's column: "If you're not afraid for our country, then you're not paying attention."

# My Cross-Town Cab Ride and a Mother's Day Message

*A man came to the Prophet and said,*
*"O Messenger of God! Who Among the people*
*is the most worthy of my good companionship?"*

The Hadith

I recently took a cab in New York. I said good morning to the driver, he said the same to me, and I told him I was going to Penn Station. He said, "I'm on the phone with my mother," so I stopped talking.

Anyone who has taken a cab cross town in New York knows that it is faster than walking, but not by much. So, when the driver was done speaking with his mother, we had time to talk.

"Where are you from?" I asked.

"Pakistan," he replied.

"Is your mother here in New York?

"No, she's in Lahore," he said. "It's evening there."

I then asked what language they were speaking, and he told me. "Punjabi."

We talked for the rest of the ride, mostly about family. He has been in the United States for seventeen years, is a citizen, and loves this country. He has five grown children, all born in Pakistan. Some live there, some are here. They are well-educated, hold good jobs, and are married.

"Did you pick who they married?" I asked.

"Yes, I did," he said, with a note of pride in his voice.

I wasn't sure about my next question, but I asked it anyway. "Did your children have any say in the matter?"

"They sure did," he told me, adding that they had rejected several of his choices before accepting one. "We all live together," he added. "I bought a house."

I told him that I know a little about Muslim family life from a book called *The Bookseller of Kabul.* "You're the boss, right?"

The driver agreed that he is but added that under Islam the mother gets "three times the respect." As for the book I mentioned, he quickly pointed out that "they're tribal," referring to Afghans, "we are not."

He has been a New York cab driver for twelve years. When I asked whether he found the work stressful, he raised four fingers and told me that he has had quadruple bypass heart surgery, takes insulin daily for diabetes, and suffers other health problems. Some of them, he thinks, are job related. Fortunately, two of the spouses he picked for his children are doctors, and "they do everything for me."

When we arrived at the curb outside Penn Station, I tapped the screen to pay by credit card, managed to complete the transaction, including tip, and thanked the driver. I told him how much I had enjoyed our conversation,

"So have I," he said.

We shook hands and then, to my own surprise, I said, "I'm Jewish."

He was looking at me over his right shoulder and, to my even greater surprise, said, "We're brothers."

> *"The Prophet said, 'Your mother.'*
> *The man said, 'Then who?*
> *The Prophet said, 'Then your mother.'*
> *The man further asked, 'Then who?'*
> *The Prophet said, 'Then your mother.'*
> *The man asked, 'Then who?'*
> *The Prophet said, 'Then your father.'"*

# ARTS AND TECHNOLOGY

## My Summer Reading and Hot Books

*The Nightingale,* by Kristin Hannah, is a very good novel. It tells the story of two sisters in occupied France during World War II. One of them, the "Nightingale" in the title, finds her life's purpose (and her estranged father's as well) by leading downed British airmen on the dangerous trek across the Pyrenees to Spain and safety.

I liked the book so much that when I was visiting my daughter in San Francisco, I told her she should read it. We went to her local branch library and asked if they had the book. The librarian consulted her computer and told us, "It's a hot book. We have fifty copies in circulation and 127 people on the waiting list." My daughter became number 128.

Then, early this summer, a friend with good reading taste told me I should read *All the Light We Cannot See* by Anthony Doerr. I went into the Jaffrey Public Library and checked it out. When I was halfway through it, the library notified me that it was overdue, and someone was waiting for it.

This posed an ethical dilemma. I was loving the book, which also takes place partly in wartime France, but slow reader that I am I still had many pages to go. The Jaffrey library does not charge fines for overdue books, so it wouldn't cost me anything to make whoever was waiting wait for however long it took me to finish the book.

Still, that sort of library lawlessness didn't seem right, so I came up with plan B. I would check the book out of the Keene Library and then return my overdue copy in Jaffrey. When I asked the Keene librarian about an available copy she did what the San Francisco librarian had done, with a similar outcome. She consulted the computer and told me, "We have five copies in circulation and fifty-eight people waiting for the book."

"I guess it's a hot book," I said, pondering my next move.

I returned the unfinished book in Jaffrey and immediately went on the waiting list. "I'll fill in with something else," I told myself, unhappily.

The next day, however, I decided to try Plan C—the Boston Public Library branch near my office. As you can see, I move around and have quite a few library cards. Of course, I could just buy the book, but the Pianist says we have no more bookcase space. So, I asked the latest in this series of librarians and she did what the others did, and this time it was even worse. "We have 127 copies in circulation," she told me, "and 538 people on the waiting list."

I'll admit it. I'm out of options, so I intend to wait my turn in Jaffrey and, meanwhile, go back to another unfinished book, *Citizens of London* by Lynne Olson. This is a book about three men who played a crucial role in persuading President Roosevelt to join forces with Churchill to save England from Hitler. One of them was three-time New Hampshire governor John Gilbert Winant. Somehow, despite growing up in New Hampshire and spending a lot of my adult life there, I had never heard of this man, much less the crucial role he played as our ambassador to the Court of St. James. Incidentally, the book includes the interesting fact that he had an affair with Churchill's daughter, Sarah.

I'm not concerned about having the library snap *Citizens* away from me. I own it.

As for *All the Light We Cannot See*, I noted that it is on President Obama's summer reading list as well. The newspaper didn't say how he got the book, but I don't suppose he will need to give it up halfway through.[32]

---

32   In 2021, I read a 2013 book called Braiding Sweetgrass, by Robin Wall Kimmerer. It is filled with wisdom, memorable stories, and quotable sentences on nearly every page. Here's one from page 296 that seems appropriate for this book: "Time as objective reality has never made much sense to me. It's what happens that matters."

# My Latest Watches and Trotting the Globe

This article is not about wristwatches or travel. It is about three, maybe four, television series that I have enjoyed and recommend to those of you who have some time on your hands.

I considered offering up some "summer reading" ideas, and if I were to do that I would begin with *Educated* by Tara Westover. It is a very good, indeed compelling, book, well deserving its status at the top of the best seller list. But truth be told, I seem to spend as much time these days watching as reading. So, I'm devoting this column to multiseason dramatic programs that I found both entertaining and informative. None of them, it happens, were made in the United States or feature American performers.

*A Place to Call Home* is a seven-season Australian production in which a nurse named Sarah (born Bridget) Adams, a Holocaust survivor played by Marta Dusseldorp, returns to her birthplace to visit her ailing mother, who insists on calling her by her birth name. As the saga unfolds, in a fictitious Australian town named Inverness with periodic detours to Sydney, we become engaged with a great many characters, including members of the Bligh family and its matriarch, the formidable Elizabeth Bligh, performed by Noni Hazlehurst; her son George, played by Brett Climo; and a host of others played by actors you've never heard of.

I use the word "saga" advisedly. This post-World War II multigenerational story combines plot with character to produce historical drama of the highest quality. Sarah owns the show, with Elizabeth a close second, but its other heroic characters include a war-damaged doctor haunted by demons, a homosexual Bligh son confronting a homophobic society, a meddlesome town gossip you will never forget, and an aboriginal war veteran who is unwelcome in his native land. The story is, ultimately, about love, forgiveness, and redemption.

The next one is *Poldark*, also a postwar story but from a different war—the American Revolution—and a different place, Cornwall, on the southwest coast of England. The principal character, Ross Poldark, played by the Irish actor Aidan Turner, fought on the losing side (the British) and returned home to find that Elizabeth, the girl he left behind, had become a woman married to his cousin. And there is Demelza, played by an English actress named Eleanor Tomlinson, a "scullery maid" at the beginning who soon turns out to be a lot more.

This six-season BBC series is based on several historical novels by Winston Graham. Watching it is like taking a course in late eighteenth century English culture—how they dressed, what they ate, what they thought about sex (they liked it), and how the "upper class" treated their "inferiors" (not very well). It also features bare-knuckled politics, assizes (courts) that hung people without batting an eye, and copper mining with hammer and chisel.

The characters in both series speak English, but unless you're Australian or British, you may find some of the dialogue challenging. That's what subtitles are for.

The third of my recommended watches comes from Canada. *Murdoch Mysteries* stars an actor named Yannick Bisson as Detective William Murdoch of the Toronto Constabulary, and Hélène Joy as Dr. Julia Ogden, a knockout pathologist who can smile and dissect dead bodies at the same time. What makes this show so interesting is the combination of clever plot twists and the frequent appearance of such late nineteenth century personages as Arthur Conan Doyle (working on his latest Sherlock Holmes mystery), Nikola Tesla (busy conducting experiments on various types of electrical equipment), and science fiction writer H. G. Wells (unsympathetically portrayed preaching eugenics as the way of the future).

I don't know whether these people actually visited Toronto in the 1890s, but they have nothing on Murdoch when it comes to being clever. The forensics of that time bear little resemblance to those of today's *CSI* and its progeny, but Murdoch proves it is possible to solve crimes with shoe leather, a blackboard and chalk, and an inquiring mind.

If you're willing to trot the globe nine thousand miles from Australia to Israel, let me add one more, a series called *Fauda*. It will bring the Israeli-Palestinian conflict into your TV room, and of the four, it is the hardest to watch, but worth it.

So, these are my recommended watches. Let me know how you like them.[33]

---

33 The Pandemic, not a good time for movie theatres, created something of a run on Netflix (and Amazon Prime, Hulu, etc.) series. I liked *Outlander*, *The Queen's Gambit*, *The Crown*, *Borgen* (Danish), and *Thou Shalt Not Kill* (Italian). *Peaky Blinders* is pretty good if you don't mind violence. *Call My Agent* (French), *Seaside Hotel* (Danish), and *Intersection* (Turkish) are all excellent.

# My Reading List and the Growing Pile

I like to read and give most of the credit to my Claremont teachers Miss Manley (Way School fifth grade) and Mr. Paquette (Stevens High, senior year). Picking a major in college was easy. English literature.

I'm not sure that such required classics as Bunyan's *Pilgrim's Progress* or Milton's *Paradise Lost* or Spenser's *The Faerie Queen*"[34] added to my enthusiasm for reading, but some of the classics left me better off. *Huckleberry Finn* and *Moby Dick* come to mind, as does Walt Whitman's book of poems that don't rhyme, *Leaves of Grass*, which is all about life and the senses. Whitman provided me with a great quote. "Do I contradict myself? Very well, then I contradict myself. I contain multitudes."

I am a slow reader, and law school compounded the problem because I was afraid that I would miss a word. I once took a speed-reading course, but it didn't help very much, so I still make my way laboriously down the page, one word at a time. So far as I know, my lips don't move.

Another problem is that I cannot seem to read just one book at a time. On any given day, books are piled on my bedside table and strewn around the house—all with bookmarks somewhere between the front and back covers. The Pianist, on the other hand, is a fast reader, finishes one book before she starts another, and keeps her books in one place.

I will confess to some literature gaps that I doubt I will ever fill. One is Proust's *Remembrance of Things Past*, sometimes called *In Search of Lost Time*, the longest novel ever written according to the Guinness Book of World Records. Another is Tolstoy's *War and Peace*, which weighs in at 1,225 pages.[35] There are others, but you get the point.

When it comes to book recommendations, I may not be the most reliable person. But if you've come this far, you might as well continue reading and see what my eyes have been up to.

---

34  J. K. Rowling, writing under the name "Robert Galbraith," has written several mystery novels featuring a detective named Cormoran Strike and his partner-in-solving-crime, Robin Ellacott. The most recent one, *Troubled Blood*, is over nine hundred pages long. Each chapter begins with a verse from *The Faerie Queene*, which remains as incomprehensible as it did the first time I read it. Even so, I loved every page of the new book.

35  The novel was first translated into English in 1886, and there have been many translations since then. I recently met a woman who had just finished reading *War and Peace* in Russian. She loved it.

First, a few books I finished pre-pandemic. *Red Notice* by Bill Browder is a chilling first-person account by an American money manager, grandson of the former head of the American Communist Party, who went into business in Russia, stood up to Putin, and paid a heavy price. The Russians killed his Moscow lawyer and stole his company. It is a must-read, as is *How Democracies Die*, by Harvard professors Steven Levitsky and Daniel Ziblatt. On the more optimistic side is Jon Meacham's *The Soul of America*. He reminds us that Lincoln's "better angels" have been with the country through hard times past and will be again.

I recently read *The Lies that Bind: Rethinking Identity* by Kwame Anthony Appiah. The book deals with five ways we identify ourselves: creed, country, color, class, and culture. The book is both short and heavy, but I liked it so much that I bought another of his books, *The Honor Code: How Moral Revolutions Happen*.[36]

Over ten years ago, Michelle Alexander published *The New Jim Crow: Mass Incarceration in the Age of Colorblindness*. It has lost none of its relevance. A good companion book is Eric Foner's *The Second Founding: How the Civil War and Reconstruction Remade the Constitution*. I switch back and forth between the two.

On the lighter side, I'm reading *Girl Intrepid: A New York Story of Privilege and Perseverance*, an autobiography by my college friend, Leslie Armstrong. Another book about someone I knew in college is George Packer's *Our Man: Richard Holbrooke and the End of the American Century*. I just took it off my bookcase, which is a start at least.

To deal with the 2020 foreshortened baseball season, I should go back and reread Roger Kahn's 1972 *The Boys of Summer*, which tells the story of Jackie Robinson, Roy Campanella, Pee-Wee Reece, Duke Snider, and all the rest. Brooklyn-born Kahn wore his heart on his sleeve when it came to the Dodgers, but I still think it is the best baseball book I have read.[37] David Halberstam's *Summer of '49*, which is about the Yankees–Red Sox 1949 pennant race, is on my bookcase. I am sorry to say that I remember how that race turned out, which may be why I haven't read it.

---

36  Appiah is the "Ethicist" in the *Sunday New York Times Magazine*. People send him ethical problems they are facing, and he provides thoughtful answers.

37  Roger Kahn died on February 6, 2020, at the age of ninety-two. He was a frequent visitor to the Monadnock region due to a close friendship between his wife, Katherine, and Ann Lunt of Temple, New Hampshire, a freelance editor and writer. I had the good fortune to meet Roger and spend many hours with him.

I just bought Erik Larson's book about Winston Churchill, *The Splendid and the Vile*. Everyone says it's a great read, and it now sits at the top of the pile. One book not on my list is John Bolton's *The Room Where It Happened*. Neither is Mary Trump's book about her uncle Donald, *Too Much and Never Enough*.

# My "Candide" and Intersecting Lives

I never heard of Barbara Cook until I was a senior in college. Susie Ross, the girl I was dating, introduced me to the singer who played the role of Cunegonde in Susie's favorite musical, *Candide*. Over the years, I have seen the play twice, in New York in 1972 with that girlfriend, who had become my wife; and in Boston many years later with the Pianist who had become my second wife.

Ms. Cook was not in either of those revivals, but I own the original cast recording and have listened to her lustrous soprano voice countless times. And we, the Pianist and I, heard Ms. Cook in concert when she was nearly eighty, and the voice was still clear, resonant, and pure.

Barbara Cook died in August of 2017 at the age of eighty-nine, singing nearly to the end. And when her voice, but not her heart, was stilled, her friends brought music to her bedside. John Pizzarelli strummed "The Way You Look Tonight," Vanessa Williams sang "Send in the Clowns," and others such as Josh Groban, Audra McDonald, and Kelli O'Hara, either serenaded her in person or sent recordings and messages of love.

And me? When I read she had died, I thought about the pleasures this woman I never met has given me. She sang from her heart and touched

Barbara Cook at the Isaac Stern Auditorium, Carnegie Hall, New York City, November 18, 2006

mine. We never touched, but our lives intersected. You may have not had the "Barbara Cook experience," but perhaps you have experienced something like it listening to Frank Sinatra, Judy Garland, or Elvis Presley. For my father, it would have been Al Jolson.

*Candide* was a flop when it opened on Broadway in 1956, but today it is one of our most enduring musicals. Based on the 1759 novella by Voltaire, it tells the story of a young man whose tutor teaches him that this is "the best of all possible worlds." Early in the play, he sings, "Life is happiness indeed" and "I love all my fellow creatures." He falls in love with Cunegonde, but her guardian disapproves and banishes him out into the world. Candide laments, "Is it true? . . . Can the heart find strength to bear it?"

Candide is shocked by what he sees in the world, a place of evil and decay that "deals more coldly than I had dreamt it would." Still the idealist, he blames himself. "It must be me," he decides.

Candide mistakenly believes Cunegonde has died. He is unaware of her unhappy transition, in Paris, "forced to bend my soul, to a sordid role" of degradation. You can understand what that means.

Yet all is not lost. To their great surprise, the two lovers are eventually reunited. Candide wonders, "How can this be so? You were dead you know." She answers with a woman's pragmatism ("That is very true, ah, but love will find a way"), praises Candide for having survived so cleverly, and asks him where he has been. "To and fro," he tells her, and "I would do it all again, to find you at last."

The play tells us that life is "neither good nor bad." And it concludes with the two lovers facing the challenge of the future. Candide proposes marriage. "Let us try, before we die, to make some sense of life." They sing the play's last song together:

> *We're neither pure, nor wise, nor good*
> *We'll do the best we know.*
> *We'll build our house and chop our wood*
> *And make our garden grow . . .*
> *And make our garden grow.*

My first wife, Susan Ross Steinfield, died in 1983. Her funeral service began and ended with the Overture from *Candide*.

# My "Annie" and When to Love

"Tomorrow, tomorrow, I'll love you tomorrow, it's only a day away."

Those famous words from the 1977 Broadway musical *Annie* were written by Martin Charnin, who died in July 2019 at the age of eighty-four. I never met Mr. Charnin, but I have felt connected to him for a long time. Here's why.

First, Dorothy Loudon. She was Miss Hannigan, the play's hateful matron at the orphanage where Annie and the other young girls led a "Hard Knock Life," another memorable song from the show. "Dot" (as my mother called her) won the Tony Award for Best Performance by a Leading Actress in a Musical. I didn't see her perform, and I don't recall ever meeting her. But, like me, she grew up in Claremont and went to Stevens High School. I took piano lessons from her mother, although you wouldn't know it today.

Second, Melissa Cannon. She lived next door to us in a Boston suburb and was best friends with my daughter Lizzie when they were young. She was in and out of our house, where she would regularly sing "Tomorrow" and other songs from *Annie*. She had a very good voice.

So good, in fact, that when Martin Charnin announced he was conducting open tryouts for the role of Annie in the first national tour, taking over from Andrea McArdle, Melissa persuaded her mother to take her to New York to try out for the part. They arrived to find hundreds of redheaded girls outside the theatre in Times Square but, somehow, they managed to get in. It turned out to be a long day.

By late afternoon it was down to a dozen talented young hopefuls, and by the dinner break the process of elimination left just two, Melissa and another redhead. They came back that evening, and back and forth it went. Finally, Mr. Charnin decided that Melissa was too tall, and he chose the other girl.

My third connection with Martin Charnin is the one that has affected me the most. It goes back to around 1980. I was attending the Jewish High Holiday services, and I heard a remarkable sermon that began with the rabbi telling us that he was going to talk about *Annie*. That got my immediate attention, given my Loudon and Melissa connections. Then he quoted the lyrics that appear in the first line of this essay, "Tomorrow, tomorrow, I'll love you tomorrow, it's only a day away."

"The song is wrong," the rabbi said. "If you really love someone, you must love them today."

"If you're over forty," he said, "you owe it to those you love to make 'arrangements' today."

What he meant, of course, was that part of being a grownup is to recognize that life is not forever, and you should do what you can to make it easier for those you love and leave behind. He talked specifically about picking out a burial plot.[38]

I have come to recognize over the years that the point of that long-ago sermon was much broader than buying a small plot of land or making some other type of funeral arrangements. It was about procrastination in general, which Charles Dickens once called "the thief of time."

There is, after all, only so much time to be had, especially if you want to have time for everything. Doing the important stuff cannot wait until tomorrow, much less the day after. If we follow the rabbi's advice, and do it today, then chances are, to quote Mr. Charnin's lyrics once again, "the sun'll come out tomorrow."

---

38   We mentioned the sermon to close friends, who invited us a few days later to come to their house that week and meet with a Sharon Memorial Park representative. We did so, and purchased two plots. It never crossed our minds that we would have need for one of them just three years later.

# My Charlie Brown and the Wisdom of Charles Schulz

It's hard to believe that Charlie Brown turned seventy in early October 2020. And the same is true of the rest of the *Peanuts* gang—Lucy van Pelt, Linus, Snoopy, Woodstock, Schroeder the pianist, and many more.

I'm no expert on Plato or Aristotle or Socrates, but I have long believed that Charles Schulz, who created *Peanuts*, is one of the great modern philosophers. He was the master of all seasons and of our national condition.

It's fall, and just as Charlie Brown is about to kick the football, Lucy snaps it away. Couldn't she make him happy and let him kick the ball just once? No, said Schulz, because "Happiness is not funny." To his great credit, Charlie Brown never stops trying.

Meanwhile, Linus stays up all night waiting for the Great Pumpkin to arrive. *It's the Great Pumpkin, Charlie Brown* should be required watching, at least the four-minute segment available on YouTube. You can see Lucy double-cross Charlie yet again, and hear Linus advise the "second place" Great Pumpkin to "try harder" if it wants to become as popular as Santa Claus.

Schulz captured the essence of the seasons. According to Snoopy, "Snowflakes are kisses from Heaven," while Lucy the contrarian complains, "Hey, all you geniuses, who said let it snow?" On this subject, she and Charlie Brown ("Winter's not for me") seem to agree.

As for spring, one of my favorites reminds me of my own childhood. Linus and Charlie Brown are standing outside wearing baseball caps and baseball gloves while the snow is falling. "Is it spring yet?" asks Linus.

Later in the season, Charlie Brown asks that universal question, "Why did I have to go and try to steal home? WHY? WHY? WHY?" Linus has no sympathy, telling him, "I have been asked to tell you that your cries of anguish are keeping the whole neighborhood awake."

The Peanuts gang in summer is a lot like us. Snoopy forgets to tell Woodstock to take "beak lotion" to the beach, while Lucy, lying next to Charlie Brown on a beach towel, complains, "You're using up all the sun." Peppermint Patty goes on her summer diet of ice cream cones, while Snoopy and Woodstock partake of their favorite flavors, black raspberry and pistachio. And Charlie Brown reminds us that "Life is like an ice cream cone. You have to learn to lick it."

There is no end to how these characters react to the circumstances of life, or to the world around them, including politics. When Pigpen decides to run for class president, Charlie Brown suggests "we should sort of clean up a bit first." Pigpen reassures him. "I have . . . I took all the old candy wrappers out of my pockets."

In one memorable strip, Snoopy sees birds campaigning for office, each carrying a sign with a punctuation mark—one an exclamation mark "!," another a question mark "?," and a third a semicolon ";". We can appreciate Snoopy's reaction: "It's hard to know what to believe."

Snoopy then goes on to become Head Beagle in New Jersey, the highest position in the dog world. He laments, "The last head beagle left things in an awful mess."

Charles Schultz brought us universal truths through the words, and often the silences, of a made-up society of children, a dog, and a bird. It says a lot about Schultz that he made Charlie Brown, the optimist who never quits, the central character in the *Peanuts* universe.[39]

---

39  After this piece appeared in the *Monadnock Ledger-Transcript*, Duncan Watson, assistant Public Works director for the City of Keene, New Hampshire, sent me an e-mail telling me that he had read the piece and agreed that the unfailing optimism of Charlie Brown is what keeps the comic strip alive after seventy years. Mr. Watson's e-mail continued, "You may know that I had the privilege of playing the voice character of Charlie Brown in several *Peanuts* TV shows and one movie. It's humbling to have been associated with something so iconic in American life and I appreciate your efforts to share your passion for all things Charlie Brown so that the coming generations can gain this important life wisdom."

Duncan Watson with a poster of "Be My Valentine Charlie Brown"

# My Fire Stick and Turning the Page

You can buy devices from Apple, Amazon, and others that enable "streaming" on your television. This is particularly useful if cable isn't available where you live, or you've got better ways to spend your money. If you do get such a device, the trick is to get it up and running.

Steve Jobs, the genius behind Apple, believed everything should be self-explanatory and intuitive. Not including written instructions was part of his mindset. That may be fine for Gen Xers and Millennials who grew up with digital technology, but it's not so easy for those of us who grew up with model airplane and sewing kits, erector sets, and all the other things that came with directions. We so-called elderly people may have mastered e-mail and do pretty well with Word but wait 'til you get one of these TV streaming devices.

The first thing you need is that necessity of life called Wi-Fi. Your children and grandchildren won't visit unless you have a password. But even if you have it, there's a catch. You need to be sure the signal from your router, a word that makes me think of plumbing, reaches the TV room.

I used to think a Fire Stick was something Boy Scouts used instead of matches, but the modern version is a small doohickey you can get from Amazon, along with a mini-remote device. I ordered one a few years ago, and it arrived without directions. That really didn't matter since our router and television room weren't on speaking terms. I wasn't about to uproot the TV for the sake of something I'd lived my whole life without. Cable is enough, even though I only know about most of the channels because I go by them on my way to CNN.

Then came the Coronavirus, meaning wash your hands frequently, practice social distancing, and stay at home. Two things occurred to me. One is that a few months ago we upgraded our Wi-Fi coverage, the other is that somewhere I still have that useless Fire Stick.

So, I set about to give it a try, which began by my looking everywhere before I found it. Then I located a vacant port on the back of the TV called HDM3. Then I figured out which end of the power cord fits into it—not the end with the power plug. That goes into a wall outlet.

At that point I gave up and went to Google where, no thanks to Steve Jobs, there are several links under "How to set up your Fire Stick device." They all say pretty much the same thing, emphasizing how simple it is. I went to my TV, pointed the remote device at the screen, hit the "Home" button, and got a televised message: "You need to replace your batteries."

I can do that, I thought to myself, until I realized that unlike a flashlight this device has nothing you can turn and unscrew. Instead, there is a barely visible arrow on the back, but nothing happens if you push it. So, back to Google, where I found several "How to change the Fire Stick batteries" links, ranging from how easy it is (push and slide) to how no one can get the thing open.

I banged on it, pushed and pulled, cursed—all with no luck. Then the Pianist took over, and the next thing I knew she had it open. Turns out all you need are a pianist and two fresh triple-A batteries. I had the pianist but no AAAs.

Back from a battery run, in they go, replace the back cover (which is a lot easier than taking it off), back to the TV room, hit the Home button on the mini-remote, and things start to liven up.

I won't advise you "Don't try this at home," since that is what you're supposed to do. But be warned. If you get to the "set up" stage, you need to be armed with the name of your Wi-Fi network, your ID, various passwords, and your blood pressure reading.

Is it worth it? I'll let you know when I get around to watching something. First, I need to finish the book I'm reading, which is a page-turner and requires no technical expertise.[40]

---

40   A few weeks after writing this piece, I started using the device, which worked well enough until the remote stopped communicating with the TV. Amazon says online that you can reset it in eight easy steps, but, like changing the batteries, it's not that easy. Then, Eureka! If you download the Fire Stick app you can turn your cell phone into a remote.

# My Drive Home and the Latest Technology

When I took my driver's test, on my sixteenth birthday, I had to roll down the window and prove that I knew the hand signals for right and left turns. Back then, cars did not come with directional signals, meaning that on that February day I had no choice but for my hand to brave the cold temperature. When the weather got warmer that year, I had another reason to turn the window handle, which was to "air condition" the car, since there was no AC either.

You could just get in and drive away without having to buckle up, because there was nothing to buckle. Cars had radios, but AM only, with a telescoping antenna. I'm not sure whether they had outside mirrors, but if they did you had to adjust them by hand, another reason to open the window.

Today's cars are different. On the low-tech side, they have cup-holders. I'm sure we used to drink while driving (I don't mean that the way it sounds), but I have no idea where we put the cup. Another innovation is that there is a place to keep change for tolls. I don't recall that there were any toll roads, but I do remember that every time you drove from West Claremont into Vermont, you had to pay either a dime or a quarter before you could use the bridge. Another low-tech improvement is that the visor now swings to the left so that driving north in the afternoon, you can block the sun. Some visors also have a little slot where you can put your parking ticket, although you'd better check first to see if you need to take it with you and pay before returning to your car.

On the high-tech side, cars have all sorts of devices and gimmicks, more than most of us need. To start, I no longer turn a key, I push a button. It's handy, but hardly essential. One feature that I do like is that the headlights go on and off by themselves, which avoids a lot of dead batteries.

Not all cars have that feature, however. The Pianist recently went to start her car on a cold morning and the battery was dead. With help from a neighbor, she brought the battery back to life, but no radio, no clock, no CD player. The readout screen said: "Insert Code," but it didn't provide the code or tell you where to find it. For that you need to visit the dealer.

A few weeks ago, I was driving to Boston after attending the Jaffrey Village Improvement Society dinner in Troy, New Hampshire, when a loud screech came out of nowhere. I slowed down below forty miles per hour and the noise went away; I accelerated, and it returned, a blood-curdling sound. I knew something was terribly wrong, but the dashboard indicators offered no clues. So, I pulled off the road, did a careful walk-around, but couldn't find anything.

I considered my options. Turn back? Call AAA? I decided to keep going, but at a reduced speed. Even then, the screech came and went, but at least I could hear my audio book, the latest David Baldacci thriller, and I was in no danger of getting stopped for speeding.

Early the next day, I called the dealer. The service representative invited me to come in right away, which is what I did. I waited for about twenty minutes, wondering how serious it was and how much it would cost. The service person came to tell me they had located the problem, and everything was fixed.

"What was wrong?" I asked.

"Your rear window was slightly open," he replied.

What do you say when you're caught doing something that stupid? It took me a minute, but then I knew. "How much do I owe you?" I asked.

# SPORTS AND HUMOR

## My Baseball DNA and What I Can't Not Do

We survived the dark, unhappy, chicken wings-and-beer 2012 baseball season. Sixty-nine wins, ninety-three losses. Red Sox management brought in a new manager, but even so we didn't expect miracles in 2013.

Then, to the surprise of the sportswriters and everyone else, we saw those bearded wonders do the impossible. Yes, less than a year ago, our last-to-first team was on top of the world, which includes the American League. Ninety-seven wins, sixty-five losses. And that doesn't include the World Series—Boston over St. Louis, four games to two.

Lester, Lackey, Gomes, Drew, Ellsbury—what great players, surely the nucleus of a successful 2014, maybe even a dynasty. Then Ellsbury left, as we knew in our hearts he would. Whenever that happens, the sportswriters remind us, "It's a business." But the rest of the team seemed solid—good pitching, solid hitting, all the ingredients for another good year.

Instead, we have witnessed the baseball equivalent of a sinkhole at Fenway Park. The pitching was fine, but the hitting stank. Without warning we went directly from a world championship into survival mode. Yet, like generations of Red Sox fans, many of us remained hopeful. We said to ourselves, "It's a long season, all they need to do is get the won-and-lost record up to .500, and we'll work from there. The division is evenly balanced, the pitching is great, and the hitters will come around."

Except they didn't, and sometime around the Fourth of July, the season started getting too long. It became clear to all that this team wasn't going anywhere.

The same cannot be said about the aforementioned nucleus. By month's end, they were all gone, along with a few others. Lester, classy as always, took out a full-page newspaper ad thanking the "best fans in the world" for their loyalty. When I saw the ad, I considered myself part of that group.[41]

Even for those of us who remember the wait-'til-next-year old days, this endless 2014 season has been painful. Mired in last place by mid-summer, with players from here and there along with the stalwart Pedroia and the ebullient Ortiz, the Red Sox had given up on the season. So had I, or so I thought.

On a Tuesday night in August, my friend and I found ourselves in Cincinnati's Great American Ballpark, surrounded by Reds players' wives and family members in the best seats in the stadium thanks to a Reds relief pitcher.[42] I was even wearing an autographed Reds hat, and I thought to myself, *Why not, just this once, root for the Reds?*

It was a good game, and the Reds were ahead, 2–1, going into the eighth inning. If they held the lead, my friend and I agreed, we would get to see the relief pitcher, our client, come out and pitch the ninth. I made a command decision. I would root for the Reds, and no one would be the wiser.

Then Yoenis Cespedes—the Red Sox got him for Lester and Gomes—hit a two-run home run to deepest center. My baseball DNA took over, and I jumped out of my seat, pointed to where the ball had just landed, and let out a shout. You can imagine the looks I got from the other inhabitants of the box containing Reds players' family members.

So, we didn't get to see the Reds closer in action, but I learned a valuable lesson about myself. I really am one of the loyal fans in Lester's ad. No matter how hard I try, I can't not root for the Red Sox.[43]

---

41 In January 2022, Lester announced his retirement after a sixteen-year career. He added a third World Series ring with the Cubs after winning two (2007 and 2013) with the Red Sox. With two hundred wins, he will be a Hall of Fame candidate. If he gets in, whose jersey will he wear?

42 The pitcher was Aroldis Chapman, whom my friend, a Spanish-speaking Florida lawyer, and I were representing at the time. We had timed our trip to Cincinnati to coincide with the baseball interleague schedule. As Aroldis was driving us to the hotel, we spotted the Red Sox team getting off their bus. Aroldis, who was Cincinnati's "closer" at the time, knew David Ortiz and asked if I would like to meet him. Ortiz was a Boston hero not only because of his clutch hitting but also because, in the dark days following the Boston Marathon bombing, he lifted the spirits of the city with a speech outside City Hall in which he said, "This is our f—ing city." When we talked that day in Cincinnati, I told him I hoped he would stay connected to Boston after his baseball career ended. He assured me that he would.

43 The next day, I asked Aroldis whether he had known Cespedes in Cuba. He had, he told me. "We played against each other in the all-star game." "Did you strike him out? I asked. "No," he replied, "He's too good a hitter. He grounded out to shortstop."

Me with Aroldis Chapman and David Ortiz

## My Red Sox Rhymes and a Return to Good Times

My grandfather, Maurice D. Firestone, came to this country early in the twentieth century with no education, no money, and no English. He lived first in Boston, where he met Lillian Gerson, who had arrived at about the same time from a village in Russia not far from where he grew up. They married and later moved to New Hampshire—first Littleton, then Berlin, and finally Claremont.

As Ken Burns observed in his 1994 *Baseball* documentary, for many immigrants, baseball was part of the process of becoming American. My grandfather embraced it as a young man and held on to it for the rest of a long life.

His words to me at a young age are still in my ears and my heart. "Joey, there are two leagues, the American and the National." My grandfather died in April 1970, forty-five years ago, long before I wrote these lines to start the 2015 Red Sox season.

OK, he's gone, we can't let it fester,
We'll just get along without Jon Lester.
Yes, spring is here, the Red Sox are playing,
Let's all give a cheer, Big Papi is staying.

What would we do without David Ortiz?
By unanimous vote he's the team's big cheese.
And this year, we think, Pedroia is healthy,
John Henry is smiling; it helps to be wealthy.

He took out his pen and wrote a big check.
Now Hanley Ramirez is again on deck.
Sandoval's at third, it's his veranda,
He's known by his nickname, "Kung Fu Panda."

In center field, once Dom DiMaggio's home,
That's where young Mookie Betts will roam.
He's ready, they say, and so is Tazawa,
The setup man for Koji Uehara.

They begin next Monday, for the pennant they'll race,
With Mike Napoli patrolling first base.
Then they'll open at home, on April thirteen;
Rest assured Fenway Park will again be green.

Will there still be snow along Yawkey Way?
"Never mind" says John Farrell, "we've come to play."
But without Moncada, the young Cuban whiz.
They've sent him to Greenville, wherever that is.

But he'll make the Show, of that I am sure;
In the meanwhile, don't worry, he'll never be poor.
Nor will Rusney Castillo, he's also from Cuba,
Unlike Xander Bogaerts, who hails from Aruba!

In right field Victorino, his first name is Shane.
The position is his, but let me explain,
As you run down the roster, the Sox seem to have a
Surplus of players, such as Daniel Nava.

There's Allen Craig and the team's antidote,
The utility player named Brock Wyatt Holt.
They got him from Pittsburgh, a good acquisition;
Last year he played nearly every position.

Jackie Bradley's another who will be competing.
As he learned last year, fame can be so fleeting.
We miss Ellsbury, how he used to please.
How could he have signed with the dreaded Yankees?

On the mound the team still needs a number one ace,
Someone who can take over Jon Lester's place;
It might be Joe Kelly, or southpaw Wade Miley,
He pitched well this spring, he's earned his own smiley ☺.

They will need five starters, not so easy to find;
An injury or two, and the team's in a bind.

There's Masterson, Buchholz, and Rick Porcello,
And perhaps Steven Wright, the knuckleball fellow.

The man on the mound will take signs from Vazquez,
From Puerto Rico, his biography says.
The back-up catcher is Ryan Hanigan,
If Vazquez falters, he'll be the signalman.

Reliever Craig Breslow graduated from Yale;
He's smart, but still looking for his holy grail.
His ERA last year was five point nine six,
This season that's something he *will* need to fix.

In the bullpen will be Escobar as well
(He's just getting started so there's not much to tell);
And a bunch of others I've never heard of,
We will see what they do when push comes to shove.

Well, that's the rundown of this year's players,
No doubt, as always, there *will* be naysayers.
But winter is past, we should have no fear,
For Red Sox Nation, it is now Next Year![44]

---

44 This was the first of my baseball poems, which I continued yearly until the pandemic shortened the 2020 season. But over the years I've also written some non-baseball doggerel, usually to commemorate a birthday or other special occasion. In 2009, at Bud Collins's eightieth birthday dinner, I read a poem that included these words: "Bud's no spring chicken, born the year of the crash, Before they invented the overhead smash. His coming out, it happens, was on Bunker Hill Day. Who won Wimbledon that year, why . . . Henri Cochet!" And Bud, my writing superior by far, once wrote a poem for the Pianist that included the lines "Chopin to Waller with ease—Faster hands than Agassi's."

# My Summer Woes and After the Snows

Here it is, my tale of woe:
No win, no place, not even show.
My hopes last May soon turned to pain.[45]
Again, it's that old Sox refrain

About next year: we now wait 'til,
And ponder the many gaps to fill;
We look back and think about those trades;
Ramirez and Sandoval get failing grades.

But hope, no doubt, will soon take over;
Next year, of course, we'll all be in clover
As the kids mature, Bradley Jr. and Betts,
And Ortiz is still as good as it gets.

We saw some changes, this year was odd,
Here in the home of the bean and the cod;
Dombrowski's in and Cherington's out,
Lucchino's gone, it's a front office rout!

Orsillo will no longer speak for the team,
He's off to the Padres, with the fans' esteem;
What will now happen to the old Remdawg?[46]
Was this season also his epilogue?

The season's done, Brady's in action;
The judge let him play—now that's satisfaction.
As Fenway fans make the Foxboro drive,
The traffic is bad, but the Pats still thrive.

---

45   The "pain" refers to the fact that the 2015 Red Sox ended up in last place.
46   Former Red Sox second baseman Jerry ("Remdawg") Remy went on to a memorable career in the broadcast booth. Despite recurring bouts of cancer, he remained the Red Sox game color commentator until 2021. He died on October 30, 2021.

So once again, the Sox finished last,
Despite Big Papi's five-hundredth blast;
This year we expected a higher placement,
But no such luck, we're back in the basement.
They showed life in September, giving us reason
To look forward to the upcoming season;
One thing is for sure, they must get a stopper,
Or again next year, they'll again come a cropper.

For the next four months we just have no choice,
But to wait for the sound of the team's new voice
From Fort Myers, and the start of the grapefruit league,
Meanwhile, it's baseball deprivation fatigue.

John Farrell will manage, his health restored,
And Tory Lovullo will still be aboard.
The grass will be green, the stands will be full,
As men, women, and kids for the Bosox will pull.

The new season will start, we'll all hear the call,
Time once again for our team to "Play ball."
"Bring 'em on," we will say, "you help keep us young!"
The snows have passed, and a new spring has sprung.

# My Fenway Friends and a Not-So-Good Ending

Taking in a Red Sox game is always a calculated risk. For one thing, it could rain. For another, the team could lose. You never know when, or how, the unexpected will happen.

Even so, the odds are that you will have a good time at Fenway Park, and when you walk up the ramp and look out at that field of green, you know you are in a different world. Here grown men play a game, while men, women, and children eat peanuts and hot dogs and sing "Sweet Caroline"—"*Good times never seemed so good . . . So good, so good!*"[47]

In the summer of 2016, I invited three friends to join me for a Yankees game. This was A-Rod's last visit to Fenway, and we hoped to see him on the field.

We decided to eat near the park, and my first victory of the day was snagging a parking place in Kenmore Square. Inserting a few quarters in the meter before and after dinner beats the fifty-dollar parking lot spaces being offered on every street within walking distance of the park. My friend Tom, who drove in from Keene, was duly impressed and helped pay for the meter.

We all showed up on time, had dinner in Kenmore Square, and joined the throngs of people walking over the bridge to Yawkey Way.[48] It was a cloudless evening, a perfect night for baseball. We took our seats behind the third base line just as the first pitch was being thrown. Sitting to my left were a tall young man and a young woman.

One thing about ballgames is that everyone talks to the people around them. I soon learned that this couple, recently wed, was visiting Boston from Alabama. He was wearing a Red Sox shirt, she had on a Red Sox hat, and they were crackling with enthusiasm, excited to be at Fenway Park and root for the Sox. He served in the military and remains on weekend active

---

47  The reference is to Neil Diamond's song, which Red Sox fans have sung during the eighth inning of home games since 1997. Not everyone likes this practice of singing a song that isn't about baseball or Boston, but it seems to have become part of Red Sox culture.

48  In 1977, the street that runs alongside Fenway Park was named after long-time Red Sox owner, Tom Yawkey. During his ownership, the team was slow to hire black players, leading to charges of racism. In 2018, two years after the story told in this piece, the City of Boston approved changing the name back to "Jersey Street." The "Jersey" refers to George Augustus Frederick Child Villiers, the Sixth Earl of Jersey who died in 1859 and who, ironically, got rich from the slave trade before Britain abolished it in 1833.

reserve. She's a nurse, born and raised in the South. When they told me what they paid for tickets through StubHub, I raised my eyebrows. He said, "It's worth every cent just to be here."

I remember thinking, "He's got just the right amount of enthusiasm."

After an inning or so, they went off and returned a half inning later with beers in hand, which happened at least twice more as the game wore on. Meanwhile, Rick Porcello pitched a great game; Andrew Benintendi, the twenty-two-year-old rookie, went 3 for 3; and Jackie Bradley Jr. threw out a Yankee runner at third, right in front of our eyes.

A-Rod did not play, or even go out on the field, but he stuck his head out of the dugout a few times, just a few rows in front of us. My new friend from Alabama joined the hooters with gusto. "He's a Yankee-hater in the best sense," I told one of my friends.

At the end of the eighth inning the Sox were ahead 5–2, and people started to leave. In came the "Closer," Craig Kimbrel, who proceeded to give up two walks, followed by a passed ball, and then two more walks. Now the score was 5–3, and no one was leaving except for Kimbrel. The Manager waved his hand, and in came another pitcher.

While all of this was going on, I stepped away for just a minute, and when I got back to my seat I noticed that the young couple from Alabama were nowhere in sight. "Where are they?" I asked.

"They're gone," one of my friends told me. "I saw him walk down to behind the Yankees' dugout. It looked like he was, shouting something at A-Rod, and the next thing I knew security was leading him out of the ballpark." I guess he had too much enthusiasm.

# My Crystal Ball and Our National Pastime

I wondered, what with the goings-on in the world,
As a new administration its flag unfurled;
Would the President issue an order ordaining
That this year there would be no spring training?

As rumors abounded, I awaited the day,
When pitchers and catchers arrived to play;
What relief I felt, how glad I was,
That again this year we could take a brief pause

From the daily tweets that you-know-who likes,
And focus instead on the balls and the strikes;
As John Farrell once again assembles the players,
And Red Sox fans say their annual prayers.

This year a new challenge the Red Sox will face,
As Big Papi's strong bat no longer will grace
The park we all know by its first name, Fenway,
I, for one, wish he'd decided to stay.

There's also the problem called "After the Pats,"
And whether our team, using nothing but bats
Can again conjure up the '04 mystique,
When they had that incredible winning streak;

And match the euphoria that all of us felt,
When Belichick shuffled and winning cards dealt;
As we looked out and saw the cool cat named Brady,
Who knows better than most about the fat lady.

Who began to sing ere the third quarter was over,
And the field turned from grass into Patriots clover;
With help from defense, Tom knew how to deflate,

Not the ball but Falcons he did disintegrate.

Which comeback was better? I'm not sure that it matters,
So long as the other team ends up in tatters.
It's now back to baseball and the season ahead,
My crystal ball says there is no need for dread.

First, we'll go around the horn,
At third, Sandoval, the Panda reborn!
Shortstop Bogaerts made the All-Stars last year,
And at second Pedroia will make it quite clear,

At age thirty–three, there's no one more scrappy.
Rub some dirt on his shirt, and he will be happy!
Someone named Moreland will be at first base,
While DH Ramirez just pitchers will face.

One more position, the one where they scratch:
Behind the plate, we need someone to catch.
It looks like either Vazquez or Swihart,
Whichever the manager says gets to start.

As for pitchers, they say that he cannot fail:
An off-season pickup by the name of Chris Sale;
Our opening day starter will be Rick Porcello,
Last year's Cy Young winner, a remarkable fellow.

Those two along with a southpaw named Price,
Three-fifths of a rotation that looks pretty nice;
And in case they fall short, out beyond right field,
There's the bullpen where we're pretty well-healed.

In center field Bradley Jr. will roam,
After last year's success, he can call it his home.[49]

---

49   After eight seasons with the Red Sox (2013–2020), Bradley was traded to the Milwaukee
Brewers, where in 2021 he batted .163, well below the Mendoza Line named after Mario Mendoza,
who consistently batted below .200. In December 2021, the Red Sox reacquired JBJ, so Fenway is
his home once again.

In right, cast your bets on a Betts named Mookie,
And in left, Benintendi, the promising rookie.

As for me, I am primed and once again ready,
For the team with which I have long gone steady.
On the field of green I will once again gaze
And reflect back on those halcyon days,

Recalling the stars who have gladdened our hearts,
In a sport that is more than the sum of its parts.
Not merely a game or occasion for rhyme,
If you ask me, it is still our national pastime.

# My Spring Song and Keeping Young

A year ago, the Pats were winners,
Deflating the charge they were pigskin sinners;
The best comeback ever, a gleeful fourth quarter,
Edelman the brick, and Brady the mortar.

Not so good this year, gone are the thrills,
Three Patriots players have gone to the hills.
Amendola departed, and so did Lewis,
Butler somehow became superfluous.

It's time once again to announce the new season,
I'm talkin' baseball, and there is good reason
For hope once again, though we're still Papi-less.
It's time to dispel our unhappiness,

There's a new DH, he goes by J. D.,
The name's Martinez, and they've said that he
Will help us forget last season's distress,
And make the new skipper a great success.

Now calling the shots is Alex Cora,
My grandmother would have said *kinehora*.
That's the Yiddish version of knocking on wood,
To wish him luck, "he should only make good."

The infield looks sound, though Pedroia won't start,
He's still in rehab, his knee fell apart.
Ramirez at first, that's where he will stand;
(In the wings we'll still have Mitch Moreland).

Nunez at second, filling in for a while;
Shortstop Bogaerts, from the Aruban isle.
The Panda is gone, no longer at third—
Rafael Devers, the last thing I heard.

The outfield is set, the same as last year:
Benintendi in left, it's his hemisphere;
The other two-thirds look pretty airtight,
Jackie Bradley in center, Mookie Betts in right.


One spot remains, it's behind the plate,
On Opening Day, Vazquez will await
The cry to "Play Ball!" amid roaring applause,
As arm-wavers remain true to their cause.


Starting pitcher Chris Sale the ball will propel,
Lydia's dad in the bullpen, the closer Kimbrel;[50]
After that come Porcello, Velazquez, and Price,
We need a fifth starter, someone who'll suffice.


Was there ever a sport that gave more pleasure?
If there is, I'd like to take its measure;
But for now, once again, my spring song I have sung.
Let's just hope they don't come undone. [51]

---

50   Kimbrel's daughter was born with a heart condition and had the first of several heart surgeries
when she was four days old. Red Sox fans were reminded that some things are more important
than that day's game, and Kimbrel's teammates wore #LydiaStrong shirts.
51   The 2018 season turned out better than I could have imagined. Under manager Alex Cora, the
team's record was 108–54, the team's best in more than a hundred years. The postseason got even
better, winning the division against the Yankees 4–0, the pennant against the Astros 4–1, and the
World Series against the Dodgers 5–1.

# My Baseball Rhymes and Opening Day

Last fall we did not sound the usual call;
The words "wait 'til next year" were not heard at all.
A mere five games and a World Series win,
We Red Sox fans had no need for chagrin.

Good players responded to the manager tricks;
The winter was quiet, there was nothing to fix.
But did you see what happened on Opening Day?
They showed up, but it seemed they forgot how to play.

Last year, was it too good to be true?
One hundred eight wins and the World Series too.
This season began, 'gainst Seattle alas.
Just as well they did not tread on Fenway's fresh grass.

Chris Sale was a bust, some say it's his shoulder;
Velocity's down and he's another year older.
Four other pitchers complete the rotation;
Despite their high pay, do they lack motivation?

Was it something about the West Coast air,
That left those five hurlers in such disrepair?
The season's still young, it's no time to quit,
But I've got a bad feeling, I must admit.

Eleven games in, it's too soon to say,
One hundred fifty-one more still to play;
But to say the least it's been rocky so far,
No high fives just yet, and no caviar.

I suggest we start over, today's the day;
The Sox open at home, it's a matinee.
Some kids will skip school to watch the team play;
Principals may not approve but do not make them pay.

For those of you there, with seats in the bleachers,
Check around, you may spot some of those pupils' teachers;
And in center field, you'll see Jackie Bradley,
He's a "junior" you know, named after his daddy.

Benintendi and Betts are the rest of the trio,
Like a pianist I know, they play with con brio;
The rest of the team is the same as last fall,
Their names I'm sure you all will recall,

Xander Bogaerts just signed for another six years,
So at shortstop we need have no immediate fears;
When the team is on defense, Martinez is a sitter.
That's what happens if you're the designated hitter.

Moreland at first, and Devers at third,
Pedroia remains disabled, his return still deferred;
At second, Brock Holt, the utility player,
Or maybe Ed Nunez, he's no giant slayer.

And neither is Vazquez, he's behind the plate,
Good on defense for sure, but his hitting's not great;
And that's the full lineup—oh I almost forgot—
We don't have a closer, which matters a lot.

Will Dombrowski find someone to come in and do closeout?
End the ninth with raised hands and give out a shout?
I'm betting he will, optimism still reigns,
It's a brand-new year for the game that sustains

Us through winter, and then in the dog days of summer,
When the heat can get bad and humidity's a bummer;
Politicians galore will surround us full time,
Thank the Lord there's still baseball, the game that's sublime. [52]

---

[52] It turned out there was a lot to fix, and the first eleven games were just the beginning of a mediocre 2019 season, with the team barely over 500 and ending up in third place, nineteen games behind the Yankees. Then it got worse, with the departure of Alex Cora (by "mutual agreement"), who was then suspended from baseball for a year because of his involvement in stealing signs as a coach for the Astros in 2017. He returned for the 2021 season as the Red Sox manager.

## My Incomplete Passes and the Glint in His Eye

Tom Brady has dominated professional football like no other player. Whatever the score, it didn't seem to matter. Tom would turn it around, even if the Pats were way behind and it was late in the fourth quarter. He had a glint in his eye—not a twinkle, which is entirely different—and the outcome belonged to him. Larry Bird had the same glint during his Celtics years, 1979–1992. It's a look that says, "Give me the ball and don't worry, I'll take care of the rest."

In my winless season as a junior varsity quarterback, I think my total yards gained passing was a negative number. Fortunately, they didn't keep such statistics back then. When the Stevens High varsity team won the 1956 state championship in the fall of my senior year, I marched downfield at halftime, playing my clarinet.

How would you describe the look on the face of Kansas City Chiefs quarterback Patrick Mahomes as he stood on the sidelines during the 2020 Super Bowl waiting for the Chiefs to regain the ball? Baby-faced? Cherubic? Determined?

I would choose the word "confident," a player who believes in himself. And when he straps on his helmet, takes the field, announces the play in the huddle, and then sizes up the defense, there is an unmistakable glint in his eye.

For much of the game the glint didn't seem to work, with Mahomes throwing two intercepted passes and Jimmy Garoppolo, late of the Patriots, seemingly leading the Forty-Niners on their way to victory. And then it did.

With only a few minutes left and San Francisco ahead by ten points, one of the announcers said, "Now the Chiefs have the Forty-Niners where they want them." He was referring, I assume, to the fact that the Chiefs had come back from behind in their last two playoff games, overcoming twenty-four- and ten-point deficits against the Texans and the Titans.

After winning the AFC championship, Mahomes had said, "We're not done yet. We're going to get it." Professional athletes (and their fans) brag all the time, "We're Number 1" and the like, but Mahomes wasn't bragging, he was predicting the future.

Did Mahomes really *know* that he would lead his team to victory in Super

Bowl LIV? Of course not. But bet against him at your peril.[53] He has more than a great arm that can throw from all angles, and more than great running legs. He can do what many people cannot, which is put intercepted passes and other mistakes behind him and focus entirely on what comes next. That's the self-confident glint in his eye.

I have never regretted my one disastrous no-win season as a quarterback or forgotten the fear I felt looking into the eyes of those gigantic Bellows Falls defensive linemen. I understood, much later, that it was good preparation for becoming a trial lawyer. And, speaking metaphorically, I like to think that in later years I completed some passes in the courtroom, with a glint in my eye.

---

53   Before the beginning of the 2021 Super Bowl, I e-mailed my sons, "Don't bet against Mahomes." Then former Patriot, Tom Brady, now of the Tampa Bay Bucs, took the field, and he still had the glint. If Mahomes had his from 2020, it seemed to have gone away the first time the Bucs defense took the field, and he never really got it back in what turned into a rout. Fortunately, neither of my sons is a betting man.

# My Parking Spots and Claremont Karma

People who live in Jaffrey or Claremont have a lot in common. One similarity is that they don't have to worry about finding a parking spot. That was also true in the 1950s, when I got my license and first drove downtown to the Pleasant Sweet Restaurant. When the space right in front was taken, I felt like I'd been skunked.

So, all my life, I have refused to worry about finding a parking place. If someone asks, "Where will we park?" my standard answer is, "Don't worry, I'm from Claremont."

One time, for example, the Pianist and I drove to New York and stayed at a midtown hotel that had "free parking." We had tickets for a show at Lincoln Center, and the question was how to get there. We were meeting friends later for dinner somewhere on the West Side, so I told the Pianist, "We'll drive." She shrugged her shoulders but knew better than to argue.

We got close to Lincoln Center, I took a right turn on one of those streets where nobody can afford to live, and a car pulled out of a legal, metered space. It was a block away from the theatre, and I apologized. "Sorry, this is the closest I can get." For me, it seems, finding a parking place is a competitive sport.

After the show, we drove off to meet our friends. I parked right outside the restaurant, shades of the Pleasant Sweet in Claremont but with a lot pricier menu, and we met them inside. After dinner, the four of us stepped outside and I pointed to our car. "You what?" our incredulous friends said. "Hop in," I replied in my best, nonchalant tone of voice, "We'll drive you home."

Until recently that was my best parking story, but no longer. On a recent July Friday, I surpassed my Manhattan success.

My daughter was visiting from California, with my 5 3/4 (he insists) year-old grandson. The Red Sox were in town to play the Tigers after a disastrous road trip, and I had tickets.

First we drove down Beacon Street, hoping to park near a restaurant called Audubon's. It was about five thirty, and I spotted a space, put quarters in the meter, and then read the fine print. "Resident Parking Only After 6." That took care of leaving it there and hiking several blocks to Fenway Park. But we chanced it, had our dinner, and got back in the ticket-free car at six thirty.

"I will drop you off near the ballpark," I said.

"Where will you park?" my concerned daughter asked anxiously.

"I'll figure something out," I answered, thinking of the parking area hawkers offering a "not blocked" space for only fifty dollars. At those prices, you'd think the Red Sox were having a good season.

I drove through construction on Park Drive and took a left on Brookline Avenue, inching my way along. As I approached Yawkey Way, I looked ahead and an apparition in the form of an on-street parking spot manifested itself in the shadow of Fenway Park. Even I was surprised, but I recovered quickly and grabbed it.

As I was once again putting quarters in the meter, a meter maid came along, and I said, "I'm legal. What do you think of this parking space?"

"Awesome," she replied. "How did you manage that?"

She looked puzzled when I gave her the answer: "Claremont karma."

# My Crystal Ball and Nineteen for 2019

This column is called "Looking Back," but just this once I've decided to look the other way. So, here are my nineteen "Looking Ahead" predictions for 2019. First sports, then politics.

1. After the Patriots don't make it to the Super Bowl, Tom Brady vows to play next season "and beyond." He doesn't say what or where.[54]

2. After the Patriots lose the Super Bowl, Bill Belichick announces that he is "stepping back." He doesn't say from what or to where.

3. Robert Kraft praises Tom and Bill with the words, "They're like family." He doesn't say whose family.

4. *Boston Globe* sportswriter Ben Volin writes, "It's over." He doesn't explain.

5. The Red Sox open the home season at Fenway Park on April 9 with Dustin Pedroia at second base. "I'm a lot younger than Brady," he mumbles.

6. Wall or no wall, in April and May America's major league baseball teams will play regular season games at the Estadio de Béisbol in Monterrey, Mexico.

8. Brexit or no Brexit, on June 29 and 30 the Red Sox will play the Yankees at Queen Elizabeth Olympic Park in London. Cricket bats will not be used.

9. By the All-Star Game, thirty-seven Democrats will have visited Iowa, forty-one will have "explored" New Hampshire, and Oregon senator Jeff Merkley will be considering a trip to Guam.

10. Chris Pappas is one of the Iowa thirty-seven, Annie Kuster is not. Paul Hodes visits Polar Caves Park in Rumney and says, "I live here."

11. World's richest man Jeff Bezos, owner of Amazon.com, goes to both Iowa and New Hampshire in August. "Just delivering packages," he exclaims while eating a corn dog at the Iowa State Fair.

12. On Labor Day, Senator Merkley takes to an otherwise empty Senate floor and announces, "I favor statehood for Guam."

---

54   Unlike most of my "predictions," this one turned out to be prophetic. Brady left New England and at age forty-three became the 2020 quarterback for Tampa Bay. He proved, during the Bucs' 2021 Superbowl victory over the Chiefs, that he is ageless.

13. Non-senator and non-judge Roy Moore drives his truck from Alabama to Manchester and is seen standing in line outside the Red Arrow Diner holding a small statue of the Ten Commandments.[55]

14. Elaine Chao resigns as Secretary of Transportation to become president of Mount Holyoke College, her alma mater. "I'm a New Englander at heart," she tells *The Washington Post*, which Jeff Bezos also owns.

15. Ms. Chao's husband, Mitch McConnell, immediately declares, "I've had enough." He does did not say of what.

16. In October, New Brunswick, whose forty-nine legislators each makes $85,000 a year, invites New Hampshire to become one of the Maritime Provinces. Governor Chris Sununu makes an "exploratory" visit to Frederickton.

17. Upon returning to Concord, the governor announces that New Brunswick is "too rich for my blood." Rumor has it that he is considering a bill to reduce New Hampshire legislators' salaries, currently one hundred dollars a year.

18. The Supreme Court orders the Mueller Report unsealed. The report does not include the words "witch hunt."

19. President Trump says he plans to read the Report after he finishes reading Proust's *Remembrance of Things Past*.

---

55 For many presidential campaigns this diner has been a mandatory destination for candidates running in New Hampshire's first-in-the-nation primary election. In 2003, Moore was removed from his position as chief justice of Alabama because he defied a federal court order to remove a Ten Commandments monument from the courthouse.

# My Crystal Ball and Twenty for 2020

Last year's crystal ball predicted that President Trump would read the Mueller Report as soon as he finished Proust's *Remembrance of Things Past*. So far as I know, neither that nor most of my other predictions came true. But here I go again, with twenty for 2020, which may or may not be the start of a new decade.

1. After a private morning phone call with Vladimir Putin, Donald Trump announces that the 2020 election will be postponed "indefinitely."

2. An "Obama Judge" enters an injunction reinstating the 2020 election, and Trump sends out a dozen tweets calling the judge "stupid," "lazy," and a "traitor."

3. New Hampshire Secretary of State William Gardner announces, "We're going ahead. It's the law."

4. Tulsi Gabbard wins the New Hampshire primary, with Andrew Yang a close second.

5. Elizabeth Warren endorses Michael Bloomberg. "He's got a plan," she says.

6. When told that the Constitution limits a president to two terms, Corey Lewandowski says, "That's fake news."

7. Trump signs bill banning presidential tweets and announces. "From now on, I will address my subjects on the radio, just like FDR, and he got elected four times."

8. The Clintons move back to Little Rock amid reports that Bill plans to follow Paul Hodes's "good example" and run for the Arkansas state senate.[56]

9. Mark Zuckerberg joins the Trump campaign as a "special adviser" on antisocial media.

10. Alan Dershowitz declines to join Trump's impeachment defense team because "I've got my hands full defending myself on Martha's Vineyard."

11. Senators McConnell and Lindsey Graham change their minds, the Senate convicts Trump, and President Pence pardons Rudy Giuliani.

---

56  Former Congressman Paul Hodes, who ran for the US Senate in 2010 and lost to Kelly Ayotte, ran for New Hampshire state senate in 2020 but lost in the primary.

12. After 103 ballots the Democratic Convention remains deadlocked, party brokers meet in a smoke-filled room, and Nancy Pelosi is nominated by acclamation.

13. The Republican Party adopts a platform plank vowing to repeal Article III of the Constitution, which establishes the Judiciary as the third branch of government.

14. Starbucks CEO Howard Schultz announces that he will run for president as an Independent, promising "a pumpkin spice latte in every car cupholder."[57]

15. Justice Brett Kavanaugh writes the Supreme Court opinion upholding Roe v. Wade. "I'm keeping my promise to Susan Collins," he tells Fox News.

16. Meghan Markle, Duchess of Sussex, tells Prince Harry, "I'd like a favor though; ask your grandmother to make my cousin, Mookie Betts, a knight."[58]

17. Melania Trump becomes the United States ambassador to Slovenia.

18. After no one responds to her posting on the Bumble dating site, Sharon Stone enters a nunnery.[59]

19. Chris Sununu promises that following his reelection he will rebuild a "smaller version" of the Old Man of the Mountain on Mount Monadnock.

20. Sir Mookie Betts hits a walk-off homerun in the seventh game and leads the Los Angeles Dodgers to a World Series victory over the Red Sox.[60]

And a Happy New Year to all. I think the new decade actually begins in 2021.

---

57 This is my twenty-first century version of "a chicken in every pot," a Republican slogan in the 1920s.

58 I stole the quoted words from what President Trump reportedly said to the president of Ukraine during the thirty-minute phone call that led to the first impeachment. And yes, Betts and Markle really are distant cousins.

59 In 2019, movie actress Sharon Stone went on a dating site called Bumble. The site locked her out for a time, thinking the posting was fake.

60 As it turned out, the Dodgers did win the 2020 World Series at the end of a pandemic-shortened season, but not against the Red Sox. They beat the Tampa Bay Rays.

# HEALTH

## My Useful Aids and the Parts that Work

Many years ago, I developed a pain in my ankle which, according to a recent article in *Smithsonian* magazine, is a "dauntingly complex part of the anatomy." In my case, braces secured by Velcro help me avoid pain and walk with a spring in my step. They have become a part of my daily life, like hearing aids and contact lenses.

Contact lens singular; left eye only. That's my good eye. The other one is lazy, meaning it does not work very well, and is not correctible. I am one of thirty-eight million Americans who wear contacts, although I don't know how many of us are of the one-eye-only variety.

Every day, I put a lens on my left eyeball, and every night I take it off. Pesky little thing a contact lens. Try finding it if you drop it on the floor, especially if you don't see so well, which is why you wear it in the first place. I'm in no hurry for cataract surgery, but I understand they can implant something called an intraocular lens which, I assume, would eliminate crawling around on the floor trying to find the thing.[61]

Hearing is another matter. It used to be that the Pianist and I would go to a movie and I would keep saying "What?" and complain about all the mumblings. Fortunately, she has good ears and would serve as my translator. I preferred foreign films where I could skip the dialogue and, with the help of my contact lens, read the subtitles.

So finally, I went to an audiologist, and now I'm on my third set of hearing aids. I remember the time I wore my first set and went outside.

"What's all that racket?" I asked the Pianist.

---

61   After several years of "not yets" from the eye doctor, I had the surgery on my "good" eye in the fall of 2019, thereby eliminating searches on the floor since the implanted lens stays put. I have thrown away all the solutions, plastic holders, and other paraphernalia that have been part of my life for many decades, but old habits die hard. My brain still thinks I'm supposed to go through the daily lens cleaning, soaking, and in and out rituals.

"Birds," she said.

Then there's my flat feet, which heredity threw in along with the lazy eye. It took me a while, but eventually I learned about orthotics, the low-tech miracle cure. Stick them in your shoes, and your feet aren't flat anymore.

I have also discovered the "Subtitles" button on the TV remote. Using it means you can watch movies in English on Netflix and read the dialogue, just like seeing a foreign language film in the movie theatre.

I recently read *Being Mortal,* in which the physician-author Atul Gawande writes about problems a lot more serious than my small inconveniences. I usually avoid "self-help" books, especially those dealing with "end of life" issues, but this one left me feeling upbeat. Like it or not, a lot of us are running the risk of making it to four score years or even beyond, "by reason of strength" according to the Bible. or just by dumb luck if you ask me.

I recommend the book, and I, for one, am glad to be in the running.[62] I have a lot of company. Today there are nearly as many old people as there are young ones. You know who they are—the ones who still wear a wristwatch and read the newspaper.

At a time in life when I am losing friends, some younger and some not much older, I think about the randomness of life and my good fortune. I am still able to walk, to see, and to hear. I can even find my car keys . . . most of the time.

---

62 I also recommend A *Bittersweet Season: Caring for Our Aging Parents—and Ourselves, by Jane Gross.* Her father, Milt Gross, covered the Yankees for the New York Post. The book is about how she brought her widowed mother back from Florida to New York and then dealt with the confusing world of assisted living facilities and elder services.

# My Ankle Braces and the Supply Chain Backup

A long time ago I developed a left ankle problem. Some sort of tendon issue, but we can fix it, the surgeon said. "No thanks," I said, and went looking for something simpler and non-invasive.

I found it, an "Aircast" brace with that word printed on the strap in turquoise green letters. Easy on and easy off, thanks to Velcro. Painless walking.

Sometime later, for symbiotic reasons maybe, the right ankle started imitating the left. This time I skipped the doctor and started wearing the "R" (for right) brace with the same lettering.

They do the job, but they wear out every six months or so, and I order a new pair. It's easy. Just go online and find the ankle brace with the right color on the strap.

Usually I order from "Better Braces," but this time I went on Amazon.com which, say what you will about the company and Jeff Bezos, does seem to deliver what you ordered—free delivery if you sign up for Amazon Prime. Like other online vendors, they include a picture of the product, so you know you're ordering the right thing. I put in my order and got an immediate confirmation.

The blue-and-white Bubble Wrapped package arrived with two braces, one "R" and one "L." The "R" one was fine, but "L" was a different brace with no turquoise lettering. Not what I ordered.

A shipping clerk's mistake, I thought. These things happen. I figured I could just go online, find the "Returns" section, get the bar-coded return coupon, and drop it off at the Amazon returns desk at Kohl's.

But that's not what happened. Instead, Amazon's message was that they were crediting my account, but I should keep the wrong brace. Why, I wondered, don't they want it back?

Well, I suppose that's Amazon's business, so I went back to the Amazon. com webpage, spotted the "L" brace with the turquoise green lettering, went to checkout, and made the purchase for the second time. Two days later the familiar package arrived.

They sent the same wrong "L" as before! I went back to "Returns," this time a bit irritated. But this time the voiceless online message said, "No returns on this product." Apparently, you can get a credit for the wrong brace once, but you can't do anything if they send it again. And now you're stuck with two of them.

I decided it was time to call Amazon on the phone. You can actually do that, and the service person was friendly and helpful. "They must be having a supply chain problem," he said, "so they made a substitution."

Welcome to the backup—thousands of unloaded containers on ships resting offshore in various harbors. Maybe my left brace is in one of them.

The Amazon representative then said he would be glad to help. It took a few minutes before he came back on the line and told me he had issued a credit. I thanked him and asked him to send me the bar-coded return so I could send it back.

"I can't do that," he replied.

"Why not?" I asked.

"Because the system says all I can do is issue a credit," he answered. "Perhaps you can give them to someone."

This story reminds me of when I went to the Stevens High School junior prom and my girlfriend told me I had two left feet.

# My Last Procedure and the Benefits of Age

Today, the word "procedure" seems to cover every medical event, from routine tests to open heart surgery. Those of you who have reached a certain stage in life may recognize the "procedure" that is the subject of this column.

It begins with a notice from your doctor that "it has been ten years" since your last time. So, you make an appointment, and they send you your "instructions." Squeamish readers need go no further.

As you go through the list, not remembering the details from a decade ago, you think to yourself, "I can handle this. I've done it before."

So, you go to the pharmacy and buy three ten-ounce bottles of an "oral solution" located at the opposite end of the store from anything actually drinkable. This "solution" comes in different flavors, so you buy one cherry, one lemon, and one grape.

And then, a few days before the appointment, you begin a "low-residue" diet. No fruits or raw vegetables or salads or cereals or bran or nuts. Also, no hot dogs or sauerkraut. I like all of those foods, but a few days without is no problem. How much sauerkraut does anyone need?

Then comes the "day before," and it's all kidding aside. Nothing but clear liquids. I bought enough bouillon, Gatorade, and apple juice to last a year, if not a lifetime. I don't recall when I last drank any bouillon, but I have quite a few leftover little cubes if anyone needs them.

Then the hard part, the not-so-tolerable, sets in. The night before the "procedure," you start drinking the stuff from the drug store, which tastes awful in all its different flavors. For those who have not had the experience, I can tell you it's the worst drink ever. It makes you want to drive over to Bedford and buy a case of Moxie.[63]

Once the first round is over, and by now it's around 8:00 p.m., you start chug-a-lugging those clear liquids. I had planned on some serious reading, or perhaps watching an episode of *Fauda* on my iPad. All such thoughts went away. Blessed sleep, until the interruptions start in what the humorist Dave Barry has labeled the "behindular zone."

---

63  Moxie, a soft drink known for its bitter taste, caused by gentian root extract, was invented by a Maine doctor as a patent medicine in 1884. It is the "official" beverage of Maine. Coca-Cola bought the company in 2018, but the Moxie Beverage Company remains located in Bedford, New Hampshire.

But that's not the end of it. The sadist who dreamed up this regimen says you need to do the whole thing over again six hours "before your scheduled procedure time," which for me was 9:00 a.m. So, at three o'clock in the morning, I embark on Round 2, another fifteen ounces of the undrinkable liquids, the same clear chasers, and sporadic sleep but mostly awake waiting for the minutes to pass.

When you show up at the hospital, they take you into an enclosed space and tell you to put all your stuff in green plastic bags. Then they ask a lot of questions, beginning with "name and date of birth." I'm usually pretty good at that, but I was hungry and tired and stumbled over the year.

The doctor, who hasn't changed much in the last ten years, arrives with a smile on his face. No wonder. He's been eating just fine and got a good night's sleep.

And then they wheel you off, dripping IV and all, and the next thing you know you're back where you started. Apparently, the procedure is over, though you don't remember it.

The doctor arrives, still smiling, and says it all "looks good." He hands you "discharge instructions," a page that includes eight color photos. I had no idea that particular part of my anatomy was so colorful. "Doctor," I say, "You haven't made getting ready for this any easier."

"That's true," he says, "but I have more good news for you. That's your last one."

The benefits of age never felt so good. If you are over fifty, I hope this article won't deter you. Despite all my complaints, it's worth it.

# My Missed Meeting and Lessons Learned

One time I was taking a plane to Washington for a meeting. We got diverted to Baltimore. Bad weather? Engine trouble? I don't remember. The disembodied voice told us we could get off the plane if we wanted but assured us we'd be back in the air soon. I believed the voice, which was a mistake. I could have rented a car, hailed a cab, taken a bus, or boarded a train, even hitchhiked. But I did none of these, and I never got to the meeting.

The memory of that missed meeting came back to me recently. I had been having some on and off pain, so I saw a specialist to get it fixed. He performed the usual examination, took some tests, and pronounced, "It's 'Something-itis,'" using a medical term I'd never heard before. And I believed him. He put me on an over-the-counter painkiller and told me maybe it would go away and maybe it wouldn't.

I didn't like that prognosis, so I decided to see another specialist for a second opinion. He ordered more tests and ultimately told me he didn't know what was causing the pain. "Maybe it's 'Something-itis,' but maybe it isn't," he opined. "Let's just call it pain."

I was willing to go along with that but calling it what it obviously was didn't seem to provide much of a plan going forward. I pondered my next step.

The equivalent of getting off the plane and taking a bus might have been to try acupuncture, but I didn't do that. Instead, I went to see my primary care doctor, who said, "I think it's anatomical." I wasn't sure what she meant, but I took her advice and saw a surgeon. He found the likely root of the problem, a hernia, and said, "I can fix that." We made a date for outpatient surgery three weeks later.

Then things got worse. I e-mailed a distress signal to my primary care doctor, she called me at home, and I ended up spending several nighttime hours in the hospital emergency room. The pain finally subsided and, after speaking with my doctor at two o'clock in the morning, they let me leave.

The next day, a Thursday, I called the surgeon's office to tell them I couldn't wait three weeks. They found a place on his operation schedule twelve days later, which was better but still not soon enough for me. "How about someone else?" I asked the surgeon. He said he would reach out to some colleagues.

Later that day I got a call back. "Dr. H. can do it tomorrow morning."

I had no idea who Dr. H. was, but at that point I would have settled for the janitor. So, I showed up early the next morning with an empty stomach, as instructed.

Dr. H. turned out to be an excellent surgeon, and he seems to have fixed it. The old pain has gone away.

There are some lessons to be learned from this medical experience, one of which is not to grit your teeth and settle for pain. I can think of at least three others.

One, see if your family doctor will give you his or her e-mail address. Mine did, long ago, and she was there when I needed help. When I arrived in the emergency room, they knew I was coming. And the reason they called her before letting me out was that she asked them to do so.

Two, see that doctor first. I have nothing against specialists, but as the expression goes, if the only tool you have is a hammer, everything will likely look like a nail. In my case, that nail was called "Something-itis."

And three, if one means of transportation isn't getting you where you want to go, don't just sit there. Get off and take another.

# My Good Fortune and Remedies for the Ills of Life

*If music be the food of love, play on.*
William Shakespeare, *Twelfth Night*

The 2021 baseball season is upon us and, to my surprise, I have gone back to the sports pages to check on the Red Sox who, after a halting start, went on a nine-game winning streak. I still haven't recovered from the Mookie Betts trade (he's hitting .323 for the Dodgers), but the Red Sox players look like a scrappy bunch, and postgame comments from team manager Alex Cora, back from a year in exile, are music to my ears.

Even so, I still keep track of the front page coronavirus statistics. Over ninety thousand New Hampshire residents have become infected, and more than a thousand of our fellow Granite Staters have perished. The Covid-19 survivors can attest to the truth of what my father used to say, "It's no fun to be sick."

New Hampshire leads the country in distributing its allotted vaccine doses, but even so, we are not yet up to 25 percent fully vaccinated, and new cases are going up, not down. To quote Governor Sununu, "We are still in the thick of it."

I suppose the best way to avoid getting infected would be to live alone on a desert island or move into a leftover 1950s bomb shelter. Short of those extremes, we can follow such commonsense practices as voluntary mask wearing and social distancing. We can also think harder about how to stay healthy in a broader sense: don't smoke, avoid fatty foods, get some exercise, watch your weight. Willpower comes easier for some than it does for others, and no matter how careful we are, luck has a lot to do with it.

I have had the good fortune to avoid serious illness so far, but I know better than to take much credit. Recent experience reminds us that even the most careful person can get sick. If that happens, we may have no choice but to see the doctor, who will likely make a diagnosis and recommend a course of treatment. Whether it's "it will go away on its own," medication, or the hospital, modern science is finding that music and poetry can help us prepare for treatment and get over our symptoms.

On April 13, 2021, *The New York Times* featured two health-related columns, one captioned "Read the Doctor's Advice, Chapter and Verse," the other "Music Shows Its Power to Soothe and Heal." Both articles resonated with me.

The Pianist has been telling me for decades that music is good for the body, not just the soul. She is a fan of the neurologist-writer Oliver Sacks, whose book *Musicophilia* promotes the idea that for patients with illnesses ranging from migraines to Parkinson's and Alzheimer's, music can "speak" in a way that words cannot. He cites case histories that prove the healing power of music.

The *Times* article about "music therapy" cites medical benefits at all stages of life, from neonatal intensive care units to oncology waiting rooms to surgery recovery rooms to hospice care. Unlike medications, music has no worrisome side effects, and listening to it requires no willpower.

A psychiatry professor quoted in the poetry article says that "Poetry can serve as a vaccine for the soul." His point is that all of us go through difficult times, and often poetry can provide a lift that pills cannot. When I read those words, I immediately thought of Robert Frost, who wrote "Whose woods these are I think I know, His house is in the village though." No matter how many times you read "Stopping by Woods on a Snowy Evening," or practically anything else he wrote, you discover something new and uplifting.

The poetry article cites Amanda Gorman's inauguration poem as an example of the emotional and social power of poetry. "Let the globe, if nothing else, say this is true; that even as we grieved, we grew." And "Being American is more than a pride we inherit, It's the past we step into and how we repair it." Like the poetry of Frost and many other poets, these powerful words do more than rhyme and inspire. They can encourage us to feel better about ourselves and about the future.

You don't have to be sick to listen to music or read a poem. You can be healthy and do it just for fun. I recommend Chopin, George Gershwin, and Dave Brubeck, along with Frost, Amy Dickinson, and Walt Whitman. But if you prefer, you can start with "Take Me Out to the Ball Game" and then turn to "Casey at the Bat."

# LIFE AND POLITICS

## My White Childhood and the Moral Universe

I never had a black schoolmate until I got to college in 1957 and met my fellow freshman, Dick Nurse. Reg Lindsay, who became my partner and friend many years later, had the opposite experience growing up in segregated Birmingham. He never had a white schoolmate until he got to Harvard Law School in the late 1960s.

How did it feel to grow up in an all-white town in a mostly all-white state? The truth is that during those formative years, when black people were known as "colored" or "Negro," I never thought about it. In grade school we sang a song with the words "You can get good milk from a brown-skinned cow, the color of the skin doesn't matter anyhow," and that is all I remember learning on the subject of racial tolerance.

When I was young, there was an annual minstrel show at the town hall auditorium, now the Claremont Opera House. The local judge, a pillar of the community, was an "end man," face blackened with burnt cork. No one in the all-white audience seemed to consider this intolerant, much less as racist stereotype.

I should point out that Claremont did have black residents before I was born. A woman from Barbados named Louisa Parris married a man named Edwards and settled in Claremont, where he worked for the town's principal employer, Sullivan Machinery. One of their eight children was a classmate of my Uncle Eddie, Stevens High Class of 1938. And one of Louisa Edwards's grandchildren, Katherine McCray, born in Claremont, was the mother of the writer Chirlane McCray, who is the wife of New York mayor Bill deBlasio.

I was a high school freshman in 1954, when the Supreme Court decided that "separate but equal" education is unconstitutional. I was a sophomore in December 1955, when Rosa Parks was arrested in Montgomery for refusing to give up her seat to a white person and sit in the rear of the bus. The year-long Montgomery Bus Boycott began a few days later. And by the middle of my senior year in 1957, Martin Luther King Jr. had become an important national figure.

Did these events make it into our classrooms? Maybe, but I have no memory of it. My best guess is that, for most people in our corner of New Hampshire, racism in America just didn't seem relevant.

I do remember the segregationist governors and senators who held out for so long for what they euphemistically called "states' rights." In September 1963, when I was in my last year of law school and Reg Lindsay was entering Morehouse College in Atlanta, white supremacists bombed the 16th Street Baptist Church in Birmingham, killing four young girls. Reg knew one of them.

We know from recent events that Jefferson's Declaration of Independence words, "all men are created equal" have yet to become a reality. But hope is hard to quench, and the words "No justice, no peace" are heard today not just in places with large black populations but everywhere. Claremont's minstrel shows are a distant memory, while the statue commemorating Union soldiers who died in the Civil War still stands in Broad Street Park. And, like citizens in cities and towns across the country, people recently gathered near that statue to protest racism.

Martin Luther King Jr., like my friend Reg a Morehouse graduate, said, "The arc of the moral universe is long, but it bends towards justice." Time will tell, but what we are seeing now gives us renewed reason to believe he was right.[64]

---

64   I wrote this piece in 2020, shortly after Minneapolis police officers killed George Floyd on May 25. On June 1, 2020, federal officials cleared away peaceful protesters so that Donald Trump could walk across the street from the White House for a photo op holding a bible in front of St. John's Church. Four days later, on orders from Mayor Muriel Bowser, the Washington, DC, Public Works Department painted "Black Lives Matter" in thirty-five-foot-tall capital letters on 16th Street NW. On April 20, 2021, a Minneapolis jury convicted Derek Chauvin, the police officer who knelt on George Floyd's neck for over nine minutes, of second and third degree murder and manslaughter.

# My Wrong Purchase and Filling the Bucket

Not for the first time, I went to the store and got the wrong thing. This time it was deck stain. I bought water-based, only to learn from an expert that I would be much better off using oil-based. So, the next day I headed back to the store, trying to think of a good excuse. I had extra thinking time, since hundreds of motorcycles, a regular New Hampshire happening, held me up from making a left turn on Route 202.

I came up with a strategy, but when I got to the paint counter my salesperson wasn't there. I forged ahead anyway. "I made a mistake," I told the new man. "I bought the wrong stain, but it's a special color so if you can't exchange it, that's OK."

He pondered this for a minute, looked inside my can of wrong stain, and then said the magic words. "I'll see what I can do."

While my new oil-based stain was being agitated in the paint shaker, we got to talking. My accommodating salesman's former employer, a well-known company, decided after thirty-nine years that they no longer needed him.

"That's not fair," I said.

"Stuff happens," he said. "They gave me a fair severance, and I had my retirement plan. But I'm too young to retire, so I took this job."

"Too young to retire," words that always give me pause. I remember when my old law firm left me by going out of business in 2002. I had been there thirty-eight years and, like the helpful stain exchanger, was "too young to retire."

Now it is a dozen years later, and people regularly ask, "Are you still working?" When I say yes, retirees usually respond in one of two ways. Either they say, "Don't ever retire," or "I only wish I had done it sooner." Some talk about their "bucket list," words having nothing to do with paint that, according to Google, refer to "10,000 things to do before you die." At the rate of one a day, that would take twenty-seven years. Somehow that isn't encouraging.

My grandfather had no bucket list. He retired at sixty-five as manager of the Metropolitan Life office in Claremont and spent the next twenty years reading, listening to Red Sox games, drinking coffee at the Pleasant Sweet

Restaurant, and enjoying his family. I don't think he was ever bored. My father, on the other hand, never retired. He just stopped going to the mill, due to poor health and other reasons. He missed it terribly.

I ran into a lawyer acquaintance recently, a man several years younger than me. I asked how he was doing, and he said, "I'm retiring and moving to Maine."

"What are you planning to do when you get there?" I asked.

"I think I'll learn to read music and take up the cello," he answered. "Do you think that's realistic?"

"No problem," I replied, thinking to myself, "that's enough to fill an entire bucket."

He asked when I was going to retire. I had no answer but admitted he wasn't the first person to ask. I'll have plenty of time to think about that when I get around to opening the can and staining the deck.

# My Downsizing and the Beautiful Deck

We bought our house in Boston's South End, just around the corner from where we had been living, in 1998. It had many nice features, including a deck off the dining area. We imagined ourselves eating breakfast out there in nice weather, watching squirrels scamper up and down our very own tree—a bit of the country in the middle of the city.

Over the years we did just that. When friends would come to visit, they would often admire the tree and say how lucky we were to have this outside space.

I've been "downsizing" in recent years by getting shorter. Last spring, we decided to downsize in a different sense by selling the house with the nice deck and the tree out back. The real estate market in Boston's South End has been "hot," we were told, and vertical living with three sets of stairs was becoming a challenge.

My daughter had recently sold her San Francisco condominium, which is how I learned about "staging." In case you're not familiar with that word, it means you hire a specialist who knows how to spiff up a house to make it more attractive to buyers. In her case it worked pretty well, so the Pianist and I thought maybe we should get some advice.

"I don't think you need to do much," our broker told us. "I can help you with the staging."

That sounded good to us, since it was part of her service at no extra cost. "What do you think we should do?" we asked.

After a thorough walk-through during which she pointed out various items—some clutter here and there, a few too many chairs, curtains hiding portions of windows—she focused on the deck. "You'll need to fix that," she said, pointing to wood that had seen better days. "And some painting out here would help too," she added.

Before listing the house for sale, we, meaning mostly the Pianist, straightened up the place, took down some curtains, and followed our broker's advice. We called our Mr. Fix-It to help us out with the deck. After all, we were avoiding the cost of a "stager," so spending some money out there would undoubtedly pay off.

When it came time to show the house, that deck looked much better. New wood, matching paint, and pots with flowers. Sure enough, within a few days we got an offer, accompanied by a letter from the prospective buyers telling us that they loved the house just as it was. That appealed to us since some other prospective bidders had talked about making major changes. But mostly it was that the "we won't change it" letter writers made the highest offer, so we sold it to them.

We signed the necessary papers, and soon the house no longer belonged to us. If the weather cooperated, we thought, the new owner could enjoy the deck before winter.

A few weeks later we were in the old neighborhood, so we drove down the alleyway behind the house, just to have a look.

The deck is gone.[65]

---

65  A while later, the tree came down as well.

# My Wannabe Presidents
# and a Pre-Inaugural Conversation

I got interested in presidential politics in 1948. My mother took me downtown and pointed to a man running for the Republican nomination. "Look, Joey," "she said, "there's the next president of the United States." She was pointing at Harold Stassen, who was making the first of what turned out to be multiple unsuccessful campaigns for the Republican presidential nomination.

After Thomas E. Dewey turned back Stassen's challenge and won the nomination, my friend Mike told me Truman would win, and I told him that was nuts, which may have been my first in a succession of wrong political predictions. I wasn't alone. The *Chicago Tribune*'s memorable day-after-election-day, egg-on-your-face headline was "Dewey Defeats Truman."[66]

My second viewing of a presidential candidate was in 1952—Tennessee senator Estes Kefauver. I don't remember whether he was wearing his trademark coonskin cap, but he lost in the primaries to Adlai Stevenson, who lost to General Eisenhower in two general elections, that year and again in November 1956.

The following January, I attended my first inauguration, marching down Pennsylvania Avenue as a member of the Stevens High School Band. The president and Vice President Nixon waved as we walked past the reviewing stand.

After Kefauver, several election cycles passed before I laid eyes on another presidential candidate. But in 1987 my friend and former Hill & Barlow partner, Mike Dukakis, who had become governor of Massachusetts, decided to run. I threw myself into that effort, gave myself the title "Senior Staff Counsel," attended the convention in Atlanta, and prepared to attend my second inauguration. Instead, I watched Chief Justice William Rehnquist swear in George H.W. Bush on television.

In 2007, after another period of campaign inactivity, I heard about a candidate named Barack Obama. I was smitten from the start, and I put a lot of time into his campaign and even got to spend some time with him, in

---

66  If anyone is interested in that historic election, there is an excellent recent book by A. J. Baime entitled *Dewey Defeats Truman: The 1948 Election and the Battle for America's Soul.*

Boston and in Puerto Rico. I endured that frigid January 20, 2009, day on the Washington mall, finally attending my second inauguration. I watched as he took the oath of office and gave his first speech as president. Like Lincoln, he quoted Scripture: "The time has come to set aside childish things," and reminded us that Americans "have duties to ourselves, our nation and the world."

Back in 1988, I had assumed that having a friend and former colleague run for president was a one-time experience, but I was doubly wrong. In 2020, Bill Weld and Deval Patrick, who had both been partners of mine at Hill & Barlow and went on to become Massachusetts governors, joined the race. The Pianist and I saw Deval and the other Democratic candidates speak in Manchester in February 2020, a few days before the New Hampshire primary. I saw Deval and asked how he was doing. "I think I'm getting the hang of it," he told me. Maybe so, but the following Tuesday the voters went elsewhere, and he wisely decided it was too late and too little.

We also saw another candidate that night in Manchester, Joe Biden. The polls had him running well behind several other candidates, and on the way home the I told the Pianist he would be dropping out soon—proving once again that I haven't lost the knack.

That was the second time I had seen Joe Biden in person. The first was in Washington on January 19, 2009, the evening before that frigid inauguration day. By mere happenstance we were walking from one function to another, just the two of us. We talked about our grandchildren.

# My First Campaign and Involuntary Bubbles

*I'm forever blowing bubbles,*
*Pretty bubbles in the air. . . .*
Song by John William Kellette and Jaan Kenbrovin
that my grandmother used to sing

Boys State, according to its website, is "the week that shapes a lifetime." New Hampshire has participated in this American Legion Program for seventy-three years, but not in 2020. Canceled, "with deep regret, due to the ongoing public health emergency."

In 1955, when the world was much safer, I was one of several Claremonters who got accepted to spend a week at Boys State learning how government works. The high point was electing a "governor," and I somehow became the campaign manager for one of the two candidates.

We gathered the night before election day to plan strategy. Someone, maybe it was me, came up with an idea. We collected enough money, two dollars to be exact, to buy 200 pieces of bubble gum and covered the wrappers with new ones bearing our candidate's name. Then, as the "voters" entered the polling place and waited in line, we stood in the balcony and showered them with our relabeled pieces of Double Bubble, and watched them blow bubbles and vote at the same time. Our candidate won.[67]

As this year's 2020 presidential election draws closer, we are not blowing bubbles, we are living in them. The old legal maxim "a man's house is his castle" has taken on new meaning. Today, home is our refuge, more than ever a place to be safe. "Stay home," the authorities warn us.

As for baseball, I saw no point in writing my annual Red Sox poem this year. Yet the season did finally get under way, with Fenway Park and other ballparks turned into fan-less bubbles. One definition of "bubble" is "something that lacks reality." I'm reminded of the old question: If a tree falls

---

67   Heather Cox Richardson's 2020 book, *How the South Won the Civil War: Oligarchy, Democracy, and the Continuing Fight for the Soul of America,* recalls the impact of Lee Atwater's 1988 "Willie Horton ad," which completely undid Michael Dukakis's substantial lead in the presidential polls and put George H. W. Bush permanently ahead. Shortly before his death, Atwater apologized for the ad. There's no comparison, but now I'm wondering whether we overstepped with our bubble gum manna from above.

in a forest and no one is there to hear it, does it make any noise? As far as I could tell, the 2020 baseball season pretty much fell on deaf ears.

Still, as Plato said, necessity is the mother of invention. In July 2020, the National Basketball Association took over much of Disney World and converted it into a quarantined basketball village. The League created an elaborate system of rules set out in a 113-page manual. That's nearly nine million dollars a page when you consider that the NBA playoffs produce a billion dollars in television revenues.

Creating bubbles for professional basketball players is one thing, educating our school-age children at home is another. Looking back to when my children were young, I had it so easy, reminding them to do their homework and helping out when I could. I remember looking helplessly at math assignments and saying, "Sorry, you're on your own."

Today, two of our children have become involuntary "home schoolers," on their own in a very different sense. And no one is paying them as they slam-dunk from one laptop to another and dribble their way through apps, codes, and links, not to mention their own jobs.

My first election at Boys State may not have shaped my lifetime, but I still remember those bubble-blowing young voters, so it did leave a permanent impression. If our grandchildren tell their children what life in a pandemic was like (I forgot to ask my grandparents about 1918), I hope they will include not just the indelible horrific parts, but also such pretty bubbles as the strength of community, the love of family, and their grandfather's latest undertaking—baking bread.

# My New Pastime and Getting to Second Base

For over seventy years I have embraced our national pastime, baseball, as my personal pastime. Back in the day, I played second base, but that day ended when I didn't make the high school baseball team. Since then, I've had to content myself with rooting for the Red Sox who, in 1967, the "Impossible Dream" year, came from ninth place the year before to first in the league; and, in 2004, overcame the "Curse of the Bambino" and won it all. For fans like myself, loyalty paid off.

During the Covid-19 pandemic, my interest in baseball has waned, and I don't feel very loyal. In times such as these, it's hard to get worked up over how much the minimum major league baseball salary should be. On the one hand, $600,000 sounds like a lot, but on the other the owners can afford the $750,000. That difference, along with some others, has the opening day of spring training up in the air.

When the current troubles started early in 2020—two years seems like a lifetime ago—people speculated about how long it would take to create a vaccine, how many people would suffer, and when the virus would go away. As for how long, drug companies moved with warp speed. As for the other two, all we know is that the number is staggering, and no one knows when it will end.

Meanwhile, most people are washing their hands more often, some are reading more books, others are taking frequent walks, and nearly all of us have learned how to "get together" with others without being with them.

As for me, I have found refuge in the unlikeliest of places—the kitchen.

Where does someone whose cooking skills consist of using an outdoor grill begin? Unlike my grandmother, who seemed to make everything out of her head, I have no natural talent in this area.

I began by taking an inventory of our kitchen, where I found measuring cups, spatula, bowls, and various other useful implements. Then I found a cornbread recipe, which I thought I could manage. Various ingredients populated the cabinet, but no cornmeal. So off I went to the market and discovered that there is an entire aisle devoted to baking. Maybe, I thought, I'm biting off more than I can chew.

Here I am, nearly two years into this new and mysterious culinary world, and I can report modest progress. When I started, I knew about salt and pepper but not such aromatic spices as cardamom, cumin, and turmeric, which I now keep in my overcrowded "spice drawer." I've moved from cornbread to other baked goods, and the occasional entrée, and have even ventured somewhat beyond the recipes' four corners, though very gingerly.

One thing about cooking something from scratch is that it offers immediate results. You spend an hour or so getting everything just so, pop it in the preheated oven or on the burner, and the next thing you know you've smoked up the kitchen.

Well, not always, and I am making progress, which is not to say that Rachael Ray or Gordon Ramsay has anything to worry about. Sometimes I think that Julia Child, whom I had the pleasure of knowing, is smiling down on me.

In other words, as a cook I've made it to first base. Fortunately, I have help from a sous-chef, also known in these pages as the Pianist. She doesn't use recipes and rounded second base a long time ago.

# Our Land and a Time to Heal

Over the last fifteen years, I have written close to two hundred "Looking Back" columns. The title of every one of them, up to now, has begun with the word "My." But it's not good to be too rigid, so this time is different, and I have changed the "My" to "Our."

As I recently wrote, I am no philosopher. I am no biblical expert either, though I have read much of both the Old and New Testaments. I particularly like the book of Ecclesiastes and have from time to time reminded the Pianist that "the race is not to the swift, nor the battle to the strong" (Ecclesiastes 9:11). Whenever I do so, she asks, "Who is it to?"

This part of the Old Testament contains other remarkable observations that challenge how we look at the world, and at life. For example, according to the wise person (or persons, as some believe) who went by the pseudonym Ecclesiastes, "it is better to enter a house of mourning than a house of feasting." That gives us something to think about as we approach the feast of Thanksgiving 2020 during a pandemic that has created over 240,000 American houses of mourning.[68] And, regrettably, this is "a time to refrain," not a "time to embrace."

The book of Ecclesiastes also tells us that there is "a time to mourn" but also "a time to dance." Even if one of these activities may be "better" than the other, fortunately there is time for both. And while there is "a time to weep," there is also "a time to laugh." So, Mr. Ecclesiastes, whoever he was, is not a complete killjoy.

Some of the sayings are quite practical and down to earth. I like "a time to keep and a time to throw away," although I have some difficulty with the latter. Not that I'm a hoarder, but I do tend to hang onto stuff and still have some clothes I started wearing back in the last century. Fortunately, most foods and medicines have expiration dates, so some decisions are out of my hands.

Then there's "a time to be silent and a time to speak." I'm not so good at the first part of that one either. One way I deal with that problem is by using my left thumb and forefinger to pinch my lips and hold them together. It sounds silly, but it works.

---

68    By early 2022, the number had exceeded the death toll from the 1918 Spanish flu and was approaching 900,000.

If some of these biblical quotes sound familiar, it may be because you have read the Old Testament. Or it may be that you are remembering the 1965 song "Turn! Turn! Turn," sung by the Byrds. Pete Seeger usually came up with his own lyrics, as he did in "Where Have All the Flowers Gone" and "If I Had a Hammer," but in this particular case he cribbed from the Bible, which has no copyright protection. The "Turn" song made it to Number 1 on the Billboard Hot 100 charts.

Speaking of Pete Seeger, another song he didn't write (Woodie Guthrie did), but that he sang more than anyone, has been rambling around in my head for the last week. "This land is your land, this land is my land . . . This land was made for you and me."[69]

Ecclesiastes' words can be understood in different ways, but what I see and hear in them is both wisdom and a degree of optimism. He believed, as I do, that there is "a time for everything, and a season for every activity under heaven."

This piece is not about "Looking Back." I'm looking ahead, and I can think of no better way to end this post-2020 election column than with two of the most important activities "under heaven"—there is "a time to build" and there is "a time to heal."

---

69  It turned out that others had the same thought. At the inauguration of President Biden on January 20, 2021, Jennifer Lopez gave a stirring bilingual rendition of the song, combining it with "America the Beautiful." On January 20, 2009, at the first inauguration of President Obama, I watched and heard Pete Seeger and Bruce Springsteen lead the crowd in a joyous rendition of the song.

# My Retraction and What Lies Ahead

This is not the column I intended to publish to start off 2021. In fact, I had already written "My 21 for 2021," once again making s series of outlandish, and hopefully humorous, "predictions" for the year just started. Then, on January 6, 2021, President Trump incited a mob, thousands laid siege to our national Capitol building, and suddenly cracking jokes about Trump no longer felt right, or even in good taste. I have decided to retract what I wrote, or at least most of it.

So, I will not mention anything about the "Mar-A-Lago White House," or about Trump issuing a self-commemorative stamp and sending out his "last" misspelled tweet saying "a leter is better." As it happens, this man's use of social media created a clear and present danger to both the English language and the country.

As I write these words, on Friday, January 8, 2021, I have no idea what the next twelve days, the remainder of what's left of the Trump administration, will bring. Despite the title of this column, I make no prediction of what lies ahead.

We have seen an attack not only on a building but on ourselves. Property has been destroyed, arrests have been made, people have died. The United States lies before the rest of the world in disgrace. Resignation, removal, impeachment—these words are in the air, along with others.

And while Trump and other elected officials bear their share of the blame, the buck doesn't stop with them. I do not accept the notion of collective guilt, that we are all somehow to blame, that we must now "reconcile our differences" and put all of this behind us. We do not just have a pandemic decimating our population; we also have an infection that threatens our democracy and, therefore, our way of life.

There is no vaccine for that infection, and it will not go away on its own. What we need, first, is accountability. The rule of law requires that the lawbreakers whom we saw on television—rampaging into the Capitol, marching through its corridors, destroying property, and threatening the safety of our elected officials and others—be held accountable for their conduct. They should be arrested, tried, and punished. Shame on us if we do anything less.

Why, as I watched the insurrection on January 6, 2021, did I think of Kristallnacht, the days in November 1938 when German Nazis killed Jews and attacked homes, synagogues, and Jewish businesses? That was another time in another country, and the two events are far from identical. But the resemblance between them, notably the fact that racist civilians were active participants both then and now, is not a figment of my imagination.[70]

On a wall on the Holocaust Memorial Museum in Washington, you can read the words of Bishop Martin Niemöller, a German clergyman who wrote about the cowardice of silence, about not speaking when "they" came—first for the socialists, then for the trade unionists, and then for the Jews—because he was none of those. "Then they came for me, and there was no one left to speak for me."

It may be true that what happened in Washington last week does not represent who we are as a nation, but the risk is that it is who we will become. Accountability of the culprits is essential, but it is not enough. None of us can afford to be indifferent or remain silent. Now is the time to heed the words of Bishop Niemöller.[71]

---

70 Unknown to me when I wrote these words, Arnold Schwarzenegger was having similar thoughts, which he expressed both knowledgeably and articulately on a January 11, 2021, YouTube video.

71 On May 28, 2021, The Senate voted 54 to 35 in favor of establishing a bipartisan commission to investigate the January 6 attack on the capitol. Because Senate filibuster rules require sixty votes, the bill did not pass. Six Republican senators voted in favor. Eleven senators, nine republicans and two democrats, did not vote.

# Our National Mourning and Remembering Tragic Dates

Every year on September 11, we pause to remember the day foreign terrorists hijacked four planes, attacked the Word Trade Center with two of them, hit the Pentagon with a third, and were aiming at Washington, DC, with the fourth when a passenger named Todd Beamer shouted, "Let's roll." He, with other heroic passengers and crew, gave their lives and saved the United States Capitol.

This month we paused on the twentieth anniversary of the day we lost our innocence. Somehow it felt different this time, but I don't think it had as much to do with the number "20" as it did with the changes we have experienced in recent years. Two stand out in my mind.

One is that we now fear domestic violence as much as we do foreign terrorism, maybe more so. Just as 9/11 has taken on a special significance in American life, so I believe will "January 6," the day the mob stormed the Capitol that 9/11 heroes saved.

The other is that American troops are no longer in Afghanistan, America's longest war. Once again, we have discovered that certain kinds of wars don't work out very well. The withdrawal was chaotic, and as I watched the televised somber arrival at Dover Air Force Base of the thirteen US service members killed in Kabul on August 26, 2021, I was reminded of the 2009 movie *Taking Chance*. It depicts how the military transports its fallen soldiers from Delaware to their families.

As you can see, this column is different from my usual monthly essay. I write it with a heavy heart. I can't help wondering what will become of us. Will we become a nation of vigilantes, free to carry unlicensed guns, turn in our neighbors for exercising their constitutional rights, and allow a minority of extremists to rule? That seems to be a possibility, something I never would have imagined while taking eighth grade civics at Stevens Junior High School in Claremont.

Or will we recover from the traumas of the last twenty years and return to a degree of normalcy and the quiet certainty that we are a law-abiding society that believes in the Constitution and the Bill of Rights and learns from our mistakes?

I wish I could say, with confidence, that it will be the latter.

Those of us old enough to remember November 22, 1963, can say exactly where we were that afternoon when we learned that President Kennedy had been assassinated. I was about to attend a law school seminar that was never held.

The same is true of September 11, 2001. We remember where we were that day as we watched in horror when the second plane hit the World Trade Center. I was in my office that morning, on the phone with someone in a midtown Manhattan office building. He was looking out the window towards downtown, and I remember his exact words. "You won't believe what I just saw."

And now we can add January 6, 2021. We watched from our homes as a mob attacked our Capitol, threatened to kill the vice president and members of Congress, and attempted to prevent the peaceful transition of power from one presidential administration to the next.

This lawlessness, whether from abroad or homegrown, has to stop. We have enough tragic dates to remember.

# Part II

# Thinking About the Law

# THE RULE OF LAW

## My Lifelong Learners and the Continuing Experiment (2017)

*The best test of truth is the power of the thought to get itself*
*accepted in the competition of the market. The Constitution*
*is an experiment, as all life is an experiment.*

Justice Oliver Wendell Holmes

In the fall of 2017, I taught constitutional law course as part of the CALL (Cheshire Academy for Lifelong Learning) program at Keene State College. When I signed up to do this, I wondered whether anyone would take the course. It turned out I need not have worried. Over the course of eight Fridays, I enjoyed the company of sixty-three lifelong learners who were eager to talk about a hot subject, the United States Constitution.

That document, created in 1789 and amended in 1791 by the first ten amendments (the Bill of Rights), has been amended seventeen more times since then. The Eighteenth Amendment made the country dry, and the Twenty-first undid the Eighteenth, so those two cancel each other out.

Of the other fifteen amendments, some have become as much a part of our constitutional fabric as the first ten. The Thirteenth Amendment outlaws slavery; the Fourteenth grants rights of citizenship, due process, and equal protection; the Fifteenth extends voting rights to all races; and the Nineteenth grants women the right to vote. In 1971, Congress passed, and the states ratified, the Twenty-Sixth Amendment, which gives eighteen-year-old citizens the right to vote.

We haven't had occasion to use all the amendments yet. The Twenty-Fifth Amendment, ratified in 1967, says that the vice president and a majority of the cabinet members can decide that the president is "unable to discharge the powers and duties of his office," in which case the vice president takes over. If the president puts up a fight, then it is up to Congress to decide. There was speculation over invoking that amendment during the Trump administration, but nothing came of it.

The first three words of the Constitution are "We the people." Not "I the King," or "In the name of the Lord," but "We," the governed. As Lincoln put it in his most famous speech, ours is a government "of the people, by the people, for the people."

Some of the Founding Fathers' names we all recognize—Washington, Jefferson, Hamilton, Franklin, Madison. Other have faded into obscurity. New Hampshire's John Langdon and Nicholas Gilman were among the Constitution signers, along with many others whose names history barely remembers.

We have been through some rocky times since they and thirty-two other Framers signed the Constitution. In 1857, the Supreme Court decided the *Dred Scott* case, effectively deciding that not all men are created equal. According to seven of the nine justices, slaves, former slaves, and anyone else of African descent, were not "citizens" of this country, a decision that Lincoln called an "astonisher in legal history."

Going back to that case remains a wrenching experience. It took a Civil War and the Fourteenth Amendment to overrule the *Dred Scott* decision and give "all persons," not just white people, the rights of citizenship. And our constitutional "experiment" continues to this day, with the country a much different place than it was in Philadelphia in 1787, or Appomattox in 1865.

For the last several weeks my sixty-three students and I have been trying to understand at least some of this "experiment," and everyday life keeps reminding us that the Constitution really matters. Unfortunately, we haven't yet met the ambitious goals set forth in the preamble, one of which is to "insure domestic Tranquility."[72]

---

72  As I was considering how best to begin this Part II of Time for Everything, the second Trump impeachment trial was taking place. There could not be a better example of our failure to ensure domestic tranquility than the events of January 6, 2021, that gave rise to that impeachment.

# Politics, Ethics, Recusal, and the Rule of Law
## (2017)

As those of you who have reached middle age will remember, we have been here before. In October 1973, President Nixon ordered Attorney General Elliot Richardson to fire the special Watergate prosecutor, Archibald Cox. Richardson refused to do so and resigned, as did his deputy, William Ruckelshaus. Third in line was Solicitor General Robert Bork, and he did the president's bidding.

Nixon then appointed a Texas lawyer named Leon Jaworski, who, from Nixon's point of view, turned out to be just as bad (for Nixon) as Cox. He subpoenaed the "White House tapes," Nixon objected, and the rule of law took over. The Supreme Court ordered Nixon to turn over the tapes, and in less than a year he resigned, taken down by his own words.[73]

According to the CIA and numerous other government intelligence agencies, Russian hackers tried to interfere with the 2016 presidential campaign. Over the last few months, word has leaked out of meetings between Russian officials and members of the Trump campaign, including former national security advisor Michael Flynn, Attorney General Jeff Sessions, campaign manager Paul Manafort, and the president's son and son-in-law, who took a meeting at Trump Tower with a Russian lawyer.

This is not conjecture or fake news. Donald Trump Jr. released the e-mails between him and the intermediary who brokered the meeting. The point was to get dirt against his father's opponent, Hillary Clinton, and Donald Jr. acknowledged, with regret, that the meeting was a "waste of time" because the Russian lawyer did not provide any useful information.

During the Watergate investigation in 1973, Senator Howard Baker asked, "What did the president know and when did he know it?" Now we have the "Russian investigation," which asks what did the Russians do and whom did they do it with? Now, in the spring of 2017, we have a special counsel named Robert Mueller, whose job it is to uncover the truth. And, once again, we appear to be witnessing a conflict between the president and the rule of law.

---

73   In January 2022, relying on the precedent set in *United States v. Nixon* (1974), the Supreme Court rejected Donald Trump's invocation of executive privilege and allowed the Select Committee investigating the January 6 attack on the Capitol to obtain documents held by the National Archives.

As a matter of both ethics and law, Attorney General Sessions had no choice but to step aside from the investigation, based on his involvement in the Trump campaign and his own conversations with Russian officials. Instead of praising him for doing the right thing, Trump told *The New York Times* that if he had known Sessions was going to recuse himself from the investigation into Russia's election meddling, he would not have appointed him in the first place. That assumes that Sessions would not have appointed Robert Mueller, as the deputy attorney general, Rod Rosenstein, did. Now we hear daily speculation about Mr. Mueller's job security.

Whether or not Sessions remains in his job,[74] firing Mueller isn't so simple. The federal regulations require a showing of "good cause," such as misconduct, dereliction of duty, incapacity, or conflict of interest. Anyone who knows Robert Mueller knows that he would never come close to such misconduct.[75]

All three branches of government play a role in maintaining the rule of law, and Congress now seems ready to do its part. Specifically, under a bipartisan bill filed early this month, the president's power to terminate the special counsel would be subject to judicial review, with Mueller remaining on the job during the process. In other words, as with legislation about the Russia sanctions, Congress seems ready to assert itself not only as a coequal branch of government but as a meaningful check on the executive branch.

The bigger picture here is reassuring. Despite the turmoil of recent months, the Constitutional structure of checks and balances remains in place. And in the United States, unlike Russia, the rule of law still applies, even to a president.[76]

---

74   He did, until November 7, 2018, when Trump fired him and, a few months later, appointed William Barr, who had served as attorney general previously under President George H. W. Bush.

75   Disclosure: Bob Mueller and I were law partners in the 1980s. He told me back then that his ambition in life was to become the director of the FBI, and he got his wish when President George W. Bush appointed him in 2001. President Obama extended the appointment in 2009 for the first two years of his first term.

76   When I wrote these words, I naively believed that Congress would take sensible steps to protect the special counsel's independence. The proposed bill was never enacted into law. The Mueller Report, publicly released on April 18, 2019, found no collusion between the Trump Campaign and the Russians. As for obstruction of justice, the report reached a legalistic double-negative conclusion that the evidence was such that Mueller could not declare that Trump had not obstructed justice. The story of the Mueller investigation is recounted by one of its insiders, Andrew Weissman, in his 2020 book *Where Law Ends*.

# Is Impeachment Without Conviction Worth It? (2019)

Since former FBI Director James Comey testified before the Senate Intelligence Committee on June 8, 2017, there has been a steady impeachment drumroll. According to the polls, 47 percent of voters think President Trump should be impeached, while 37 percent think he is doing a good job.

An impeachment is like an indictment. The process is the same under both the federal and New Hampshire Constitutions. The House accuses, the Senate decides.

Defining just what acts put a public official at risk is a good question. If we drive on the highway, we know the speed limit. There are signs that tell us. Neither the federal nor the state Constitution posts such signs.

Instead, they contain vague, elastic language. The federal words "corruption" and "treason" may be relatively straightforward, but the United States Constitution also says that a federal official is impeachable for "high crimes and misdemeanors." It does not say what offenses are covered by those words.

The impeachment clause of the New Hampshire constitution also includes the word "corruption," but instead of the other federal grounds it specifies "bribery" and then two more, "malpractice" and "maladministration."

Most lawyers never get to participate in an impeachment case, but in April of 2000, I became an exception. House Speaker Donna Sytek invited me to drive from Boston to Concord, New Hampshire, to meet with her and a bipartisan group of elected officials.[77] The issue at hand was how the Court had handled the selection of substitute justices to hear the appeal of one of its members, Justice W. Stephen Thayer III, who was a party to a contentious divorce proceeding. The House had passed a resolution directing the Judiciary Committee to investigate the chief justice and other members of the state Supreme Court in connection, and it was up to the Speaker to implement that directive.

Speaker Sytek called the day after the interview and offered me the position

---

77  This call came about thanks to Peter Burling, my Hill & Barlow associate in the early 1970s, who moved from Boston to Cornish, New Hampshire, where he and his wife Jean still live. Jean became New Hampshire's first woman judge in 1973, initially on the state district court and then on the Superior Court. Peter served for many years in both the New Hampshire House of Representatives and the New Hampshire Senate.

of Special Investigator. I asked for a day before giving her my answer, just to get my thoughts in order. I then turned for advice to retired Massachusetts chief justice Edward Hennessey. He told me I should take on the challenge but added, "Joe, remember this is not the ordinary case. The Court is an institution, and part of your job will be to protect it."[78]

My clients, the twenty-four members of the House Judiciary Committee, asked for my help understanding the meaning of the constitutional words "malpractice" and "maladministration," and how to apply them. Despite many hours of research, the best I could come up with was the dictionary definition and the legislator's own conscience, neither of which added much clarity. A few committee members thought that if the chief justice wasn't doing a "good job," that would be "malpractice." I explained that "independence of the judiciary" means that legislators don't have the right to look over judges' shoulders. As for "maladministration," I told the committee members, "it means something very serious and not just a mistake of judgment."

The Committee voted to recommend impeachment, and in August of 2000 a substantial majority of the full House of Representatives voted to impeach the chief justice, David Brock.[79] Speaker Sytek, who kept her distance during the investigation phase, then asked me to stay on as Special Prosecutor. I agreed and asked that our contract spell out that I would not be allowed to speak to the press; I figured I had enough to deal with.

At that point, the chief justice switched lawyers[80] and retained a Washington attorney named Mike Madigan. State Senate President Beverly Hollingworth hired former US Senate Majority Leader George Mitchell and impeachment expert Bob Bauer as her legal advisers.[81]

Madigan and I met with Senator Mitchell to discuss the rules that would govern the proceedings. The first question was whether conviction required

---

78  I had known Chief Justice Hennessey (1919–2007) from my early days as a lawyer, when we often rode the train together from Needham to Boston. Being with him was always a privilege, and his advice was never out of my mind during my once-in-a-lifetime stint as an "impeachment" lawyer.

79  With four hundred members, New Hampshire has by far the largest state legislature in the United States. Pennsylvania, with 203 House members, is in second place.

80  Brock's lawyer up to that point had been an eminent Maine lawyer named Ralph Lancaster (1930–2019), a former president of the American College of Trial Lawyers. He was my friend both before and after the impeachment case.

81  Bauer went on to become counsel to the president in the Obama administration and principal legal adviser to Joe Biden during the attempts by Donald Trump to overturn the results of the 2020 election. On April 9, 2021, President Biden appointed him as cochair of the Presidential Commission on the Supreme Court of the United States, a body created to analyze the merits and legality of various possible reform proposals.

a simple majority vote or a "super-majority" of two-thirds, a question on which the New Hampshire constitution is silent. I argued that a majority should suffice, Madigan argued for a two-thirds vote, and Senator Mitchell agreed with him, pointing out that the federal Constitution requires two-thirds to convict, and that it should not be easy for elected politicians to get rid of appointed judges or elected officials.

At that moment, I knew that any possibility of "winning" the case had just evaporated. The supermajority requirement means, as a practical matter, that whenever a public official faces impeachment, the outcome, absent an overwhelming one-party majority, rests with members of his or her party. In other words, impeachment may be a little bit legal, but it's mostly political.

Various senators, unencumbered by judicial restraints on public comment, had already made their views known. Knowing that the New Hampshire Senate would not vote to convict Chief Justice Brock was, in a sense, a liberating experience.[82] And in October of 2000, the New Hampshire Senate acquitted the chief justice on all counts.

Our country's circumstances following Comey's testimony and later events involving President Trump and Ukraine are entirely different from what we faced in New Hampshire in the year 2000, and the stakes are much higher. But they resemble each other in one important respect, and Chief Justice Hennessey's words remain timely. Whether it's a state court judge or the president, an impeachment proceeding challenges a governmental institution whose protection and preservation, as envisioned by the Founding Fathers, should be our uppermost concern.

I believed then, and still do, that at least in my case impeachment without conviction was worth it.

---

82 My instincts as a trial lawyer did not disappear. With the help of my Hill & Barlow partner Peter Ball and our paralegal Abigail Gordon, and several others, I marshaled the evidence and put in the best case I could. The trial took three weeks and was televised on New Hampshire Public Television. My goal was to help the members of the New Hampshire Senate, and more importantly the public at large, understand how the New Hampshire Supreme Court had been conducting the public's legal business.

# The Senate Rules and the King Can Do No Wrong (2020)

An old Latin legal maxim says *rex non potest peccare*: "The king can do no wrong."

America was founded on the very opposite principle. The preamble of the United States Constitution begins with the words "We the people," which are in sharp contrast to the first words of the Magna Carta, which begins "JOHN, by the grace of God King of England." You can tell a lot about a country by how its documents begin. Or so we thought.

The Framers knew what they were doing when they wrote that preamble, and (for the most part) when they wrote the rest of the Constitution and the Bill of Rights. They envisioned that, in the words of John Adams, ours would be "a government of laws and not of men."

For many of us, it has been less than a lifetime since 1973, when President Nixon said, "People have got to know whether or not their president is a crook. Well, I am not a crook." He made that proclamation before the Supreme Court rejected his claim of executive privilege and ordered him to turn over the secret White House tapes. Four years later, Nixon told interviewer David Frost, "When the president does it, that means that it is not illegal."

According to a Gallup poll at the time, most Americans pooh-poohed Nixon's statement as un-American, but times have changed, and immutable principles have become mutable. During the 2016 campaign, candidate Donald Trump boasted that he could "shoot somebody on Fifth Avenue" and not lose any of his support. No one could believe he meant to be taken literally.

Or could they? Last summer, President Trump tweeted proprietarily, "I have an Article 2, where I have the right to do whatever I want as president." Shades of Richard Nixon, and a lot like France's King Louis XIV as well: *L'état, c'est moi* ("I myself am the nation").

Since becoming president, Trump has not mentioned shooting someone on Fifth (or Pennsylvania) Avenue, but in October of 2019 his lawyer told a federal court of appeals that if the president were to commit such an act, the local authorities could not do anything about it.

The impeachment trial of Donald Trump ended a few days ago, and times have changed again—not because the Senate acquitted Trump, which we always knew it would, but because it did so without hearing witnesses or seeing documents. That refusal effectively turned what was supposed to be a constitutional trial process into a different proceeding than that contemplated by Article I, Section 3, which says that the Senate "shall have the sole Power to *try* all Impeachments."

What that means, according to Hamilton's Federalist Paper No. 66, is that the Senate acts as "a *court* of impeachments." And that is exactly what it did in the first two presidential impeachments, the trials of Andrew Johnson in 1868 and Bill Clinton in 1999, and in every other federal impeachment trial in American history.

This time, however, it did not. Fifty-one senators voted to deprive the rest of the Senate, and the American people, of relevant evidence, thereby redefining the words "try" and "court."

What we have just witnessed reminds me of what Juror Number 10 says in the movie *Twelve Angry Men*—"Don't give me any of the facts. I'm sick and tired of facts."

It is not as if the House of Representatives didn't try to get more facts. The president stonewalled subpoenas, and evidence was not obtained until a later time. Senators then said it was "too late" for such evidence to be presented, even though its existence wasn't known during the House impeachment hearings. The workings of the United States Senate get curiouser and curiouser.

The "executive privilege" argument on which Trump's refusal to cooperate ostensibly rested (and which Nixon tried to invoke) is equally specious. Like any privilege, the specific circumstances will dictate whether certain evidence may be withheld. But first you need a witness (or a document), then the lawyer asks a question, then the opposing lawyer objects, and then the presiding judge makes a ruling. In other words, a legal privilege does not exist on paper but in real time, and whether it can be successfully invoked depends on the context and is up to the judge, not the person who claims it.

Executive privilege, failure to get the facts sooner, not turning square corners—the reasons varied, but it didn't matter. What Trump wanted to do was control the proceedings, and with the help of Mitch McConnell and others, he succeeded. The impeachment "trial" was not about truth; it was about political party and fear.

History will not look kindly on this latest episode in our unraveling democracy, not necessarily because of the outcome but because of how the Senate conducted the proceedings. Time will tell whether Yogi Berra was right that "It ain't over till it's over."

# Can Attorney General Barr Un-ring a Bell? (2020)

As early as Roman times, the law has recognized the doctrine of *non bis in idem* ("an issue once decided must not be raised again"). It is enshrined in the Fifth Amendment as the double jeopardy clause. If a defendant goes to trial and is acquitted, the case is over. and the Government cannot ask for a do-over. That is how the system works.

We now have the unusual, if not unique, situation where a defendant named Michael Flynn twice pleads guilty in open court to a federal crime—lying to the FBI—and the federal judge, after determining that Flynn is acting voluntarily and understands what he is doing, accepts the plea. The guilt-or-innocence phase of the case is over, and all that remains is for the judge to determine the appropriate punishment. Flynn's recourse at that point would be to ask President Trump to pardon him under Article II of the Constitution.

Does Flynn have another way out? Can Attorney General Barr un-ring the bell unilaterally and tell the judge, "We've changed our minds, he didn't do anything wrong (or at least we can't prove he did), so we're dismissing the case."

The answer should be "No." According to the Federal Rules of Criminal Procedure, "The government may, *with leave of court*, dismiss an indictment, information, or complaint." The rule says nothing about dismissing a case after a conviction, whether by guilty plea or otherwise, but the final say rests with the presiding federal judge, Emmet G. Sullivan, an appointee of presidents from both parties (Reagan and Bush 41 to District of Columbia courts, Clinton to the federal court).

A brief review of the case: Flynn served for two years as director of the Defense Intelligence Agency under President Obama. He later joined the Trump campaign and became Trump's national security advisor, a position he held for two weeks following Trump's inauguration. He "resigned" after it came out that he had misled both the FBI and Vice President Pence about his conversations with Russian ambassador Sergey Kislak.

Flynn then came under the scrutiny of Special Counsel Robert Mueller, with whom he reached a plea agreement. On December 1, 2017, he pleaded guilty to a felony—"willfully and knowingly" lying to the FBI—and he agreed to cooperate with the Mueller investigation.

What followed were a series of delays and claims for leniency by Flynn's lawyers, who claimed that the FBI had tricked their client and had not advised him that lying to the FBI is a serious crime. At a hearing before Judge Sullivan, the lawyers backtracked on whether the FBI had done anything wrong, and Flynn admitted in open court that he knew when he gave his initial interview that lying to the FBI is a crime. [83] Judge Sullivan looked Flynn in the face and said, "Arguably, you sold your country out."

A year ago, Flynn fired his lawyers, and his new lawyer moved to hold the prosecutors in contempt.[84] When that motion failed, and Judge Sullivan scheduled sentencing for January 28, 2020, the prosecutors requested jail time of up to six months. A week later, Flynn moved to withdraw his guilty plea, again accusing the government of misconduct, and a new sentencing date was set.

In February, Attorney General Barr appointed a United States Attorney from Missouri to investigate the matter, and sentencing was delayed yet again. Flynn then charged his former lawyers from the firm of Covington & Burling with providing inadequate counsel.

Meanwhile, Trump was calling for the charges against Flynn to be dropped, and on May 7, 2020, the Justice Department, acting through a Trump political appointee, announced that it was dropping the case. The career Justice Department lawyers who had been handling the case then withdrew from any continuing involvement.

The following week, Judge Sullivan made it clear that he, not the attorney general, is running this case. First, he issued an order on May 12 soliciting amicus curiae ("friend of the court") submissions. Some two thousand former federal prosecutors have already called on Barr to resign over this.

The next day, the judge appointed a former federal judge from Brooklyn,

---

83 I am reminded of a case where the defendant claimed he didn't know you shouldn't create a fake company in order to get discounts from the manufacturer. During closing argument, I said to the jury, "Some things you just know."

84 The new lawyer, a woman named Sidney Powell, went on to become an enthusiastic Trump supporter, among other things advancing frivolous conspiracy theories and making speeches about the "stolen" 2020 election. She attacked a company named Dominion, manufacturer of voting machines used in Georgia and many other states. In January 2021, Dominion filed a 124-page complaint against her in District of Columbia federal court, alleging defamation and seeking damages of over $1 billion.

now in private practice, to oppose dismissal of the case. Judge Sullivan's choice, John Gleeson, knows his way around the criminal law. Before becoming a judge, he successfully prosecuted Mafia boss John Gotti.

No one should be surprised by the judge's reaction to the DOJ's effort to un-ring its own bell and thereby turn the double jeopardy clause inside out, effectively "un-jeopardizing" Michael Flynn. Under straightforward separation of powers principles, the Justice Department cannot dictate how a federal judge decides cases. A prosecutor can decide not to file a case, but as Federal Rule 48(a) says, in plain English, once a case is in court the judge decides whether to grant "leave of court."

Predictions about court outcomes are hazardous at best. But looking at the history of this case, Flynn's repeated acknowledgements of guilt, and the judge's in-court statements, my crystal ball tells me that the Department of Justice will lose, as it should.[85] Such an outcome will vindicate the rule of law, and the public will be the winner.[86]

---

85   This article, published in the *Concord Monitor*, produced several responses, not all complimentary. My favorite came from an anonymous reader who expressed doubt that I had ever attended law school and, if I did, whether I studied criminal law.

86   The government tried to short-circuit the sentencing process by taking the case to the Court of Appeals for the District of Columbia, where a three-judge panel initially sided (2 to 1) with the Justice Department. But then, on further appeal to all the Court's active members (known as hearing en banc), the case came back to life and was returned to Judge Sullivan. On December 1, 2020, with the case still pending, President Trump pardoned Flynn of "any and all possible offenses," thereby ending the case in Judge Sullivan's court and absolving Flynn, it appears, not only from charges to which he had twice pleaded guilty, but also for anything else he had ever done up to that time. After the pardon, however, Flynn challenged a subpoena from the House January 6 Committee, and the next day the Court ruled against him. As the investigation unfolds, Flynn's problems arising out of his post-pardon activities may not be behind him.

# The Second Impeachment Trial
# and What Trump Failed to Do (2021)

If the forthcoming second impeachment trial of Donald Trump were taking place in a courtroom, the prosecutors could invoke the "law of the case" doctrine. What that means, in a real lawsuit, is that the Senate's decision to allow the impeachment case against the former president to proceed would be the "law of the case," and all one hundred senators, including the forty-five who voted not to go forward with the trial, would be under a jural duty to consider and decide the case based on the evidence.

That is not what we are about to see. Rand Paul and others will refuse to accept the majority vote and take no for an answer. He will continue to insist that the Senate has no power under the Constitution to consider the impeachment of a "private citizen." A majority of senators will then vote again that a former president who is impeached for acts conducted during his presidency remains subject to trial in the Senate, and the House Managers will present the evidence. Senators are required to remain silent during the hearings, but it is doubtful whether any of the "we shouldn't be here" Republicans will be open to persuasion.[87]

But facts matter, and much of the evidence will be in the form of social media video. The senators have already seen the mob approach, destroy, injure, and kill, and—unlike any trial in recent memory—they were present while the attack on the Capitol took place. However, this impeachment trial is not about the insurrection itself; it is about the House's accusation that President Trump "engaged in high Crimes and Misdemeanors by inciting violence against the Government of the United States."

The single article of impeachment cites Trump's refusal to accept the election results, his January 2 phone call urging the Georgia Secretary of State to "find" the exact number of votes necessary to make him the

---

This time I was right. On February 13, 2021, the Senate acquitted Donald Trump by a vote of 53 to 47. Mitch McConnell was one of the forty-seven who voted to acquit, but minutes after the proceedings ended, he condemned Donald Trump in no uncertain terms. He agreed with the House Managers that Trump had provoked the insurrection but explained his vote on the grounds that the Senate had no power to try a former president. In other words, he refused to follow the Senate vote upholding its jurisdiction to hear and decide the case. McConnell's justification for his vote is no different from refusing to follow a Senate Rule, properly enacted, because a senator doesn't agree with it. Senators, it seems, can defy their own rules with impunity.

"winner" of that state's electoral votes,[88] and his January 6 "stop the steal" exhortation to the crowd that "if you don't fight like hell you're not going to have a country anymore."

The impeachment trial evidence will likely go back to September 2020 when Trump told the Proud Boys to "stand back and stand by." It will surely include his December 19, 2020, tweet, "Big protest in D.C. on January 6th. Be there, will be wild." And on January 6, Trump told the crowd that if the election of Biden were to go forward, "our country will be destroyed and we're not going to stand for that." Trump went on, "We're going to walk down to the Capitol, and I'll be there with you."

If the evidence of Trump's conduct stopped at that point, would Trump be guilty of inciting his followers to commit a crime? I have my doubts. Ever since he lost the election, he has behaved recklessly, but reckless conduct alone may not rise to the level of "high crimes and misdemeanors." And when he gave his marching orders on January 6, he added the words "peacefully and patriotically."

Trump did not join the march down Pennsylvania Avenue but stayed behind and watched the insurrection unfold on television in real time. Every case has a tipping point and, in this instance, it came when many members of his crowd of listeners turned into a violent mob of insurrectionists. He was watching the mayhem with his own eyes, and for 187 minutes he did not lift a hand to quell the riot.

That is not an opinion, it is a fact. Trump did not speak up when after rioters, many in combat gear and carrying weapons and Confederate flags, breached the Capitol. When he finally spoke, he told them it was time to "go home in peace." He did not criticize or condemn the rioters, a reprise of his statement following the white supremacists' 2017 rally in Charlottesville that there were "very fine people on both sides." This time, he told the crowd, "We love you, you're very special." Later that day, Trump urged these "great patriots" to "remember this day forever." (Many of these "great patriots" will likely have ample time to do so while serving prison sentences.)

When Trump did not utter a word, did not send a tweet, did not signal those whom he had just dispatched to the Capitol to "stand back" and allow members of Congress and his own vice president to perform their constitutional duties, he violated the oath he took when he became

---

88   In January 2022, the Atlanta district attorney convened a grand jury to consider whether Trump should be charged with a crime under Georgia law.

president, to "support and defend the Constitution of the United States against all enemies, foreign and domestic."

Trump denies any culpability. According to him, "People thought what I said was totally appropriate." But he has yet to explain or defend his failure to act when the march turned into an assault and his own vice president's life was in danger. My guess is that Trump, in his disillusioned fog of anger, hoped the mob would succeed in preventing the certification of the electoral votes, thereby "stopping the steal."[89] If that explanation is correct, Trump put his inability to admit that he lost ahead of both the democratic process and the safety of every person inside the Capitol on January 6, 2021.

For those senators willing to accept the law of this case—that a House vote to impeach may be heard even if the official is no longer in office—the evidence of guilt is compelling. In the words of Rep. Liz Cheney (R-WY), "The president could have immediately and forcefully intervened to stop the violence. He did not."[90]

---

89  On February 13, 2021, at the last minute of the second impeachment trial, lead House Manager Jamie Raskin (D-MD) read into the record evidence from a member of Congress, Jaime Herrera Beutler (R-WA). She stated that while the Capitol was under siege, she heard a telephone exchange between House Minority Leader Kevin McCarthy (R-CA) and Donald Trump. McCarthy "asked him to publicly and forcefully call off the riot," to which Trump responded, "Well, Kevin, I guess these people are more upset about the election than you are."

90  By the spring of 2021, Trump's tight grip on the Republican party remained intact. Kevin McCarthy paid homage to Trump at Mar-a-Lago, while Liz Cheney refused to back down. On May 12, 2021, the House GOP members voted to remove her as conference chair, the third highest party leadership position by a "voice vote." Trump, no longer allowed on Twitter or Facebook, issued a statement criticizing Cheney for denying that the election was "stolen" and called her a "warmonger" and "socialist nightmare."

# The Post-Presidency and Title 18
# of the United States Code (2020)

I recently heard an interview with Andy Card, who served as Chief of Staff for President George W. Bush and later as president of Franklin Pierce University in Rindge, New Hampshire. In his opinion, soon-to-be president Joe Biden should "respect" his predecessor, soon-to-be ex-president Donald J. Trump. In other words, he should not seek retribution and should leave him alone.

In a recent *New York Times* op-ed column, Andrew Weissman, a senior prosecutor in the Mueller investigation, takes a different view. He says that a president should be held *more* accountable to the rule of law, not less. In his opinion, the next attorney general should not hesitate to investigate Trump.

Who has the better case? On the Andy Card side, I can almost hear some Trump supporters say: "First they win the election by fraud, and now they want to put him in jail."

But others, and not just people who voted for Trump, might follow a different route to the same conclusion. "It's not a good idea," their argument might go, "for the federal government to go around prosecuting former presidents." They might add, "No matter how strongly you feel or how much you dislike Trump, it would further divide us when what we really need is to come together."

The contrary Weissman position can be framed in the form of a question: If an ordinary citizen should be prosecuted for violating the law, is there a good reason why a former president should not be held to the same standard? The argument might also consider the precedent inaction would create, and whether we want future generations to look back on this period as a time when we looked the other way.

Both points of view have some merit. Of course, we don't want to sow further divisions in our country. And besides, this is not necessarily a choice between not having your cake and not eating it too. The New York State authorities are looking into Trump's business activities before he became president, and the Supreme Court has upheld their right to do so. The federal government can therefore stand down, so to speak, and leave it to the State of New York to do the investigating and the prosecuting. That may be a bit of a cop-out, but it's not the worst outcome.[91]

---

91   In March 2021, a state prosecutor in Fulton County, Georgia, opened a criminal investigation to consider whether Trump had improperly attempted to influence the outcome of the 2020 Georgia general election. On May 19, 2021, the attorney general of New York announced that she was joining

Still, if Trump's former lawyer-fixer Michael Cohen could be convicted and sent to federal prison for tax evasion and campaign finance violations, should his unindicted co-conspirator, referred to in Cohen's indictment as "Individual-1," be let off the hook?

During his 2016 campaign, Trump famously boasted that he could shoot someone on Fifth Avenue and not lose any votes. Assume, just for the sake of argument, that Trump walked down Pennsylvania Avenue and shot someone while he was president. That is purely hypothetical, but as a law professor of mine used to say, "it's my hypothetical." How many of us would believe that he should not be held responsible starting on January 21, 2021, the first full day of his post-presidency?

If, as John Adams said, ours is "a government of laws and not of men," then the rule of law necessarily applies as much to a former president as it does to the rest of us. What that means, absent a valid presidential pardon, is that we should follow the evidence wherever it takes us. It is not as if this would be a fishing expedition. The Mueller Report cites ten instances that could support obstruction of justice charges.

Prosecution cannot be justified for petty offenses, only grave ones. As defined by 18 US Code, Section 1503, the words "obstruction of justice" refer to an act that "corruptly . . . or by any threatening letter or communication . . . endeavors to influence, obstruct, or impede, the due administration of justice." An important element of this grave crime is an *intent* to obstruct an existing federal proceeding, meaning that the bar to conviction, and possible imprisonment, is set very high.

I come to my opinion reluctantly, fully aware of the media spectacle that would inevitably take place. I still think it's worth it. If Trump were to be charged, he would have all the protections afforded by the Constitution, including the presumption of innocence. Conviction would require a unanimous jury to find him guilty beyond a reasonable doubt. These are bedrock principles of our justice system.

Despite its imperfections, I believe in that system. So should the American people.

---

the Manhattan District Attorney's office in its criminal investigation. And on May 25, 2021, District Attorney Cyrus Vance announced that he has convened a special grand jury to consider whether to hand down indictments. Trump responded that this "greatest Witch Hunt in American history" was "purely political and an affront to the almost 75 million voters" who supported him.

# There Are Laws for a Criminal Assault on America (2021)

I do not ordinarily begin my monthly column by quoting federal law, but January 2021 is not an ordinary month.

18 US Code § 2385, makes it a felony to "advocate, abet, or advise" overthrowing the government. Whoever "helps" or "encourages" anyone to do so, can go to prison for up to twenty years. If "two or more persons" conspire to commit these offenses, that is yet another crime.

Section 2384 of the Code, entitled "Seditious conspiracy," calls for up to twenty years in prison for people who get together to interfere with the execution of any law of the United States or use force to take any property of the United States.

The "rebellion or insurrection" law (§ 2383) prohibits giving "aid or comfort" to, or being any part of, "insurrection" against the laws of the United States. Violate that section and you can be punished by up to ten years.

This column is not about senators or members of Congress who voted to ignore state-certified electoral votes. Federal law does not make elected officials into criminals for being wrong-headed. I am writing about those who advised, aided, or "comforted" the criminals who battered down the Capitol doors, took over the House chamber and the Speaker's office, and stormed the electoral process.

What they did looks a lot like sedition. I will leave it to you to identify who fits into this group in addition to Donald Trump himself ("Be there, it will be wild"), but among the names that come to mind are Donald Trump Jr. ("we're coming for you, and we're going to have a good time doing it"), Rudy Giuliani ("let's have trial by combat"), Michael Flynn ("we will not stand for a lie"), and George Papadopoulos ("there are but two parties right now—traitors and patriots").[92]

I am also writing about the men and women whom we saw listen to Trump's and his lackeys' exhortations, follow Trump's instructions to march

---

92  A name that did not come to mind when I wrote these words is Stewart Rhodes, a graduate of Yale Law School and founder of a group called Oath Keepers. On January 13, 2022, federal prosecutors charged him with seditious conspiracy, the first alleged January 6 insurrection leader so charged. According to constitutional law expert Lawrence Tribe, the crime of sedition "is, in effect, treason's sibling."

down Pennsylvania Avenue (he said he would join them but of course he did not), and then commit violent crimes. The First Amendment protects freedom of assembly and of free speech, even the speech that we hate, but it does not protect thugs who set out to take over the Capitol, prevent Congress from carrying out its constitutional duties, and overthrow the government.

You don't have to be a lawyer to know a felony when you see one with your own eyes. What we saw on January 6, 2021, was a whole raft of crimes— gun-related offenses, assault on federal law enforcement officers, unlawful entry, and trespass, to name a few. There is at least one more offense that law enforcement officials need to consider—murder.

The "felony murder rule" is an ancient legal doctrine that holds a person who participates in certain types of crimes responsible for someone's death while the crime is being committed, even if he or she didn't pull the trigger. The common example is the bank robbery where one of the robbers kills someone inside the bank and the driver of the getaway car is charged with murder.

In this case, someone turned a fire extinguisher into a weapon and used it against Brian Sicknick, a forty-two-year-old Capitol Police officer doing his job. This federal employee, ironically a Trump supporter according to *The Wall Street Journal*, is dead. The person who committed the deed is obviously culpable and will, I assume, face homicide charges.[93] But the felony murder rule sweeps more broadly.

I do not suggest that the rioters should all be charged with murder. But the ringleaders who instigated the attack, and those who committed violence inside the Capitol, have blood on their hands. Even if none of them is charged with felony murder, the judge sentencing those convicted of lesser felonies should consider the death of Officer Sicknick as an aggravating factor.

In sum, law enforcement must now look at two distinct groups—those who broke into the Capitol, and those who incited them knowing they were creating a risk of immediate harm. As for the group of public officials and

---

93  On April 19, 2021, the medical examiner for the District of Columbia issued a report concluding that Officer Sicknick suffered strokes the day after the attack and died of natural causes. So, it appears that my understanding was incorrect and my homicide assessment premature. Yet the medical examiner also ruled that what transpired during the riot "played a role in his condition." In such a case, the common law "eggshell rule" holds a perpetrator responsible on the basis that we take our victims as we find them.

others who did not march and maraud, but who encouraged and promoted lawlessness or "gave comfort" to the insurrectionists, the Biden Justice Department will need to make some difficult decisions. What is needed, what the rule of law demands, is accountability.

Meanwhile, the Capitol flag flies at half-staff, Officer Sicknick's family members mourn their loss, and we collectively hold our breath.[94][95]

---

94   The 2021 inauguration took place peacefully, but it bore little resemblance to the ones I attended in 1957 as part of the Stevens High School Marching Band, or in 2009, as an Obama campaign volunteer. The pandemic promised a much different event, but the January 6 attack required a radical transformation of Washington, DC, which, with twenty-five thousand National Guard members plus thousands of law enforcement officers, resembled a fortress more than a cradle of liberty. And the crowd size was a few thousand at most. But the event went off without a hitch, and everyone could breathe a sigh of relief.

95   On January 29, 2021, House Speaker Pelosi and Senate Majority Leader Chuck Schumer announced that on February 2, Officer Sicknick would lie in state in the Capitol Rotunda. He was buried at Arlington National Cemetery.

# Did Trump "Cause" the Injuries to Two Capitol Police Officers? (2021)

Not long after I got into law school, I decided I should read something about the law. Someone suggested "The Nature of the Judicial Process," by Judge Benjamin Cardozo. According to that book, judges legislate "interstitially," meaning that they fill in the gaps. It is how the common law operates.

The law of torts is a required first-year course, and I soon learned that a tort is a "civil wrong" for which the law provides a remedy. I also learned that Cardozo, along with Learned Hand and a few others, filled in many gaps and laid much of the groundwork for modern tort law. Ask anyone who has gone to law school to name a Cardozo opinion, and you will get an immediate response: the *Palsgraf* case.

In 1924, Mrs. Palsgraf was standing on a platform waiting for the train to Rockaway Beach when another train started to pull away from the station. A last-minute passenger carrying a package ran towards the moving train, and a railroad employee helped him get on. The man dropped the package, which exploded, causing a coin-operated scale on the platform to tip over and injure Mrs. Palsgraf. The jury found the railroad employee negligent and awarded damages of $6,000 (over $88,000 today).

The case ended up in New York's highest court, where Judge Cardozo accepted the jury's finding of negligence, as judges usually do, but went on to "legislate." "Negligence in the air, so to speak, will not do," he wrote, adding that "the risk reasonably to be perceived defines the duty to be obeyed." In other words, the Railroad's negligence was not the "proximate cause" of Mrs. Palsgraf's injuries. It could not have foreseen such a string of events.

The dissenting opinion argued that once there is negligence, the careless party should be held responsible for whatever harm results. "Everyone owes to the world at large the duty of refraining from those acts that may unreasonably threaten the safety of others."

Many courts have adopted Cardozo's view, requiring "foreseeability," while others have taken the broader view. In either case, the general principle is that "negligence in the air" is not enough, which leads to the interesting question of whether Donald Trump committed a tort on January 6, 2021.

We may find out in a case brought on March 30, 2021, by Capitol police officers James Blassingame and Sidney Hemby. In their federal complaint, they allege that Trump "committed torts" when he "inflamed, encouraged, incited, directed, and aided and abetted" the insurrectionist mob and then failed to take "timely action" to curtail the violence.[96]

The complaint goes back to such earlier statements as Trump's refusal to give an unequivocal "yes" at the presidential debate when CNN's Chris Wallace asked whether he would urge his supporters to "stay calm" and not

Judge (later Justice) Benjamin Cardozo

engage in "civil unrest" after the election, and his "Stand back and stand by" instructions to the Proud Boys. The complaint also quotes from Trump's numerous post-election tweets, including "people are not going to stand for having this election stolen from them," and "big protest in D.C. on January 6th. Be there, will be wild!"

While Officers Blassingame and Hemby were at their assigned Capitol positions, Trump gave his noontime speech at the Ellipse, exhorting the crowd to "fight like hell" to "stop the steal." "We will not take it anymore. When you catch somebody in a fraud, you're allowed to go by very different rules."

While trying to protect the Capitol, Officer Hemby was "crushed against the doors" and "attacked relentlessly," while Officer Blassingame was slammed against a stone column and struck all over his body. Meanwhile, Trump rejected House Minority Leader McCarthy's urgent phone call to do

---

96 Like the second impeachment case against Trump, the officers' 195-paragraph complaint alleges that during the 2016 campaign, and throughout his presidency, Trump "encourages his followers to commit acts of violence . . . including white supremacists and right-wing hate groups."

something and said, "I guess these people are more upset about the election than you are." Later in the afternoon, he released a video calling them off, while telling the insurrectionists, "We love you. You're very special."

This is a civil case, so the criminal requirement of proving guilt "beyond a reasonable doubt" does not apply. The civil requirement for proving proximate cause is "a preponderance of the evidence," and the jurors will have to consider whether Trump's conduct and words were "more likely than not" responsible in part for the officers' physical and emotional injuries.

There are other January 6 cases pending against Trump, including one brought by Representative Eric Swalwell (D-CA) claiming civil rights and other violations. Various civil and criminal investigations are underway in New York, Georgia, and the District of Columbia.

But none of these has quite the immediacy and appeal of the Blassingame/ Hemby case, which boils down to a straightforward garden-variety lawsuit that anyone can understand. These officers suffered real injuries, and the question is whether Donald Trump should have understood that words have consequences and, to paraphrase Judge Cardozo, "perceived the risk." Did his words at the Ellipse create a risk that these government officers would be placed in harm's way?

Representative Liz Cheney says that Trump "lit the flame" for the attack on the Capitol, and "everything that followed was his doing." Senate Minority Leader Mitch McConnell believes that Trump is "practically and morally responsible." And former House Speaker John Boehner writes in his new book that Trump "incited that bloody insurrection."

I know better than to predict what a jury will do, but Trump is fortunate that these Republicans will not be on the jury.

# EXECUTIVE POWER

## Court Upholds Travel Ban, and Our Country Is the Poorer for It (2018)

Article II of the Constitution begins with the words "The executive Power shall be vested in a President of the United States of America." It does not explain what that means.

On February 19, 1942, President Franklin D. Roosevelt signed Executive Order 9066, entitled "Authorizing the Secretary of War to Prescribe Military Areas." Notably, the Order did not mention Japanese Americans. It simply authorized "Military Commanders" to exclude "residents" from their communities in order to protect the western part of the country "against espionage and against sabotage."

Acting under this authority, the military "relocated" over 110,000 Americans of Japanese ancestry to concentration camps. The order remained in effect for nearly three years.

The words "executive power" have always carried great weight, but they have taken on new meaning in the Trump administration. On September 24, 2017, President Trump issued Proclamation 9645, "Enhancing Vetting Capabilities and Processes for Detecting Attempted Entry into the United States by Terrorists or other Public-Safety Threats." Popularly known as the "Trump Travel Ban," this document, while several times lengthier than Roosevelt's order, resembles that now-discredited document in at least one respect. Just as Roosevelt's order said nothing about those whom it targeted, Japanese Americans, Trump's proclamation says nothing about Muslims.

In December of 1944, in *Korematsu v. United States,* the Supreme Court voted, 6 to 3, to uphold Roosevelt's order. On June 26, 2018, in *Trump v. Hawaii,* the Supreme Court upheld the Trump Travel Ban by a vote of 5 to 4. Chief Justice Roberts wrote the majority opinion; Justice Sonia Sotomayor wrote the principal dissent. You can almost boil down their contrasting views by saying that Roberts takes the proclamation according to its words, while Sotomayor takes Trump at his word.

What I mean is that Roberts's textualist opinion considers the proclamation as if it arrived out of the blue. True, Roberts acknowledges that President Trump has said and tweeted any number of anti-Muslim statements, but according to Roberts the text of the proclamation is what counts, and "it says nothing about religion." And federal law "exudes deference" to the president's power to exclude non-citizens.

Here, the opinion says, the president has "found" that allowing the entry of "aliens" from certain countries, most of which are predominantly Muslim, would be "detrimental to the interests of the United States." Applying the so-called "rational basis" test and noting the elaborate "world-wide review" process built into the proclamation, the decision ultimately rests on the president's power to protect national security.

Most of the chief justice's opinion is devoted to the details of the proclamation, but he also considers whether Trump acted "for the unconstitutional purpose of excluding Muslims," thereby preferring one religion over another. He indirectly chides Trump by citing as an example of the president's "extraordinary power to speak to his fellow citizens," President Washington's 1790 letter to the Jews of Newport, Rhode Island, assuring them that the Government "gives to bigotry no sanction." The implication is clear.

At this point, Roberts does what judges do. He "balances" the competing factors: the president's authority, on the one hand, his intemperate remarks on the other. Yes, he says, the Court may consider extrinsic evidence, but the "rational basis" issue is whether the president has given what looks like a legitimate reason.[97] And here he has, so executive authority wins,

The opinion then takes a remarkable turn. In what might be described as a fig leaf, the Court overrules *Korematsu* as "gravely wrong the day it was decided" and having "no place in law under the Constitution."

Justice Kennedy wrote a brief concurring opinion, his last as a member of the Court. In response to the Government's position that the Court had no power to review Trump's proclamation, he says that in some instances the Court may overturn presidential action where there is no explanation other

---

97   The quoted words refer to the applicable standard of review when the constitutionality of governmental action is being challenged. "Rational basis" is the easiest one to meet, while "strict scrutiny" is the hardest. Which standard applies depends on the nature of the right at issue.

than hostility to a particular religion. I suppose that is reassuring to some degree, but it is hard to imagine a case where the evidence of "animus" could be stronger than in *Trump v. Hawaii*.

There is a straight line between Trump's beliefs and the travel ban. In June 2017, Trump tweeted, "what we need is a TRAVEL BAN," and in September, just days before Proclamation 9645, he doubled down, going so far as to retweet inflammatory anti-Muslim videos.

In her dissent, Justice Sotomayor accuses Roberts of rendering a "highly abridged account" of Trump's public statements. She connects the dots by citing Trump's reliance on FDR's 1942 Executive Order as justification for his campaign promise of a "total and complete shutdown" of Muslims entering the United States. As she sees it, "a reasonable observer would conclude "that the Proclamation was driven primarily by anti-Muslim bias." To her, it isn't even close, and the Court has merely replaced "one gravely wrong" decision (*Korematsu*), with another."

The Supreme Court is not in the business of making national security policy, so whether the Trump travel ban is a bad idea, as many foreign policy experts believe, is not for the Court to decide. But if a candidate promises to keep Muslims out and then, upon becoming president, issues the first of three travel bans, the question becomes whether he can "cure" the bias problem by telling his advisers to come up with a way of doing it that's "legal."

Sotomayor's answer is that a pretext is a pretext, and Trump's third order is simply more of the same, clothed in bureaucratic legalese but motivated by anti-Muslim bias.

Justice Kennedy can remind the president all he wants that he should "adhere to the Constitution" and assure an "anxious world" that the United States remains committed to our constitutional liberties. In the context of this case, however, the words ring hollow, and Justice Sotomayor has the better argument.[98]

---

98 One of President Biden's first acts, upon assuming office on January 20, 2021, was to revoke the travel ban.

# The Power of Inquiry (2019)

The power of inquiry goes back at least to the 1600s, when Parliament authorized committees to "send for persons and papers" in order to conduct investigations. In other words, it is older than our Republic, and Congress wasted little time in carrying on the British tradition. In 1792, following the defeat of General St. Clair's army in the Northwest Indian War, the House of Representatives appointed a committee "to inquire" into how such a disaster could have happened and to "call for" all necessary "persons, papers, and records."

And that is how it has gone ever since, during both the nineteenth and twentieth centuries. As watchers of *Boardwalk Empire* know, there was a lot of corruption in the 1920s during the administration of President Harding, most notably a bribery scandal involving Attorney General Harry Daugherty and oil reserves in Teapot Dome, Wyoming. Upholding subpoenas of Daugherty's brother's bank records, Supreme Court Justice Willis Van Devanter, an extremely conservative and narrow-minded justice, wrote for a unanimous court that the "power of inquiry" is an "essential and appropriate auxiliary to the legislative function."

In our time, many Congressional committees have conducted investigations, including Iran-Contra and Whitewater. And the granddaddy of them all, at least until recently, was the Senate Watergate Committee investigation. In 1974, while the House was investigating "illegal, improper, or unethical activities" during the 1972 election, President Nixon resisted the committee's subpoena of White House tape recordings on the grounds of "executive privilege." The Court of Appeals for the District of Columbia held that such a privilege was far from absolute and could be overcome if the "public need" so required. In *United States v. Nixon* (1974), also a unanimous decision, the Supreme Court agreed. Chief Justice Warren Burger, a conservative Nixon appointee, wrote that a claim of executive privilege did not override the validity of a subpoena for the White House tapes in the criminal case against Attorney General John Mitchell and several other Nixon henchmen.

In April 2019, three different Congressional committees, including the House Committee on Oversight and Reform, issued subpoenas to Deutsche

Bank, Capital One Financial, and an accounting firm named Mazars USA, all seeking financial records of Donald J. Trump, his companies, and members of his family. The Committee's stated purpose was to address possible changes to our ethics-in-government laws. Trump sued in the District of Columbia federal court to avoid compliance with these subpoenas, claiming the investigations served no legitimate purpose.

This case is not to be confused with the New York grand jury's investigation of the Trump Organization and others arising out of "hush money" paid to two women before the 2016 election and other possible financial improprieties. In that case, the Second Circuit Court of Appeals in New York has upheld the Manhattan district attorney's power to obtain Trump's financial documents from Mazars USA. The court did not rule on whether Trump is immune from investigation but based its decision on the narrow grounds that the subpoena is directed not to him but to Mazars. Trump petitioned the Supreme Court for review.

The District of Columbia Court of Appeals ruled that the congressional committee acted within its power of inquiry. The Supreme Court then gave Trump time to seek review, which he has now done, arguing that the "profoundly serious" constitutional question is whether Congress "can exercise dominion and control over the Office of the President."

In their thirty-eight-page petition, the seven lawyers representing Trump correctly point out that Congress is not a law enforcement agency. Its role is to legislate, and it has no right to inquire into purely personal matters including, they say, the president's finances. So, the issue before the Court will be whether Congress is acting within its constitutional authority.

That authority is derived from Article I, which grants various enumerated powers to Congress and then includes a catchall authority to "make all Laws which shall be necessary and proper" to carry out its duties. The first interpretation of those words appeared in *McCulloch v. Maryland,* the 1819 decision in which the Court unanimously agreed that Congress had the power to establish a national bank. Chief Justice John Marshall wrote, "Let the ends be legitimate . . . and all means which are . . . plainly adopted to that end . . . are constitutional."

Just to be clear, this is not an impeachment investigation. Nor is it about the motives behind the subpoena—they are beside the point, constitutionally speaking. It is, rather, about whether Congress "needs" the information to perform its power to investigate and to legislate as may be appropriate. The specific legislative question is whether the Ethics in Government Act of 1978 needs to be strengthened. According to the Second Circuit, an individual's conduct may well offer a "valid point of departure for remedial legislation."

And it is here that the Congressional subpoena and the impeachment count alleging "Obstruction of Congress" intersect. The Constitution requires the president to "take care that the laws be faithfully executed." And a president's obligation to make truthful financial disclosures, as required of every president since Jimmy Carter, is very much part of our law.

All Supreme Court cases are important. But this one will tell us whether the power of inquiry, and therefore our system of checks and balances, survives.[99]

---

99 The Supreme Court result was a July 9, 2020, split decision. In *Trump v. Vance*, the Court unanimously rejected Trump's absolute immunity claim. And seven of the nine justices concluded that the Manhattan District Attorney's subpoena was enforceable. On February 22, 2021, the Supreme Court rejected Trump's last-ditch request, and the tax records were turned over to the prosecutors. *Trump v. Mazars* was more favorable to Trump, addressing the separation of powers issues raised by the House subpoena and returning the case to the lower court for further proceedings. On February 25, 2021, the House Oversight Committee reissued the subpoena for the same documents it had previously requested.

# The 2020 Census
# and a Smorgasbord of Broken Rules (2019)

Article I of the Constitution provides that members of Congress shall be apportioned among the states "according to their respective Numbers." That Article also requires a census every ten years to count how many "persons" reside in each state.

Originally, the words "respective Numbers" referred to "free Persons" plus "three-fifths of all other persons," the latter referring to slaves. After the Civil War, the Fourteenth Amendment eliminated the notorious "three-fifths" clause and established the requirement that the apportionment of congressional members from the states be determined "according to their respective numbers, counting the whole number of persons in each State."

The words "whole number of persons" seem clear enough. When the Constitution refers to "citizens" or "the right to vote," it uses those words. For example, the Nineteenth Amendment, ratified in 1920, says that the right of citizens to vote may not be denied on account of sex. Within the same paragraph, The Fourteenth Amendment uses the word "citizens" when granting birthright citizenship to persons born in the United States, and the words "any person" when prohibiting the states from denying life, liberty, or property without due process of law, or denying equal protection of the laws.

The Census Bureau is part of the Department of Commerce, and Trump's Secretary of Commerce is a man named Wilbur Ross, a former banker who in private life specialized in buying and reselling bankrupt companies. Ross will not be doing the population count himself, but he is the person in charge, and that has led to a remarkable conflict over including a citizenship question in the Census Bureau's questionnaire for the 2020 Census.

For much of our history, the Census Bureau's questionnaire did include such a question, but in 1960 the Bureau took it out based on data showing that including the question caused an undercounting of "hard-to-count" groups, especially noncitizens and Hispanics. Now, over the objections of the Census Bureau, six of its former Directors, and countless groups from all sides of the political spectrum, Secretary Ross wants to reinstate that question.

The stakes are high because the 2020 census will determine which states gain, and which states lose, congressional districts. This, in turn, will apportion the 435 members of Congress among the fifty states. It will also affect the allocation of billions of dollars of federal aid to the states.

On January 15, 2019, Judge Jesse Furman, a federal judge in the Southern District of New York, issued a decision in *State of New York v. Department of Commerce*, a lawsuit brought by eighteen states, the District of Columbia, fifteen cities and counties, and several nongovernmental organizations. Judge Furman's decision, a mind-numbing 277 pages including eighty-eight footnotes, describes government run amok.

In a scathing opinion, Judge Furman found that Secretary Ross "blatantly" violated the federal census law by failing to follow the proper procedures and by failing to notify Congress, as the law requires, that he intended to include the citizenship question. Ross's actions were, in the judge's words, arbitrary and capricious "several times over." He "ignored, cherry-picked, or badly misconstrued the evidence," "acted irrationally," and concealed the true basis for his decision—all of which the judge called a "veritable smorgasbord" of federal law violations.

Moreover, the trial record included undisputed evidence that the Department of Justice did not initiate this brouhaha, as Ross claimed, but the very opposite. The evidence established that Ross went looking for cover, and he ultimately found a Justice Department political appointee willing to write a letter requesting the addition of the citizenship question. Shades of President Trump asking Deputy Attorney General Rod Rosenstein to write a letter justifying the James Comey firing, only to have Trump acknowledge the pretext by telling Lester Holt on NBC News that his real motive for getting rid of Comey was "the Russia thing."

The Trump administration is doubling down. Describing the case as one of "imperative public importance" that simply cannot wait, it asked the Supreme Court to bypass the Court of Appeals, take the appeal directly, hear the case in April, and issue a decision in time for printing the census questionnaire in June. On February 15, the Court granted that request and scheduled oral argument for late April 2019.

Judge Furman's decision rests on federal administrative law, but the Wilbur Ross citizenship question has profound constitutional ramifications. The government's own data show that if the question becomes part of the 2020 census, the result will be a serious undercount of "the whole number of persons," largely minorities and immigrants who tend to live in urban areas. Such an undercount would benefit rural Republican-leaning states.

The Constitution points the other way. Members of Congress represent not just citizens but all persons who reside in their districts, and it is a constitutional imperative that we count every man, woman, and child irrespective of citizenship. If the Framers and those who wrote the Fourteenth Amendment had wanted them excluded from the count, they would have used different language. We allow the executive branch to tinker with the fundamental principles of our democracy at our peril.[100]

---

100  On June 27, 2019, in *Department of Commerce v. New York*, the Supreme Court rebuffed Secretary Ross and the Trump administration. By a 5 to 4 vote, Chief Justice Roberts providing the decisive fifth vote and writing the majority opinion, the Court agreed with Judge Furman that the stated rationale for adding the citizenship question was "contrived," and that the evidence did not support the claim that this was just a matter of one department of government acting on a "routine request" from another. The Court's decision was based on the Administrative Procedures Act, which requires a "reasoned explanation" and not a "distraction" for such agency action. Justice Thomas, joined by Justices Gorsuch and Kavanaugh, chastised the majority for questioning Ross's "sincerity," lamenting the "din of suspicion and distrust" that typifies modern discourse.

This decision did not end the matter. The Court left open the possibility that the Department of Commerce could come up with a "non-pretextual" rationale. The Trump administration soldiered on, looking for some way to exclude non-citizens from the 2020 census. In July 2020, the president sent a memorandum to Secretary Ross entitled "Excluding Illegal Aliens from the Apportionment Base Following the 2020 Census." On December 18, 2020, in *Trump v. New York*, the Supreme Court issued a 5 to 3 per curiam opinion (meaning that no justice put his or her name on the opinion), with Justices Breyer, Sotomayor, and Kagan dissenting. The majority avoided deciding whether the administration could exclude "illegal aliens" from the process of reapportionment on the grounds that the case was "riddled with contingencies and speculation that impede judicial review" and was therefore "non-justiciable."

Early in his presidency, President Biden issued an executive order that canceled Trump's orders to keep track of the citizenship status of every US resident and to exclude people here illegally from the apportionment numbers used by the states. On April 26, 2021, the Census Bureau released the first results showing Congressional reapportionment. Six states gained seats (Colorado, Florida, Montana, North Carolina, Oregon, and Texas); seven states lost seats (California, Illinois, Michigan, New York, Ohio, Pennsylvania, and West Virginia).

# Donald Trump and the Power to Pardon
## (2021)

Will he, or won't he? Pardon himself, that is.

The last president who considered pardoning himself, so far as we know, was Richard Nixon. However, according to an August 4, 1974, Justice Department opinion, "the fundamental rule that no one may be a judge in his own case" means that the president cannot pardon himself. Nixon decided not to take the risk and chose to resign and hope for the best. Thanks to his successor, Gerald Ford, that worked out.

Article II of the Constitution gives the president "Power to grant reprieves and Pardons for Offenses against the United States, except in Cases of impeachment." This was not a new idea. The Founding Fathers simply constitutionalized a power long held by the Crown of England. According to Blackstone, the eighteenth century authority on common law, "The effect of a pardon is to make the offender a new man."

In July 1865, soon after the assassination of President Lincoln, President Andrew Johnson pardoned an Arkansas lawyer named A. H. Garland for the crime of participating in the "Rebellion against the United States," an offense that had kept him from practicing law. In the 1866 case called *Ex Parte Garland*, the Supreme Court said that the pardon power "extends to every offence known to the law," bestowing upon the president the "benign prerogative of mercy." So, thanks to Johnson's merciful signature on a piece of paper, Garland was, at least according to Blackstone, a "new man," once again free to practice law.

President Trump has exercised this power mostly for his friends and political supporters, pardoning not only Michael Flynn, who had twice pleaded guilty to lying about his contacts with Russians, but also Roger Stone, Paul Manafort, his son-in-law's father, former congressmen who committed misuse of campaign funds and insider trading, and Blackwater security guards who killed fourteen Iraqi civilians. These pardonees had all been charged and convicted.

Trump claims he has the "absolute right" to pardon himself. The Supreme Court would likely reject that wrongheaded view, as it did last July in *Trump v. Vance*, when the Court held that Trump, like "every man," has no immunity from a grand jury subpoena.

New York authorities have retained forensic accountants to assist them in their investigation of Trump and various Trump entities, which shows just how serious they are. However, whether Trump is at risk of federal prosecution is another matter, and the Biden Justice Department may conclude that pursuing him for obstruction of justice or other possible federal offenses would do more harm than good.

A self-pardon will not impede the State of New York from moving ahead, but as of January 20, 2021, without a pardon at the federal level, Trump faces a risk that became even more serious after the sorrowful events at the Capitol building on January 6. In light of calls for his resignation and condemnations from across the political spectrum, the likelihood that Trump will try to pardon himself remains a distinct possibility. In that event, the Biden administration will face a dilemma.

Doing nothing could be seen as a tacit admission that a self-pardon is constitutional. Doing something, on the other hand, would subject the country to years of litigation, beginning with a court challenge from Trump. And who knows, he might win that challenge, turning what might otherwise be considered a yellow light for future presidents into a green one.

There are both practical and legal reasons for Trump to pause before he hits the "self-pardon" button. Just as it is better not to poke a bear, so the wiser course may be to leave well enough alone.

In *Burdick v. United States*, decided in 1915, the Supreme Court ruled that for a pardon to become effective, the pardoned person must accept it. And, the Court added, a pardon carries with it "an imputation of guilt, acceptance a confession of it." Whereas Burdick was being investigated for a specific offense, making the "imputation" and "acceptance" somewhat tangible, just how the Court's language would apply in Trump's case is murky at best.

There are various arguments regarding the invalidity of a presidential self-pardon. An "originalist" view might look at what the Framers had in mind and conclude that they were rejecting the idea that "the King can do no wrong." From that perspective, the presidential power to pardon is necessarily limited to others. The constitutional word "grant," suggesting something given by one person to another, may provide some etymological support.

To this one might add the Court's requirement that anyone receiving a pardon cannot simply remain passive. So long as the *Burdick* case remains good law, a self-pardon would become effective only if Trump were to "accept" it and thereby admit wrongdoing. Given what we know about Donald Trump, that seems unlikely.

Finally, there is the "fundamental rule" that no one can be his or her own judge—"*nemo judex in causa sua.*" Those words are not in the Constitution, but they are an essential component of the rule of law. And if, as the Court has said, not even the president is above the law, then that ancient axiom may yet be the strongest argument against allowing the president to pardon himself.[101]

---

101  As it turned out, Trump did not pardon himself, his family members, or even Rudy Giuliani. He did issue last-minute pardons to Steve Bannon, his former chief strategist; Elliott Broidy, one of his top fundraisers; and Albert J. Pirro Jr., ex-husband of Trump apologist and Fox News host Jeanine Pirro.

# Executive Privilege and Finding the Truth
## About January 6 (2021)

Former president Donald Trump brought a lawsuit to prevent the National Archives from turning documents from his presidency over to the House Committee investigating the January 6 attack on the Capitol. These include notes, memos, and other papers that may shed light on the extent to which Trump, or members of his administration, were complicit in that attack. He claims that "executive privilege" allows him to prevent Congress from getting the documents.

Trump's lawsuit raises two important questions. Does a former president have the right to claim executive privilege, or does the right belong only to the current occupant of the White House? If Trump does have such a right, does that mean that the papers will remain under lock and key, unavailable to the Committee?

The Watergate Nixon Tapes case provides a starting point. In 1974, a grand jury indicted seven individuals—all high-ranking members of the Nixon administration—of conspiracy to obstruct justice and to defraud the United States. At the Special Prosecutor's request, a federal judge issued a subpoena directing Nixon to produce the tapes in advance of the trial.

On July 24, 1974, the Supreme Court, three of whose members Nixon had appointed, unanimously ordered him to turn over the tapes. Chief Justice Burger, one of the three appointees, wrote that the president does have such a privilege, especially where military or diplomatic secrets are involved, but the privilege is not absolute. Where the claim is based simply on a generalized assertion without showing a strong governmental interest, it must yield if the reason for the subpoena outweighs the interests of presidential confidentiality. The Court ordered Nixon to deliver the tapes, he did so, and sixteen days later he resigned.

In the case of the January 6 documents, the stakes are huge. Trump wants to keep 724 pages away from Congress. What we know is that those documents include Chief of Staff Mark Meadows's notes about the attack on the Capitol, Trump's daily schedule, visitor logs and call records, and documents about trying to overturn the election.

Under the Presidential Recordings and Materials Preservation Act of

1974, Congress gave ownership of a president's official records to the public and created a system whereby Congress could gain access to those records in order to conduct its business. Under that law, a former president can make the claim, but the current president has the last word. President Biden has rejected Trump's claim as "not in the best interests of the United States," thereby setting the stage for this lawsuit.

Just to be clear, Trump is challenging the constitutionality of the 1974 Presidential Records Act, arguing that under the Constitution he has the right to prevent disclosure in perpetuity. The is a "case of first impression"—the Supreme Court has never before faced the question, which has implications not only for the January 6 investigation but for the separation of powers and governmental transparency as well.

On November 9, 2021, Judge Tanya Chutkan, a District of Columbia federal judge, issued a thirty-nine-page opinion denying Trump's request for an injunction against the House Committee and the National Archives. Judge Chutkan ruled that Trump had failed to show a likelihood of success, which is one of the requirements for a preliminary injunction. She also ruled that he had not demonstrated "irreparable harm," which is another requirement.

The case moved swiftly to the Court of Appeals, which rejected Trump's claim without regard to his status as a former president. Even if he were still president, the Court held, he would have no grounds to keep the National Archives from turning over the documents or the House Committee from receiving them.

On January 19, 2022, the Supreme Court issued a one-paragraph order upholding the lower court's ruling. Unlike the unanimous 1975 Nixon Tapes decision, this ruling was 8 to 1. Justice Clarence Thomas, the opinion tells us, "would grant the application."

Notably, the three justices whom Trump appointed—Gorsuch, Kavanaugh, and Amy Coney Barrett—were among the eight-justice majority. As was true in 1974, so now. This is not a partisan dispute, or a contest between liberals and conservatives. As Judge Chutkan wrote, "Presidents are not kings."

# THE FIRST AMENDMENT

*The United States is a land of free speech. Nowhere is speech freer.*
Winston Churchill

## In a Democracy We Do Not Allow Prior Restraints (2020)

During the eighteenth century, a man named Blackstone wrote *Commentaries on the Laws of England*, the definitive treatise on English law. According to him, freedom of the press "consists of laying no previous restraints on publication."

We took on this common law rule against censorship when we adopted the Constitution in 1787, and when the states ratified the First Amendment in 1791.

In 1931, the Supreme Court staked out how essential this rule is to American law. Jay Near, owner of a Minneapolis newspaper called *The Saturday Press*, published antisemitic, anti-Catholic, anti-black articles, and the local authorities tried to shut down the paper under the state's "public nuisance" law. By a 5 to 4 vote, *Near v. Minnesota* decided that Near had a constitutional right to publish his paper, hateful speech and all. The greater harm, said the Court, would be to allow public officials to decide what can and cannot be published.

In 1952, the Court unanimously decided the case of *Burstyn v. Wilson*. Under New York law at the time, a film distributor had to get approval from the state educational department before exhibiting a movie. Cardinal Spellman denounced as sacrilegious a Federico Fellini film called *The Miracle*, starring Anna Magnani. Diocesan priests followed their leader, and the state revoked the license. The Supreme Court said a resounding "No"—movies are protected by the First Amendment, and you can't condition showing them on the whim of a government censor.

In 1971, the Supreme Court decided the "Pentagon Papers" case, *New York Times v. United States.* A man named Daniel Ellsberg leaked an exposé of the Vietnam War to the press, and the Nixon administration sued to prevent publication. The Supreme Court ruled for the *Times* on the basis that the Government had failed to show publication would create a "grave and irreparable" danger.[102] The *Times* and *The Washington Post*, then published the papers.[103]

What these and other cases establish is that the "no prior restraint" rule is at the heart of the First Amendment, and exceptions are rare. The classic example is that a court could prevent a newspaper from disclosing the whereabouts of American ships in wartime—a matter of legitimate national security.

President Trump has made it clear that he has no use for the press. He calls reporters "scum" who print and broadcast "fake news." But it isn't just the press that he dislikes; it is the First Amendment itself, including the "no prior restraints" doctrine.

I refer to his lawsuit against John Bolton, a classic barn-door case if ever there was one. On June 16, 2020, Trump's Justice Department sued in District of Columbia federal court to prevent Bolton from publishing his tell-all book, *The Room Where It Happened.* The DOJ claimed that Bolton was making classified information public. Trump went on Twitter to denounce the author as "Wacko John Bolton" whose book is "full of lies." One of those "lies" is Bolton's opinion that Trump is "not fit for office."

By the time this lawsuit was filed, the book had already been printed, and the publisher had distributed advance copies to news media and others around the country in advance of the scheduled June 23 publication date. The media has already provided the public with some of the juicy parts.

The judge assigned to Bolton's case, a Reagan appointee if that matters, has refused to halt publication. In a country that values freedom of the press, the Department of Justice should be ashamed of itself for wasting the taxpayers' money on such an ill-conceived case.

---

102   This is an example of "strict scrutiny," the standard employed when the government tries to suppress speech.

103   The story is winningly told in the 2017 Steven Spielberg movie *The Post,* starring Meryl Streep and Tom Hanks.

# From Nixon to Trump: Freedom of the Press
# in Difficult Times (2017)

*If the freedom of speech is taken away, then dumb and silent*
*we may be led, like sheep to the slaughter.*

George Washington

It hardly needs to be said that a free press is essential to a free America. Thomas Jefferson wrote that if he had to choose between government without newspapers or newspapers without a government, "I would not hesitate a moment to prefer the latter." Of course, that was many years before he became president and changed his mind.

We do have a historical stain, the Anti-Sedition Act of 1798. That law, signed by President John Adams, made it a crime to speak negatively about the government. The Act expired by its own terms, and President Jefferson pardoned those who had been convicted.

Most presidents have had run-ins with the press, but Richard Nixon raised press-hating to an art form and a political strategy. After his election in 1968, he started calling the press the "media," wiretapped reporters' phones, and sent the IRS after reporters he didn't like. Nixon got reelected in 1972, but in August of 1974 he resigned in disgrace, brought down by a vigilant press.

Presidents since Nixon have criticized the press, but until Donald Trump none has questioned the basic rights and responsibilities created by the First Amendment. According to him, the press is "the enemy of the American people." He recently told the Conservative Political Action Conference that the press "doesn't represent the people . . . *and we're going to do something about it.*"

He didn't say what he has in mind, but those italicized words should give all of us the shudders. The freedom to criticize government without fear of reprisal is fundamental to our way of life. Tension between the Presidency and the Fourth Estate is supposed to happen. It is healthy for America.

The Anti-Sedition Act never made it to the Supreme Court, but Justice William J. Brennan's landmark 1964 opinion in *New York Times v. Sullivan* says that the Act has been rejected in the "court of history." Justice Brennan's opinion includes the much-quoted pronouncement that under our

Justice William J. Brennan

Constitution, the United States has "a profound national commitment to the principle that debate on public issues should be *uninhibited, robust, and wide-open*." Such speech, he went on, may include "vehement, caustic, and sometimes unpleasantly sharp attacks on government and public officials."

Since then, in case after case, the Supreme Court has upheld our right of free expression, even for the "thought that we hate," to quote Justice Oliver Wendell Holmes. Unlike some areas of constitutional law, this is not a matter of "liberal" versus "conservative" values. Justice Antonin Scalia, a conservative "originalist," was a strong defender of freedom of speech and press. It appears that Supreme Court nominee Neil Gorsuch is cast in the same mold and will be a strong supporter of the First Amendment.

One of President Trump's campaign promises was to "open up those libel laws." Someone should tell him about the ill-fated Anti-Sedition Law and *New York Times v. Sullivan.*[104]

---

104  No sitting president of the United States had ever sued the press for libel until 2020, when, during the election campaign, Trump did so at least three times, first against *The New York Times* in February, then in short order against *The Washington Post* and CNN.

## Lying About the 2020 Election
## Produces Massive Lawsuits (2021)

*A good name is rather to be chosen than great riches.*

Book of Proverbs

Over my fifty-six years as a trial lawyer, mostly representing parties in civil cases, I have seen parts of the legal system from the inside. Like all human institutions, it is far from perfect. But the courts are often the only place you can go when you believe you are the victim of a wrongful act. That includes defending your good name against unfair and false attacks.

Defamation law deals with false statements of fact that are likely to harm the reputation of a person or a corporation. The law creates a very steep hill for libel plaintiffs to climb, but it is not an insurmountable one. In recent times, the 2020 presidential election and defamation law have come together in three remarkable lawsuits brought by manufacturers of voting machines, one named Smartmatic and the other named Dominion.

On February 4, 2021, Smartmatic went to New York state court and sued Fox News, its on-air personalities Maria Bartiromo, Lou Dobbs, and Jeanine Pirro, and Trump-affiliated lawyers Sidney Powell and Rudy Giuliani. The complaint begins with these words: "The Earth is round. Two plus two equals four. Joe Biden and Kamala Harris won the 2020 election for President and Vice President of the United States. The election was not stolen, rigged, or fixed. Defendants knew the election was not stolen . . . was not rigged or fixed . . . just as they knew the Earth is round and two plus two equals four."

That is an unusual way to start a lawsuit, and it is followed by 754 paragraphs taking up 276 pages. The last paragraph asks for an eyepopping damages award of "no less than $2.7 billion (the "b" is not a typo) plus punitive damages.[105]

In January, Dominion filed two one-hundred-plus-page libel complaints in the District of Columbia federal court, one against Powell and the other against Giuliani. The essence of these cases, like Smartmatic's, is that these

---

105  Lawyers know that the ad damnum is just for show; the jury will never see the complaint. Even so, plaintiffs' lawyers often include a very high dollar number where state law permits. The complaint is a public document, and it can make for good press.

individuals, one a member of the Texas bar and the other a member of the New York bar, peddled out-and-out falsehoods claiming that the company's voting machines shifted Trump votes to Biden and created non-existent votes for Biden. Dominion is asking for damages of $1.3 billion.[106]

Smartmatic's business operations are focused on elections in the Philippines and other foreign countries. Its voting machines were used in last November's presidential election in Los Angeles County and nowhere else. Dominion voting machines were used more widely, in nearly half the states. Both companies are now scrambling to deal with the results of defendants' smear campaigns, and from the face of the complaints it appears that they have sustained real economic and reputational harm.

These are private lawsuits, but they serve a public purpose. The courtroom is not only where a party can go to get its reputation back. It is also where you can go to send a message, not just to those you are suing but also to those who are watching. In that sense, the targets are more than a news network, its employees, and a couple of lawyers.[107] Be warned, media outlets and others who would use their platforms to poison the public well with disinformation.

Just as product liability lawsuits against makers of dangerous machines have helped improve safety in the workplace and the home, so these cases may encourage those who engage in promoting falsehoods to think twice before calling anyone a crook.

Winston Churchill's words to the effect that "Nowhere is speech freer" than in the United States do not mean that the sky is the limit. And Justice Brennan's assurance that under the First Amendment, we may engage in "robust, uninhibited, and wide open" speech about public issues has its boundaries. The critical question in defamation law is not simply whether the speech in question was false, but also whether the speaker was at fault. The First Amendment does not create a right to make up defamatory and injurious fictions and then avoid accountability for the foreseeable results. The statements challenged in the Smartmatic and Dominion lawsuits have hardly anything to do with freedom of speech.

---

106  On March 26, 2021, Dominion sued Fox News for defamation in Delaware Superior Court, alleging that Fox knowingly spread false claims that its machines altered vote counts, taking a "small flame" and turning it "into a forest fire." According to the complaint, "The truth matters."
107  Giuliani has been suspended by the New York and District of Columbia bars. Powell faces possible disciplinary action by the Texas bar based on her post-election activities on Trump's behalf.

If these cases go to trial, it will be up to these companies, which will likely be considered "public figures," to prove that the statements are defamatory, not just protected opinions; that they are false; and that those who made them did so knowing they were false or with reckless disregard for the truth.[108] It will be up to a jury to decide whether they have met that burden and made it to the top of the hill. In my experience, juries know how to add, and they usually get it right.

Individuals and corporations can bring libel cases, but the law does not permit countries to do so. If the law were otherwise, the United States could sue private citizen Donald Trump for lying about our country and damaging its reputation.

---

108   This "knowing falsity" standard is the test where the plaintiff is a public official or a public figure. A "private person" suing for libel is also required to prove fault, but in most states under the more forgiving standard of negligence, meaning that the defendant should have been more careful before publishing a defamatory falsehood.

# Freedom Not to Speak and Using
# the First Amendment as a Weapon (2018)

On December 5, 2017, the Supreme Court heard arguments from Jack Phillips, the Colorado baker who refused to bake a customized wedding cake for a same-sex wedding celebration. In 2015, the Court decided that same-sex marriage is protected by the Equal Protection clause of the Fourteenth Amendment. Jack argues that First Amendment freedom of religion should protect him from having to participate in, and as he sees it condone, a wedding that is against his religious beliefs. Like a lot of Supreme Court cases, this one highlights the tension between constitutional rights.

Jack's argument that his cakes are a form of expression represents a twist on the usual free speech case. Such cases usually arise where someone claims that the government is telling him he cannot express himself as he wishes. Here, Jack says he has a "negative" right, meaning the right not to be compelled to speak.

He did not invent this theory. In 1943, the Supreme Court held that the state could not require elementary school students to salute the American Flag, and there have been other such cases. In other words, school children, and the rest of us, have a right, at least in some circumstances, to remain silent.

*The New York Times* recently called this a "rear guard action" by religious objectors who, having lost the same-sex marriage battle on equal protection grounds, have moved to the free speech playing field. This is not a simple issue, but even if an artistic wedding cake can be considered a form of expression, free speech is not an absolute right. Some things you may not say, such as shouting "Fire" in a crowded theatre when there is none. And some things you may be required to say, for example that taking a particular prescription drug creates certain risks.

This is not the only negative speech problem coming before the Supreme Court during the 2017–2018 term. California has a law that requires religiously motivated, licensed pro-life "crisis pregnancy centers" to post a notice providing contact information for free or low-cost abortion services. According to the National Institute of Family and Life Advocates, "Under the First Amendment, you can't make anyone say that."

Here, as in the wedding cake case, the First Amendment is being used as a shield to avoid complying with a state law. Yes, the argument goes, a woman has a constitutional right to obtain an abortion, but if we oppose the exercise of that right, we should not have to post a notice that might lead someone to exercise it.

Using the First Amendment in this way is clever lawyering. But it overlooks an important principle, which is that, as in life, accommodations must be found in the Constitution. In the wedding cake case, the first question should not be whether, when you go to a wedding party, you look at the cake and say to yourself, "That cake is a type of expression." Rather the commonsense question is whether you think to yourself, "Whoever baked that cake approves of this marriage." I don't think so, at least so long as no one is telling Jack that he must inscribe a pro-same-sex marriage message on the frosting.

In the California case, similarly, no one is forcing the clinic to tell the patient, "You should get an abortion." The clinic is free to tell its clients, "The law requires me to give you this information, but I'm against abortion and hope you don't go there." Such an accommodation in no ways undermine the clinic's pro-life beliefs.

When the Supreme Court outlawed school segregation as a denial of equal protection of the law, many citizens were upset. Did they ask the Supreme Court to exempt their children under a First Amendment negative right of association, arguing that their children had a right not to be in the same classroom as black children? No, and if they had, they would have been laughed out of court.

Jack the Baker and the California pro-life organization are no doubt sincere in their religious beliefs, but so were those who opposed integration of public facilities and housing and lots of other rights we now take for granted. The whole point is to accommodate one right with another, even if that leaves some people disappointed.[109]

---

109 The Supreme Court ruled in favor of Jack the Baker, but not based on the First Amendment freedom-of-speech principles or free exercise of religion. The Court's June 4, 2018, ruling criticized what Justice Kennedy called the "religious hostility" of a member of the Colorado Human Rights Commission. During the state administrative hearings, that local official said that freedom of religion has historically been used to justify "all kinds of discrimination," citing slavery and the Holocaust, and none of his fellow commissioners had voiced any objection. Such failure to maintain "religious neutrality" so infected the process, according to Kennedy, that Jack did not receive a fair and impartial hearing. Notably, the court majority of seven justices included Justices Breyer and Kagan. Justice Thomas would have gone straight to the merits and ruled that Jack had a First Amendment right not to create a cake that aligns himself with same-sex marriage.

# Freedom of Assembly Is Not a Privilege
## —It's the Law of the Land (2020)

I went looking through the Constitution for a place where it says the president can break the law, but I couldn't find it. What I did find, tucked in the First Amendment between freedom of speech and the right to petition the Government for a redress of grievances, is "the right of the people peaceably to assemble."

Like so much of the Constitution, the right of assembly was a reaction to the abuses committed by the Crown, including how British authorities treated "the people out of doors." The Riot Act of 1714 provided that local officials could disperse groups of more than twelve by reading certain words concluding with "God save the King." Failure to heed the warning was a felony.

James Madison was aware of this history when he wrote the First Amendment, but Americans valued the right to protest long before then. As we all learned in grade school, in 1773 the Sons of Liberty reacted to "taxation without representation" by getting together and dumping tea into Boston Harbor.

Just as freedom of religion, speech, and press are subject to so-called "time, place, and manner" restrictions, so too the right to assemble is not absolute. We need look no further than the Covid-19 public health emergency, which has prompted state and local governments to limit the size of gatherings. The Supreme Court recently upheld California's restriction on the number of people who could assemble in church. Chief Justice Roberts, joining the four liberal justices, declined to second-guess elected state officials, noting

---

On June 26, 2018, in *National Institute of Family and Life Advocates v. Becerra*, the Court ruled in favor of the California faith-based crisis pregnancy center. On behalf of the five conservative members of the Court, Justice Thomas wrote that the state could post public notices but requiring a pro-life organization to post the notices about abortion availability was a form of "compelled speech" prohibited by the First Amendment.

The third case "weaponizing" the First Amendment is *Janus v. American Federation of State, County and Municipal Employees*, decided on June 27, 2018. Unlike the other cases in this long footnote, the *Janus* case had nothing to do with religious beliefs, but rather dealt with public employee unions. Proving once again that "money talks," the Court held that requiring non-members such as Janus to pay a so-called "fair share" fee to the union is a type of forced speech because the union uses the money to speak on behalf of employees.

that similar or more severe limits were also placed on lectures, concerts, movies, sports, and other events where people gather in close proximity for extended periods of time.

That case deals with the right to assemble to worship, protected by two different parts of the First Amendment, and 2020 produced many other instances where people assembled in large numbers for non-religious purposes. When a Minneapolis police officer killed George Floyd on May 25, 2020, millions of people saw the video, heard the words "I can't breathe," and took to the streets. "Black lives matter" has become part of the national consciousness, just like "we shall overcome."

Not to sugarcoat our recent experience, some demonstrators crossed the line and committed vandalism, looting, and random acts of violence. Hooligans in Washington set fire to the basement nursery of St. John's Episcopal Church on H Street. That is the ugly side of what we have been living through, and it is unlawful and inexcusable.

But at the same time, no one should excuse the president's shameful removal of demonstrators from Lafayette Square, just across Pennsylvania Avenue from the White House, on June 1. That Monday night, June 1, 2020, Trump announced from the Rose Garden that "we need to dominate the streets" and, with help from Attorney General Barr, had the public square cleared of peaceful demonstrators. Police on foot and on horseback pushed the protesters out of the park and down H Street, using smoke canisters, pepper spray balls, and flash-bang grenades.

All this so that Trump, accompanied by his daughter Ivanka and several flunkies, could walk over to H Street and stand outside St. John's for a photo op holding a bible.

It would be one thing if police had been called to deal with demonstrators who were not assembling "peaceably." But that was not the president's concern, and if anyone told him that the demonstrators were exercising their constitutional rights either he didn't listen or didn't care, or both. He decided to "dominate" a public space, and that was that.

The First Amendment right of assembly doesn't take sides. It protects demonstrators protesting police brutality and KKK members promoting white supremacy in equal measure. Exercising the right doesn't cost anything. All it takes is a person's physical commitment, what New York University law professor Burt Neuborne calls "First Amendment sweat equity."

Such physical commitment is as active now as at any time since the 1970s, and it shows no signs of abating. Crowds continue to gather everywhere, in New York and Washington, in cities and towns and villages across the country, and even abroad, holding "Black Lives Matter" signs. In Keene, New Hampshire, where I live, no constable showed up to read the Riot Act. Instead, local police officers held "I can hear you" signs.

Maybe we need new laws, but we already have some good ones, beginning with the "experiment" that is the Constitution. The president and the attorney general might want to read the First Amendment and then look at Article VI, Clause 2, which states, "This Constitution, and the Laws of the United States . . . shall be the supreme Law of the land."[110]

---

110  On April 19, 2021, Florida governor Ron DeSantis signed an "anti-riot" bill that grants civil and criminal immunity to anyone who runs over a protester who is blocking the road. According to DeSantis, "It's the strongest anti-rioting pro-law enforcement piece of legislation in the country. There's nothing even close." On April 21, Oklahoma governor Kevin Stitt signed a bill that grants immunity from both civil and criminal responsibility to drivers "fleeing from a riot" who "unintentionally" injure or kill "an individual," apparently including bystanders as well as individuals who are part of the "riot." These overbroad laws unconstitutionally encroach on the right of assembly under the guise of protecting the public.

# One Nation Under God and Jefferson's Wall (2019)

During the Civil War, a man named George Thatcher Batch wrote the Pledge of Allegiance, and Congress adopted it in 1942 as part of a law called the "Flag Code." Since then, it has been changed once, in 1954, with the insertion of the words "under God" between "one nation" and "indivisible." The added words were not original. Lincoln used them in 1863 in the Gettysburg Address, resolving "that this nation, under God, shall have a new birth of freedom."

Religion and the Pledge have not had an entirely smooth relationship. In *West Virginia State Board of Education v. Barnette,* a 1943 Supreme Court case brought by Jehovah's Witnesses, the Court held that mandatory recitation of the pre-"under God" pledge in public schools violated the First Amendment. Government may not compel anyone to "prescribe what shall be orthodox in politics, nationalism, religion, or other matters of opinion." No exceptions.

The First Amendment enshrines separation of church and state with the words, "Congress shall make no law respecting an establishment of religion," followed by the words "or prohibiting the free exercise thereof." The words "respecting an establishment of religion" are less than crystal clear, but we do have some historical guideposts.

In 1802, Thomas Jefferson wrote a letter to the Danbury Baptist Association, stating that the purpose of the words was to "build a *wall* of separation between Church and State." In 1803, James Madison, author of the First Amendment, wrote a letter objecting to the use of public land for churches, stating that the purpose of the Establishment Clause was to "keep from these shores the ceaseless strife that has soaked the soil of Europe in blood for centuries." John Adams said that "the government of the United States is not, in any sense, founded on the Christian religion."

In recent times, our national attention has been focused more on Trump's wall than Jefferson's. But the place of religion in public life seems to be flowing more than ebbing, and this year's Supreme Court term will tell us whether, and to what extent, government can use public funds in a way that many see as supporting religion.

The case is called *The American Legion v. American Humanist Association.*

And it deals with a World War I memorial located at a busy intersection in Bladensburg, Maryland. The problem is that this forty-foot-high marble and cement memorial in the shape of a cross is maintained at public expense. According to the Fourth Circuit Court of Appeals, the average citizen "would fairly understand the Cross to have the primary effect of endorsing religion." As such, the court majority concluded, the cross "excessively entangles the government in religion."

The word "entangles" comes from a 1971 case, *Lemon v. Kurtzman*, where the Court applied the Establishment Clause to strike down a state law allowing the use of public funds to reimburse private (mostly parochial) schools for salaries paid to teachers of non-religious subjects. The late Justice Scalia later compared the so-called "*Lemon* entanglement test" to "a ghoul in a late-night horror movie."

One can sympathize with Scalia's colorful comparison. The word "entangle" doesn't provide a lot of guidance, and the later "Ten Commandments" cases simply add to the confusion. On the very same day, June 27, 2005, the Supreme Court, in back-to-back decisions, held that the public display of the Ten Commandments both is and is not constitutional. In *Van Orden v. Perry*, the Court decided that a Ten Commandments statue donated by the Fraternal Order of Eagles to the State of Texas, installed on the Capitol grounds in Austin, was more secular than religious. In *McCreary County v. American Civil Liberties Union*, the Court held that displaying the Ten Commandments at a public courthouse in Kentucky was motivated by a religious "purpose" and therefore violated the Establishment Clause.

If, as Emerson said, "a foolish consistency is the hobgoblin of little minds," Justice Stephen Breyer passes the test. He was in the majority in both of these 5 to 4 decisions. Justice David Souter, on the other hand, dissented in *Van Orden* and wrote the Court's opinion in *McCreary County*.

The issue raised by the Bladensburg cross comes down to where to draw the First Amendment line when it comes to "religion in the public square." Here the cross, a monument to forty-nine local soldiers who died in World War I, has stood for over ninety years. Does the passage of so much time make it "secular?" And, unlike the forced recitation of the Pledge, not to mention a non-denominational school prayer (forbidden by *Engel v. Vitale*, the "school prayer" case), here the question is about a "passive" monument. No one is being asked, much less required, to do anything—unless you count unavoidably seeing the cross as you drive by the intersection.

One way of looking at the First Amendment is to say that the Establishment Clause simply prevents government from dictating religious beliefs or telling anyone what or how or where to worship. At the other extreme, Jefferson's "wall" could be understood as requiring an absolute prohibition against any governmental role, whether active or passive, that might be taken to be an endorsement of religion.

I have little doubt that the Court will reverse the lower court's ruling. Justices Thomas, Samuel Alito, and Gorsuch are sure votes for the monument, and I expect Justice Kavanaugh and Chief Justice Roberts will join them. Who knows, Justice Breyer may make it six.

But the wisdom of such a decision is open to doubt. Even if the government has a "secular" motive, intending only to honor those who gave their lives, a significant portion of the public may regard the Bladensburg monument as endorsing religion, just as a Star of David on someone's front lawn would be seen as supporting Judaism. If government erects, displays, or pays for a religious symbol, whether it be a cross, a Star of David, a star and crescent, or the wheel of dharma, should the constitutional outcome depend on the subjective intent of public officials? It all depends on the meaning of the First Amendment word "establishment."

Now might be a good time for the Supreme Court to remind all of us that the Constitution supports all religions but favors no one faith over another. One way to do so would be to affirm that Jefferson's wall still stands and that the cross in Bladensburg should not.[111]

---

111 On June 20, 2019, the Court ruled that the cross on public land did not violate the Establishment Clause. According to Justice Alito's majority opinion, this cross may have been religious when it was dedicated but, by reason of the passage of time, it "has also taken on a secular meaning." Justice Breyer joined the five conservative justices, and so did Justice Kagan. But the seven justices wrote six separate opinions, taking different paths to the same constitutional destination. The guiding principle seems to be that the passage of nearly a century gave a secular meaning to a Christian symbol. The dissenting justices, Ginsburg and Sotomayor, argued that a cross is a cross, and the passage of time does not make it any more constitutional than if it had just been erected.

## How Separate Are Church Schools and State Funds? (2021)

When I was growing up in Claremont, parents had a choice. They could send their kids to Stevens High for free, or, if they wanted their children to attend parochial school, they could send them to St. Mary's and pay.

I doubt that it ever occurred to anyone that the city should pay for St. Mary's any more than it should pay for kids who went to any other private school. But now Maine is poised to become the involuntary bellwether testing whether church and state are as separate as the Framers intended, or at least so we thought.

In Maine, more than half of its 260 school administrative units are located in rural areas and do not operate their own public secondary schools. The State's solution is to provide tuition assistance to parents who send their children to a public school in a nearby district or to nonsectarian private schools.

But what if the parents prefer a religious school over a nonsectarian one? Are they entitled to the same level of financial help from the state? Three sets of parents whose children attend Christian schools in Bangor and Waterville filed a lawsuit claiming that, under the First Amendment, excluding them from the tuition assistance program violates their constitutional rights. They lost in the lower federal courts, but the Supreme Court granted review and heard oral argument on Wednesday, December 8, 2021. The name of the case is *Carson v. Makin*.

In the 1947 case of *Everson v. Board of Education*, all nine justices accepted the Jeffersonian principle that the First Amendment creates a "wall of separation between church and state," a wall that, in the Court's words, "must be kept high and *impregnable*." Before 2017, the Court had never required government to provide financial assistance to religious organizations. But that year, the Court decided *Trinity Lutheran Church of Columbia, Inc. v. Comer*, holding that if Missouri used public funds to repave public preschool playgrounds, the First Amendment's Free Exercise clause requires that it do the same for church school playgrounds.

Then, in 2020, the Supreme Court held in *Espinoza v. Montana Department of Revenue* that a state tax credit program could not provide scholarships to nonsectarian schools unless it did the same for church-affiliated schools.

The Court's trajectory could not be clearer. To quote from the Book of Daniel, "the writing is on the wall."

On Wednesday, December 8, the Maine case played out before the Supreme Court. The lawyer representing the Maine parents, no doubt mindful of the biblical proverb that a truth speaker gives honest evidence, told the justices, "Religious schools teach religion. It is part of what they do . . . who they are."

If the justices' comments during oral argument are any indication of their sentiments—and they usually are—then it looks like the parents will win. According to Justice Kavanaugh, the parents are simply saying "don't treat me worse because I want to send my children to a religious school." If you do, he went on, "That's just discrimination on the basis of religion."

The First Amendment protects the "free exercise" of religion and prohibits laws "respecting an establishment of religion." Those words provide governing principles but do not answer the question now before the Court.

For the life of me, I don't understand how limiting public spending to nonsectarian use qualifies as unlawful "discrimination." Indeed, as Justice Elena Kagan pointed out at the hearing, it is the schools who are "proudly discriminatory" in what students they will accept and what teachers they will employ, specifically no LGBTQ need apply. How, she rhetorically asked, will other people understand why tax dollars are going to schools that discriminate. She might also have asked how such discriminatory policies square with Saint Peter's statement that "God shows no partiality" or Mark the Evangelist's second commandment to "love your neighbor as yourself."

In a speech two years ago, Justice Alito told the Federalist Society that the right to free exercise of religion "is fast becoming a disfavored right." He said nothing about the Establishment Clause, and it now seems that he and other conservative justices are choosing to treat separation of church and state as a principle to be "more honored in the breach than the observance."

Justice Alito and his like-minded colleagues need have no concern about religion being relegated to second-class status. If anything, the opposite is fast becoming true. Religion is becoming a "superior" constitutional right. Once our highest court decides that the wall is pregnable, who knows what lies ahead?

*The New York Times* recently published an op-ed column in support of the parochial school parents. If Maine is permitted to enforce its law, the writers contend, then the state will be penalizing parents "who want a school that provides both academic and spiritual nourishment."

They may be correct—such parents will be incurring an expense—but no one is forcing them to do so. That's not a penalty, it's a choice.

The next thing you know, Claremont will be required to pay St. Mary's tuition.

# THE INTERNET

## Clear and Present Danger in the Twenty-first Century (2016)

January 7, 2016, marked the first anniversary of the killings at the *Charlie Hebdo* office in Paris. Terrorists struck in that city once again in November 2015, killing 130 people and wounding a great many more. Then, just a few weeks later, husband and wife terrorists struck in this country, killing fourteen and injuring twenty-two in San Bernardino.

Do our principles of free speech play into the hands of the terrorists? Should we reconsider whether certain kinds of speech should be subject to punishment?

During the twentieth century, the Supreme Court struggled with the question of when the government may punish words. In a 1919 case called *Schenck v. United States*, the issue was whether the distribution of flyers urging draft resistance went too far. The Court said that it did, at least in time of war. Justice Holmes wrote an opinion in which he coined the phrase "clear and present danger" to explain the circumstances when the government may punish speech. He illustrated the point by saying that the right of free speech "would not protect a man falsely shouting fire in a crowded theater and causing a panic." Ten years later, Justice Holmes had moved in a different direction. Dissenting in *United States v. Schwimmer*, in which the Court upheld denial of citizenship for a woman who said she would not be willing to take up arms in defense of the country, Holmes wrote that the Constitution protects "freedom for the thought that you hate."

In 1969, in *Brandenburg v. Ohio*, the Supreme Court moved away from its rulings in the 1920s and held that advocacy in the abstract in not enough. Inflammatory speech can only be punished if it is "directed to inciting . . . *imminent* lawless action." The word "imminent" leaves little or no room for a balancing of interests or risks; it means "about to happen."

The use of twenty-first-century technology in furtherance of terrorism has expanded the concept of "speech" beyond anything Justice Holmes could have imagined. Facebook, Instagram, Twitter—these and other social media provide platforms that enable terrorist groups to recruit volunteers and promote violence over a communications network that knows no geographic boundaries. As President Obama said in his State of the Union Address, they use the Internet to poison the minds of individuals inside our country. Free speech, in their hands, is a weapon.[112]

The president also spoke of the importance of protecting an "open Internet," and of course it would be difficult, if not impossible, to control Internet speech even if we wanted to. That does not necessarily mean we are completely powerless to address the problem. Should the First Amendment protect the "republishing" of calls to join violent jihad and murder innocent people? In former times it was not so easy to pass on a message, and you usually had to do so one person at a time. Today, just hit "Forward," and you can reach an unlimited number of people.

One way to look at this is to reject any suggestion that we should curb our nearly limitless right of free speech just because ISIS, Al Qaeda, and other extremist groups take advantage of it. Such an absolutist approach has an immediate appeal—why should we give in to these criminals?

On the other hand, restricting our ability to deal with real threats unless they are "imminent" may not be the only way to preserve essential freedoms. As Harvard Law School professor Cass Sunstein has written, such words as "clear and present danger" and "imminent lawless action" may be ill-suited to twenty-first-century conditions.

James Madison left no record of just what he intended when he wrote the First Amendment words, "Congress shall make no law . . . abridging the freedom of speech, or of the press." The Supreme Court has been left to its own devices, and for at least the last fifty years it has been uncompromising in its protection of free speech. As one example, in 1989 the Court ruled, in *Texas v. Johnson,* that burning an American flag is a form of protected speech. As another, in the 2011 *Snyder v. Phelps* case, the Court upheld the right of members of the Westboro Baptist Church to picket a soldier's funeral from a public sidewalk, carrying signs bearing hateful homophobic, anti-American messages. These and other speech

---

112   When I wrote these lines, I was thinking about international terrorism. From the January 6, 2021, attack on the Capitol, we know that the same holds true for domestic terrorists.

cases make it unlikely that Schenk's conviction would hold up today.

Yet, if Madison's words are understood to mean that the United States is completely powerless to deal with foreign or domestic terrorist organizations' use of today's communications technology to promote death and destruction, then it may be time to reconsider the requirement that the peril created by such speech be "imminent." The risks of not doing so may be more than we can afford to take.

## The Internet Is Today's Wild West of Speech (2019)

The Internet is a lot like the Wild West, but with at least one important difference—it is not entirely lawless. Section 230 of the Communications Decency Act of 1996 provides internet service providers ("ISPs"), the companies that connect all of us to the Internet, with protection from being considered the "publisher or speaker of any information provided by another information content provider."

This law, passed when there was no such thing as Facebook or Twitter, and less than 1 percent of the world population used the Internet, created what lawyers call a "safe harbor," meaning that these companies, as well as Google, Yelp, and countless others, are not required to screen what people say. In that sense, they are treated like a bookstore or a magazine stand, whose owners are not legally accountable for the contents of the books or magazines they sell.

Newspaper publishers, broadcasters, and other media are "content providers" legally responsible for what they publish. They risk exposure to libel and other kinds of lawsuits even if what they publish or broadcast are accurate quotations from another publication, or even letters to the editor. Under what is known as the "republication rule," if you publish it, you own it.

Under Section 230, the opposite is true. The ISP does not "own" what appears on its website.

The preamble to this federal safe harbor law says that Congress has found that interactive computer services offer the public "a great degree of control over the information that they receive" and "a forum for a true diversity of political discourse." The authors of those words may have believed that ISPs would engage in self-regulation, thereby protecting the public interest. More than twenty years later, one can fairly ask whether they were overly optimistic.[113]

If it weren't for Section 230, we would live in a different world. Today, Justice Brennan's words that debate on public issues should be "uninhibited,

---

113 Facebook has created an Oversight Board whose international membership consists of academics, human rights activists, journalists, and former elected officials. Facebook has essentially outsourced the ultimate say over what content will or will not be allowed. On May 5, 2021, this Oversight Board upheld Facebook's ban on Donald Trump for his role in the January 6 Capitol riot. The Board took issue with making the suspension "indefinite," leaving it to Facebook to decide whether it was permanent or for a specific period.

robust, and wide open" carry a certain irony. According to Georgetown Law Professor Rebecca Tushnet, the safe harbor law has given big companies "power without responsibility."

Access to information online is extremely useful: think Wikipedia, or Google. But there is a dark side to the Internet, populated by cyber criminals, terrorists, and, we now know, foreign governments intent on influencing our elections.

The problem is where to draw the line, and perhaps that is just part of the American constitutional condition. In many countries, "freedom for the thought that we hate" does not exist. Here it does, and examples are plentiful—*Hustler* magazine's vulgar parody directed against Southern Baptist pastor and televangelist Jerry Falwell; funeral protests by members of the Westboro Baptist Church carrying hateful posters; and yes, Alex Jones, who tells his millions of radio listeners that the Sandy Hook school shooting never happened, or at least did so until he found himself in court facing the victims' parents.

The issue is not whether online speech should be protected, but whether Section 230, as it now exists, strikes the right balance. When the law was passed in 1996, there were 36 million Internet users in the world; in 2020 the number had grown to 5.1 billion. As a result of this astonishing growth, Facebook, Google, Twitter, and other online platforms have acquired extraordinary, virtually unchecked power, although the use of the Internet to offer not-so-thinly veiled messages offering "personal" services prompted Congress to amend the law by passing the "Allow States and Victims to Fight Online Sex Trafficking Act of 2017" (FOSTA). This led to the demise of Backpage.com, which had previously avoided liability thanks to Section 230.

The role of the Internet in our society, and in our political system, raises profound legal and social questions. Even in a country where censorship is forbidden in all but the most extreme situations, and where punishment for speech is greatly disfavored, not all speech is free. The difficult question is how to tame those who would be outlaws without infringing on "wide open" debate on public issues. [114]

---

114  One way to curb social media would be to repeal Section 230, thereby eliminating the umbrella of immunity. Senator Josh Hawley (R-MO) introduced such legislation in 2019, describing Section 230 as a "sweetheart deal" for tech companies. The Trump administration got behind this and, during 2020, various bills were introduced, one called the "Limiting Section 230 Immunity to Good Samaritans Act." The problem, as is often the case when Congress tries to legislate speech, is that by throwing the baby out with the bath water, the supposed cure may be worse than the disease.

# THE FOURTEENTH AMENDMENT

## The Fourteenth Amendment Still Searches for Justice (2017)

In 1958, President Eisenhower declared May 1 to be Law Day, and in 1961 Law Day gained federal legal status as a day to celebrate the "ideals of equality and justice under law."

Law Day 2017 was devoted to the Fourteenth Amendment, which says a lot in a mere fifty-two words. First, it says that "all persons born . . . in the United States" are citizens of this country. Second, it tells *states* that they cannot deprive "any person of life, liberty, or property without *due process of law*, nor deny to any person . . . the *equal protection* of the laws."

This amendment was not part of the Bill of Rights. It is one of the so-called "Civil War" amendments, and on July 6, 1866, New Hampshire became the second state to ratify it, following Connecticut by just a week. It took another two years before the amendment became a part of the Constitution on July 9, 1868.

Through a process of judicial interpretation known as "incorporation," the Supreme Court has found a lot more in the Fourteenth Amendment than meets the eye. In a series of decisions going back to the 1920s, the Court has held that this amendment takes the personal rights guaranteed by the first ten amendments—the Bill of Rights—and makes them applicable to the states through the due process clause. So, for example, the First Amendment says that "*Congress* shall make no law" limiting freedom of religion, speech, press, and so forth. Since 1925, however, these rights have been "incorporated" into the Fourteenth Amendment, thereby making them binding not just on Congress but on the states as well.

There is so much to like about this subject that it's hard to know where to begin. In 2016, candidate Trump challenged the citizenship of children born in this country to undocumented parents (he calls them "anchor babies"), thereby ignoring the plain constitutional birthright citizenship language. But for this column, I will focus on the Sixth Amendment, which guarantees trial "by an impartial jury." Like the First Amendment, this guarantee now applies, by way of the incorporation doctrine, to all fifty states, along with Puerto Rico, the US Virgin Islands, American Samoa, the Northern Mariana Islands, and Guam.

The right to an impartial jury has had its twists and turns. As recently as 1942, only twenty-eight states allowed women to serve as jurors, and New Hampshire did not join that group until 1947. In 1880, the Supreme Court ruled that a state could not exclude blacks from juries, but the "all white" jury remained part of the southern way of life throughout much of the twentieth century. In 1982, the Court took an important step when it decided that a defendant's right to equal protection under the Fourteenth Amendment was denied when prosecutors used peremptory challenges to exclude jurors because of their race.

In a 2017 case called *Peña-Rodriguez v. Colorado*, the Supreme Court confronted a major conflict between two principles. One is known as the "no impeachment" rule, which says that what goes on in the jury room stays in the jury room. The other principle is that jurors should be impartial.

After the trial in which a Mexican man was convicted of a sex offense, two jurors signed affidavits stating that during deliberations a juror said, "I think he did it because he's Mexican." The question before the Supreme Court was whether that man had been denied his Sixth Amendment right to an impartial jury? By a vote of five to three, the Court answered "Yes." Justice Kennedy's majority opinion says that where there is "compelling evidence" that a juror voted to convict based on racism, such misbehavior goes beyond ordinary misconduct. Rather it implicates "unique historical, constitutional, and institutional concerns." In such circumstances, the right to an impartial jury has been denied.

Chief Justice Roberts, Justice Alito, and Justice Thomas, disagreed. Justice Alito argued that "jurors are ordinary people" who sometimes say things they shouldn't, but that's no reason to change an "age old" rule that prohibits taking a second look at impartiality based on what went on in the jury room. According to Justice Thomas, the common law "no impeachment" rule was constitutionally frozen in the Sixth Amendment as of 1789, remained there

**14th Amendment**

when the Fourteenth Amendment was ratified in 1868, and should not be changed today.

As we celebrate the Fourteenth Amendment, it is reassuring to know that our system of justice continues to evolve, but the decision raises as many questions as it answers. Suppose someone is charged with a hate crime and a juror says, "He's a Muslim, and as far as I'm concerned that makes him guilty." Or in a financial fraud case, the juror says, "He's a Jew and that's all I need to know." Or a woman is charged with vehicular homicide, and the juror says, "Women are lousy drivers. She was probably looking at herself in the mirror putting on lipstick."

My guess is that the Court will draw the line at "race" which, according to the Court, includes Hispanics. Just who else fits into that category I will leave to geneticists.[115]

---

115　The federal Office of Management and Budget distinguishes between race and ethnicity. As in previous censuses, the racial categories used in the 2020 Census consist of White, Black, American Indian, or Alaska Native. Hispanic or Latino origin is placed in the separate ethnicity category.

# The Profound Marriage Union (2015)

*No union is more profound than marriage, for it embodies*
*the highest ideals of love, fidelity, devotion, sacrifice, and family.*

Justice Anthony M. Kennedy

As of mid-2015, I had been married for forty-six years of my life, twenty-two years to my late wife, Susie, and twenty-four years to the Pianist, Virginia. There were seven years between those marriages, but still it feels like I have always been married.

James Obergefell was also married, but the length of his one period of wedlock was brief, a mere three months. After two decades together, he and John Arthur, his terminally ill partner,[116] flew from Ohio to Maryland, where they exchanged vows. Three months later, James was a widower.

Or was he? According to Ohio, he was not. The space for "surviving spouse" on Arthur's death certificate remained blank. They were, in the eyes of the state, strangers even in death. James brought a lawsuit to correct the record. On June 26, 2015, he accomplished his goal.

Some things the state may not do, and according to the Supreme Court one of them is to deny the legal status of marriage to same-sex couples. Justice Kennedy's opinion, distancing himself from the Kalahari people whom he brought up during oral argument, teaches us that the constitutional rights of "liberty" and "equal protection of the laws," are not static. They evolve as the nine justices, or at least five of them, come to understand the full dimension of those words in the circumstances of our times.[117]

When you think about it, the idea of an evolving "living" Constitution makes sense. We used to have slavery in this country, and "liberty" was for white people. And we had segregated schools until the Court decided in 1954 that "equal protection" under the Fourteenth Amendment applies to black children.[118]

---

116  He had Amyotrophic Lateral Sclerosis (ALS), commonly known as Lou Gehrig's Disease.

117  Following the death of Justice Ginsburg and the appointment of Justice Barrett in 2020, it appears that "originalists" now make up a majority of the Court. If so, decision-making such as Obergefell will likely yield to a different, and narrower, view of how the Court should interpret the Constitution.

118  The term "originalism" didn't exist when Chief Justice Roger Taney wrote the Dred Scott

Now the Court has decided that the Fourteenth Amendment also applies to the union of James and John, and to countless other couples throughout the country, including my daughter and daughter-in-law. Insofar as marriage is concerned, they are no different than anyone else.

Many poets have written about marriage. A famous Shakespeare sonnet begins with the words, "Let me not to the marriage of true minds admit impediments." Robert Frost wrote that married life "is only life forevermore, together wing to wing and oar to oar." And Elizabeth Barrett Browning asked, "How do I love thee? Let me count the ways."

Justice Kennedy's opinion in *Obergefell v. Hodges* is not just about a constitutional right of marriage between people of the same sex, but about the institution of marriage itself:

"Marriage responds to the universal fear that a lonely person might call out only to find no one there. It offers the hope of companionship and understanding and assurance that while both still live, there will be someone to care for the other."

Justice Scalia, dissenting, said he would sooner "hide my head in a bag" than adopt what he called Justice Kennedy's "mystical aphorisms of the fortune cookie." I have no idea what he was talking about, but I do know a sore loser when I see one.

I also know that something none of us even imagined either time I got married is now the law of the land.

---

decision in 1857, but that decision could well be deemed "originalist." And when the Court issued its Brown v. Board of Education nearly a century later, the Court was departing from how the Constitution was understood in 1787, or even when the Fourteenth Amendment was ratified in 1868.

# The President Has No Power
# to Undo Birthright Citizenship (2018)

Dred Scott was born into slavery in 1795 and lived as a slave in Missouri. His owner, a military man named Emerson, took Scott with him when he was transferred first to Illinois and later to the Wisconsin Territory, neither of which had slavery. As a result of several moves, Scott ended up back in the slave state of Missouri. After Emerson died, his brother-in-law Sanford, who lived in New York, assumed control of his property, and Scott sued for his freedom in New York federal court.

The Founding Fathers were concerned that citizens from another state might not get a fair shake in a state court subject to local bias. They therefore included the "diversity of citizenship" clause in the Constitution, which permits an out-of-state citizen to have his legal grievance heard in federal court. That clause was the basis for Scott's choice of the federal court in New York.

In 1857, the Supreme Court decided *Scott v. Sandford* (the court documents misspelled Sanford's name), widely regarded as the worst decision the Court has ever made. According to Chief Justice Roger Taney, whose name has become synonymous with the case, Scott had no right to sue in federal court because "a negro, whose ancestors were imported into [the United States], and sold as slaves . . . could not be an American citizen." Taney, himself a slaveholder, went so far as to describe black Africans brought here as slaves as "beings of an inferior order . . . unfit to associate with the white race."

Frederick Douglass, a former slave and a leader of the abolitionist movement, was undaunted. The "highest authority" had spoken, he acknowledged, but he was optimistic that the "National Conscience" would not, in his words, be "put to sleep."

He was correct, though it took a Civil War, the Civil Rights Act of 1866, and a constitutional amendment to right the Supreme Court's wrong. The Fourteenth Amendment, which overruled the *Dred Scott* decision, says, "All persons born or naturalized in the United States, and subject to the jurisdiction thereof, are citizens of the United States and of the State wherein they reside."

Wom Kim Ark

Dred Scott may be a familiar name in American history, but Wong Kim Ark is not. In the case that bears his name, the Supreme Court described his parents as "persons of Chinese descent," aliens living in California who remained "subjects of the Emperor of China." The question before the Court in 1898 was whether their son, born in San Francisco in 1873, was an American citizen.

This was a time of strong anti-Chinese feelings, codified in the Chinese Exclusion Act of 1882. Wong Kim Ark was returning from a visit to China to visit relatives, including his parents who had moved back, when customs officials barred him from getting off the boat in San Francisco Bay. The Chinese Benevolent Association had a prominent lawyer named Thomas Riordan on call, and he obtained a court order upholding Mr. Wong's birthright citizenship. The government appealed on the theory that Wong Kim Ark was not a citizen but was, "by reason of his race, language, color and dress, a Chinese person," adding that he was also "a laborer by occupation."

The Court's answer was that Mr. Wong was born on American soil and therefore he, and "all other persons of whatever race or color," are in the "clear words" of the Fourteenth Amendment, entitled to "citizenship by birth." To hold otherwise, the Court added, would be "to deny citizenship to thousands of persons of English, Scotch, Irish, German, or other European parentage" who have always been considered citizens.

On October 29, 2019, President Trump announced that he intended to issue an executive order overruling the *Wong Kim Ark* case and repealing the birthright citizenship clause of the Fourteenth Amendment. He stated, incorrectly, that no other country makes you a citizen just because you were born there; in fact, Canada, Mexico, and many other countries grant automatic birthright citizenship. According to Trump, "It's ridiculous and it has to end."

Those who agree with him point out that when Wong Kim Ark was born, his parents resided in this country but remained Chinese subjects. They argue that the Fourteenth Amendment words "and subject to the jurisdiction thereof" excludes anyone whose parents' "allegiance" is to another country.

Neither of those arguments holds water. The Supreme Court made no such distinction, and in any case such parents are "subject to the jurisdiction" of the United States, including American courts. Those words refer to Native Americans, whose exclusion from birthright citizenship was cured by the Indian Citizenship Act of 1924, and to foreign diplomats.

I doubt that Trump will attempt to carry out his threat to turn the clock back and undo the citizenship of millions of Americans. That is not to say that the rules of citizenship cannot be changed. The way to do that is by amending the Constitution, a prerogative that Article V grants to two-thirds of both houses of Congress or to two-thirds of the states, subject to ratification by three-fourths of the state legislatures. Article V does not mention the president.

Somehow, I don't think that is likely to happen.

# Roe v. Wade and a Jurisprudence of Doubt
## (2021)

Chief Justice Charles Evans Hughes once said, "The Constitution means what the judges say it means." A better way to put it might be, "The Constitution is what a majority of five justices say it is." Or even more accurately, "The Constitution means what five justices say it means until five justices say it means something different."

So, for example, in 1896 the Supreme Court decided in *Plessy v. Ferguson* that the Constitution permitted segregation so long as the segregated facilities were "separate but equal." In 1954, the Court held in *Brown v. Board of Education* that separate educational facilities are inherently unequal. The Court was nearly unanimous the first time and unanimous the second, when it said just the opposite. The Constitution didn't change during the intervening fifty-eight years, the Court, and society, did.

*Plessy* is not the only wrongheaded decision in Supreme Court history. In *Korematsu v. United States* the Court upheld the relocation of Japanese-Americans from their homes to internment camps during World War II. Three years ago, in *Trump v. Hawaii*, the Court declared that the *Korematsu* decision was mistaken.

The Court doesn't always take a half century or more, or a complete membership turnover, to recognize constitutional error. In 1986, in *Bowers v. Hardwick*, five justices upheld a Georgia law that made consensual sexual acts between adults of the same sex a crime. Seventeen years later, in *Lawrence v. Texas*, five justices agreed that the similar Texas antisodomy law violated due process. Justice Kennedy, writing for the majority, didn't mince words. "Bowers was not correct when it was decided, and it is not correct today." (Justice Sandra Day O'Connor, who had been in the majority in Bowers, made it six, but on narrower grounds.)

These "corrections" have a common theme. When the Court has recognized that an earlier group of five or more justices has failed to apply the Constitution to protect personal human rights to equal protection, due process of law, and liberty, it has used its jurisprudential flexibility to make amends. That is a good thing.

What, then, of *Roe v. Wade*?

As everyone knows, that 1973 decision protects a woman's right to have an abortion, subject to certain limits. What is less well known is that *Roe* was not a bare five-justice decision. Seven members of the Court made up the majority. Nor was it the Court's last word on the subject.

In *Planned Parenthood v. Casey* (1993), the Court changed the rationale from the Roe trimester analysis to one where governmental restrictions are permissible so long as they do not impose an "undue burden" on a woman's right to a pre-viability abortion. The breakdown of votes was complicated, with four justices ready to overrule Roe, meaning that five were not.

Among that latter group, Justices O'Connor, Kennedy, and Souter crafted a plurality opinion that affirms the "essential holding of Roe." Their opinion includes these wise words: "Liberty finds no refuge in a jurisprudence of doubt."

Last month, the Court agreed to review a Mississippi law that bans most abortions after fifteen weeks, thereby erasing the viability threshold (around twenty-four weeks) established in *Roe* and upheld in *Planned Parenthood*. The case, *Dobbs v. Jackson Women's Health Organization*, will test not only the Court's existing abortion jurisprudence but also whether respect for precedent, known as stare decisis, will yield to the originalist inclinations, or personal predilections, of at least five current justices.

This is not like *Plessy* or *Korematsu* or *Bowers*, all of which denied important individual liberties. Rather, this is about conflicting values and beliefs, in other words cultural disagreements. Before jumping too quickly, the Court would do well to go back to the O'Connor-Kennedy-Souter explanation of why following precedent usually makes sense, particularly so when it comes to the issue at hand.

Those three justices noted that the *Roe* decision, while not universally popular, "has not been unworkable;" that an "entire generation" (remember, this was in 1993) has come of age understanding that liberty includes the right of women to make reproductive decisions; and that no "erosion of principles" has occurred that would leave the *Roe v. Wade* holding "a doctrinal remnant."

I appreciate the views of those who are opposed to abortion. Their beliefs, often if not always grounded in sincere religious faith, are entitled to respect, and the same can be said about other controversial rulings. People who think nonsectarian prayer should be allowed in schools, or who consider marriage to be the union of a woman and a man, are entitled to express their opinions.

They have a constitutional right to promote constitutional amendments.

Still, a "jurisprudence of doubt" does none of us any good. It is one thing for the Court to decide that racial discrimination, anti-Japanese sentiment, and laws prohibiting consensual adult relationships have no place in our heterogeneous society. It is quite another to turn the Constitution into a vacillating document whose meaning depends on the untethered whims of five justices.

# CONSTITUTIONAL ISSUES IN THE TIME OF CORONAVIRUS

## A Public Health Crisis Does Not Suspend the Constitution (2021)

*You shall love your neighbor as yourself.*

Leviticus 19:9–18

In *Schenck v. United States* (1919), the Supreme Court upheld punishment for circulating flyers urging men not to register for the draft. In that case, Justice Holmes wrote that "when a nation is at war" the government can impose rules that would not be allowed "in time of peace."

*Korematsu v. United States* (1944) applied the same thinking to a different war. Justice Black's opinion upheld internment of Japanese Americans on the grounds that "proper security measures" must be allowed when "we are at war."

*Schenck* is still on the books, though its precedential value has diminished due to an enlarged understanding of the First Amendment following the Supreme Court's 1964 *New York Times v. Sullivan* ruling, affirming the right to criticize government. Thus in 1969, the First Circuit overruled the convictions of Dr. Benjamin Spock and others for signing a letter opposing the Vietnam War. And in 2018, in *Trump v. Hawaii*, the Court expressly overruled *Korematsu*.

We come, now, to the Covid-19 pandemic. If you look at recent governmental restrictions on everything from group gatherings to church services to road trips, you may wonder how far the Government can go. It is not a frivolous concern, raising any number of constitutional questions.

According to an 1868 case named *Crandall v. Nevada*, travel is a fundamental right. As explained in *Williams v. Fears* (1900), this right is "an attribute of personal liberty . . . secured by the Fourteenth Amendment." A half century later, in *Kent v. Dulles* , the Court held that the right to international travel is part of the Fifth Amendment right to "liberty." "Freedom of movement," wrote Justice William O. Douglas, "is basic to our scheme of values."

The current pandemic has tested this expansive concept of liberty. When New Yorkers and others decided it was safer elsewhere, some states, including Rhode Island, imposed quarantines on people entering from out of state. Such "license plate profiling" (as one legal scholar calls it), even if permissible under the First and Fifth Amendments, may yet run afoul of the Privileges and Immunities Clause, which says that a state cannot treat people from other states less favorably than it treats its own. According to that theory, Rhode Island would have to impose similar rules on its own citizens returning from out-of-state.

Government is not allowed to abridge "the right of the people peaceably to assemble." Nonetheless, many governors have limited the number of people allowed to gather in one place, starting in New York at 500 and going down in many places to ten.

In *Binford v. Sununu*, plaintiffs challenged New Hampshire governor Sununu's fifty-person limit on "societal, spiritual and recreational activities" as a violation of their constitutional rights of assembly, worship, and free speech. Superior Court Judge John Kissinger dismissed the case on the grounds that the governor acted within his power to protect public health. The judge wrote, "It would be irrational to find that the governor must wait for the health care system of New Hampshire to be overwhelmed . . . before he is authorized to declare a state of emergency and take preventive measures."

Church attendance and funerals are also victims of the pandemic. And defiance has raised both social and political problems, as the limit-defying Hasidic community in Brooklyn found out when Mayor de Blasio sent the police in to disperse a large crowd attending a rabbi's funeral.

"Contact tracing" raises yet another privacy issue. In 2018 the Supreme Court held, in *Carpenter v. United States*, that the Fourth Amendment protects cell phone location information, at least when it comes to a criminal investigation. Today, public health officials are considering widespread testing followed by tracing the contacts of those who test positive. There are nearly 260 million smartphone users in the United States, and Bluetooth technology offers a potentially effective way to locate and isolate carriers of this highly transmissible disease. Just download an app and your contacts can be identified.

Striking the right balance between constitutional rights and public health necessitates a factual basis for governmental intrusion. In his *Binford* decision, Judge Kissinger found that the governor had satisfied this requirement and, importantly, had limited the order to twenty-one days. The judge added that the order remained subject to further judicial review should circumstances change. On May 7, 2020, by contrast, Massachusetts federal judge Douglas Woodlock overturned Governor Charlie Baker's closing of gun shops for failure to provide a sufficient factual basis for burdening Second Amendment rights.

Not everyone agrees with Judge Kissinger. A judge in Illinois overruled Governor J. B. Pritzker's stay-at-home order, and a Virginia judge overruled Governor Ralph Northam's order closing an indoor gun range. Republican lawmakers in Wisconsin have sued that state's governor over his stay-at-home order, Californians are challenging restrictions, and dozens of other cases have been brought around the country.

In the words of Attorney General Barr, "The Constitution is not suspended in times of crisis." I agree with Barr's constitutional sentiments, though probably not with how he would apply them. Most constitutional rights are not absolute and must yield to an overriding governmental interest so long as restrictions are responsive to a demonstrated need, narrow in scope, and limited in time.

Government has an important role to play, but the book of Leviticus, and the New Testament as well (Luke 6:31), remind us that public health is not just about constitutional line-drawing. How we treat each other has a lot to do with staying safe.[119]

---

119  The Biden administration's efforts to impose vaccine or test mandates on private employers with over one hundred employees ran into a whirlwind of opposition. On January 13, 2022, the Supreme Court blocked enforcement of the directive, while letting stand a vaccine mandate for public health facilities that take Medicare or Medicaid. In both instances the Court was badly divided. Meanwhile, during the first quarter of 2022, many states have taken steps to legislate in the opposite direction by prohibiting private corporations from adopting their own employee vaccine requirements. The fact that such legislation has been proposed by conservative Republicans presents a striking irony, since historically the Republican Party has stood for the right of private enterprise to be free from government interference.

# Face Masks Should Be the Law of the Land (2020)

When I got my driver's license in 1955, seat belts had been invented, but not until 1968 did federal law require them in new cars. Beginning with New York in 1984, states passed laws requiring seat belt usage, and today every state but one has such a law. New Hampshire only requires you to use a seatbelt if you are under eighteen.

The widespread use of cell phones did not begin until the 2000s, creating a new hazard known as "distracted driving." Today, nearly every state has some sort of law controlling the use of cell phones by drivers, and New Hampshire prohibits all drivers from using handheld devices. According to the National Highway Traffic Safety Administration, distracted driving accounted for 2,841 deaths in 2018.

While New Hampshire is out of step when it comes to seat belts, there is at least a plausible distinction between that subject and cell phones. In the one case, the immediate risk is mostly on the person who chooses to drive (or ride) without restraint, while the driver jabbering or texting away while holding a cell phone endangers both himself and the rest of us. One is mostly one directional, while the other goes both ways.

Unsurprisingly, lawsuits have challenged these laws, claiming they interfere with individual freedoms. Courts around the country have for the most part rejected such objections on the ground of protecting public safety.

In August of 2020, the Keene City Council adopted a mask ordinance requiring everyone age ten or older to wear masks in all indoor public spaces and some outdoor spaces as well. This law doesn't have a lot of teeth—it imposes modest fines beginning with the third offense. But even a difficult-to-enforce rule is better than nothing, and this one has gained widespread public acceptance.

Keene is not alone. Several cities and a handful of smaller New Hampshire towns have enacted mask mandates. The problem is that the virus doesn't respect city or county lines, or any other geographic boundary. And while the pandemic is a lot worse in the Midwest and West, and while a vaccine may be on the not-too-distant horizon, New Hampshire has moved from yellow to orange on the map, meaning that new cases per 100,000 people have increased.

The Center for Disease Control (CDC) recently announced that face masks protect not just other people but the wearer as well. In that sense, a law mandating mask-wearing has a two-directional benefit, like the handheld cell phone law. But to stave off what seems inevitable over the coming months, public health requires more than a local ordinance.

More than a hundred years ago, the Supreme Court rejected the claim that a mandatory vaccination law offended the Fourteenth Amendment. "The liberty secured by the Constitution," the Court said, "does not import an absolute right in each person to be . . . wholly freed from restraint." And, the Court went on, "a community has the right to protect itself against an epidemic of disease." The New Hampshire Supreme Court followed that decision in 1937 when it upheld a school vaccination law. And this past July a Superior Court judge did the same and upheld the Nashua mask ordinance.

Meanwhile, cases are pending in Wisconsin and elsewhere challenging the state's power to require people to wear masks in public places. These cases are likely to fail. But what we really need is a nationwide mandate, not a state-by-state hodgepodge of conflicting rules. There are two ways this might be done, one by the Executive Branch, the other by Congress. The latter approach would likely rest on firmer constitutional footing.[120]

Would a national law hold up against a challenge that it inhibits the constitutional right to worship, or that it forces people to convey a message they don't believe, or that it compels individuals to engage in a particular activity in violation of the commerce clause? These theories carry varying degrees of plausibility, but at the end of the day they should fail. Until we have an effective, universally administered vaccine, this public health crisis is a lot more serious than distracted driving.

---

120   On January 20, 2021, the first day of his administration, President Biden signed an executive order requiring face masks on all federal property.

# Religion and the Supreme Court
## During the Pandemic (2020)

In July 2020, by a vote of 5 to 4, the Supreme Court rejected the petition of a Nevada church seeking to overturn the governor's fifty-person limit on attendance at religious services. Chief Justice Roberts joined the then-four liberal justices—Ginsburg, Breyer, Elena Kagan, and Sotomayor. Justice Alito dissented on the grounds that the governor's order violated the First Amendment right to worship by allowing more people to gamble in casinos than to pray in church.

This was the second case dealing with state-imposed limitations on church service attendance. The first was a California challenge to Governor Gavin Newsom's order limiting houses of worship to 25 percent of capacity but not more than one hundred attendees. The lineup of justices was the same, with the chief justice writing for the five-member majority. He explained that the California restrictions on church attendance were consistent with those on "comparable secular gatherings" such as lectures, concerts, and sports events. As such, he wrote, they did not violate religious freedom under the First Amendment.

he chief justice stressed that when it comes to public health, an "unelected federal judiciary" lacks the necessary scientific expertise and should not "second-guess" those who are responsible for protecting the public. He cited a 1905 case called *Jacobson v. Massachusetts*, where the Court upheld a Cambridge, Massachusetts, ordinance requiring smallpox vaccinations.

In his dissent, Justice Kavanaugh asked, "Why can someone safely walk down a grocery store aisle but not a pew," or "safely interact with a brave deliverywoman but not with a stoic minister?" He suggested that the state could have taken other means, for example requiring social distancing, or imposing "reasonable occupancy caps" across the board.

Policy disagreements can rarely be solved by asking rhetorical questions, and that is especially true here. When I walk through the grocery store, I keep on going and exit as fast as I can. By contrast, if I enter a church or synagogue, I don't walk down a pew, I sit on it for an extended period of time. I have no idea what my encounters with a "brave" delivery person have to do with interactions with a "stoic" clergyman. More often than not, UPS or FedEx just leave the package at the door. And what if the clergyman is not stoic?

Justice Alito refused to take those decisions lying down. He devoted much of his November 12, 2020, Federalist Society speech to his concern that "religious liberty is fast becoming a disfavored right." In language echoing the style of his late colleague, Justice Scalia, he pointed out that "you will not find a craps clause or a blackjack clause or a slot machine clause" in the First Amendment. And Alito snarkily criticized Roberts's reliance on the *Jacobson* case. "I'm all in favor of preventing dangerous things from issuing out of Cambridge and infecting the rest of the country," he said. "It would be good if what originates in Cambridge stayed in Cambridge."

Justice Ginsburg, who voted with the majority in both the Nevada and California cases, died on September 18, 2020, exactly halfway between the Nevada ruling and the New York case that was to come in late November. During the interim, on October 27, 2020, Amy Coney Barrett was sworn in as Ginsburg's successor.

The Nevada and California cases are so yesterday, and so is Chief Justice Roberts. On November 25, 2020, in a case called *Roman Catholic Diocese of Brooklyn v. Andrew M. Cuomo, Governor*, a majority of the Court sided with the Roman Catholic Diocese of Brooklyn, and Agudath Israel of America, an organization of Haredi Orthodox Jews featured in last year's Netflix series *Unorthodox*. The Court enjoined the enforcement of Governor Cuomo's ten- and twenty-five-person occupancy limits on houses of worship located in "red" and "orange" zones.

Justice Gorsuch, having now moved from the losing to the winning side, expressed his concern that the governor's order would cause irreparable harm to orthodox Jewish women, a group not often mentioned in Supreme Court opinions. Orthodox Judaism requires ten men for a minyan (the quorum for Jewish public worship), he explained, so those women might be unable to attend Shabbat (Sabbath) services. He went on to say, "Even if the Constitution has taken a holiday during this pandemic, it cannot become a sabbatical." Isn't that a non sequitur, meaning a conclusion that doesn't follow from the first part of the sentence?

The constitutional issue raised by these state-imposed church attendance quotas is what lawyers call a close question on which reasonable people can take either side. But while clever phrases such as "no blackjack clause" and "no sabbatical" may liven up court opinions, they do not necessarily make good law, or for that matter good epidemiology. To be sure, the New York facts are not identical to the Nevada or California facts, but the differences are not enough to account for a different outcome.

There is something unseemly about the Supreme Court going one way in the spring and the opposite way in the fall. During a public health crisis, when so much responsibility rests on the shoulders of governors and local health officials, there is a lot to be said for stability in the law.

The reason for this flip-flop isn't hard to find, and Justice Alito need not worry that the constitutional right to worship will be "disfavored." The game has changed, and Justice Barrett, a product not of Cambridge but of the University of Notre Dame in Indiana, is the game-changer.

# Jurisprudence in the Age of COVID (2022)

On November 4, 2021, the Biden Administration issued two safety rules covering over one hundred million employees. One came out of the Occupational Safety and Health Administration (OSHA), which—relying on the federal law charging the agency with protecting employees' health and safety and on substantial evidence of widespread workplace breakouts—issued an emergency order giving employers of one hundred or more people two choices: Either have their employees fully vaccinated, or make sure they are tested weekly and wear masks at work.

The other rule, issued by the Centers for Medicare & Medicaid Services (CMS), requires healthcare workers employed at facilities participating in Medicare and Medicaid to be fully vaccinated.

A combination of business interests, labor unions, and Republican-led states sued to prevent these measures from taking effect. They argued that the mandates violate various constitutional limits on federal power and abridge religious rights as well.

On December 17, 2021, a divided three-judge panel of the Sixth Circuit Court of Appeals upheld the one hundred-employee rule based on OSHA's statutory authority "to assure safe and healthful working conditions for the nation's work force." The majority concluded that the mounting number of deaths and hospitalizations, and the heightened risk of exposure, have created "grave danger in the workplace."

On Friday, January 7 the Supreme Court devoted more than three hours to hearing the two challenges. In the OSHA case, *National Federation of Independent Business v. Department of Labor*, one of the objections is that OSHA's "economy-wide mandate" will cause workers to quit in droves. After noting that "catching COVID keeps people out of the workplace," Justice Sotomayor asked why, if OSHA can require masks in workplaces where machines give off sparks, can't it do the same when the "sparks" come from other human beings.

Chief Justice Roberts drew the distinction that ultimately carried the day. It's one thing, he said, for OSHA to deal with risks that are unique to the workplace, it's another to regulate those not so confined. Unlike a hard-hat requirement at a construction site, or masks around workplace machinery, this mandate "is not a workplace issue," he said, "it's an out-in-the-world issue."

I went looking for where the OSHA statute limits the agency's protection power to risks that exist only at work. I couldn't find it. Even so, according to Justice Gorsuch (the only mask-less justice in the courtroom), it's "traditional." Justice Alito thinks that the Biden administration is "trying to squeeze an elephant into a mouse hole."

This past Thursday, the six conservative justices found what I could not. In an unsigned opinion, they decided that OSHA's authority is limited to "occupational dangers." So much for OSHA's finding that the workplace rule would prevent 250,000 hospitalizations.

In their dissent, the three liberal justices—Breyer, Kagan, and Sotomayor—wrote that wisdom often takes the form of deferring to those who know something about the matter at hand, in this case the department of government whose job is to protect the public in a public health emergency. "Today," they wrote, "we are not wise."

When the January 7 hearing turned to *Biden v. Missouri*, the case dealing with Medicare and Medicaid providers, the tide seemed to turn in the Administration's favor. The arguments were similar—that the CMS had pulled a "bureaucratic power move" and that healthcare workers would quit rather than get vaccinated. Justice Kagan had a simple answer, "The one thing you can't do is kill your patients." She might have added the physician's oath that medical students learn early on: Primum non nocere, or, First do no harm.

On January 13, the Court upheld the CMS requirement on the grounds that Congress had authorized the secretary of Health and Human Services to impose conditions on the receipt of Medicare and Medicaid funds. The government prevailed only because two justices, Chief Justice Roberts and Justice Kavanaugh, switched sides. Dissenting Justices Thomas, Alito, Gorsuch, and Barrett complained that the majority was forcing healthcare workers who want to keep their jobs to undergo "an irreversible medical treatment." Until now, I had not heard anyone call vaccination "treatment," but that is the word Justice Alito used.

How has it come to pass, one might ask, that a national effort to prevent illness and death has become a political question? What's needed here is at least a dash of common sense. OSHA was not requiring vaccination; workers could choose weekly testing and wearing a mask instead. The fact that Congress didn't mention vaccines or pandemics when it created OSHA fifty-two years ago is not much different from saying that the Civil Rights Act of 1964, which prohibits discrimination by employers "because of sex," didn't refer to gay and transgender workers. Yet just a year ago, in an opinion by none other than Justice Gorsuch, the Court ruled that such employees are protected.

One problem with this legal debate is that it casts judges in the role of making public health decisions. Courts have no epidemiology expertise, and they are not politically accountable. Meanwhile, the number of Covid cases in the United States is over sixty-two million, the number of deaths is fast approaching one million, and the infection maps no longer have different colors. Every state is red and, thanks to the Court's OSHA decision, likely to get redder.

# ELECTIONS

## "Airy-Fairy" or "Sociological Gobbledygook?"
## Gerrymandering and the Precious Right to Vote
## (2017)

*Gill v. Whitford*, the gerrymandering case heard in October 2017 by the Supreme Court, involves two lines. One is an actual line, meaning the contours of voting districts within a state. The other is the abstract line known as "justiciability," meaning whether this voting question should be decided by the court ("justiciable") or left to the legislature ("political").

Gerrymandering is nothing new. In 1812, the governor of Massachusetts, Elbridge Gerry (who in 2013 became vice president under James Madison), redistricted the state to benefit the Democratic Republican party. The result was a district north of Boston shaped like a salamander. Thus, the word "gerrymander" (substituting a soft "g" for a hard one).

Electoral districts for Congress, state legislatures, and perhaps other elected offices change every ten years following the census. Boundaries need to be redrawn to reflect population shifts so that every person's vote gets equal weight, more or less. That requirement of proportional representation comes from *Baker v. Carr*, the Supreme Court's 1962 "one person one vote" decision.

Who draws these boundaries? The answer is "politicians," meaning state legislatures, and therein lies the problem. Following Governor Gerry's example, part of our bipartisan political heritage is that the majority party makes "adjustments" that will tip the scales in its favor, to the detriment of the opposing party. Today's gerrymandering technology is so algorithmically sophisticated that it can virtually guarantee that the party in power stays in power.

Following the 2010 census, the Republican Party of Wisconsin, which controlled both the legislature and the state house, drew new boundary lines. And, in 2012, republicans won 60 percent of the house seats even though democrats won a majority of the statewide vote.

To explain it in simple terms, if you create districts in dense urban areas, democrats win by large margins. If you draw district lines in more rural areas to include roughly the same number of people, you can stack the deck in favor of republicans, whose candidates win by smaller margins. That is what Wisconsin did, predicting with stunning accuracy what the new map would accomplish.

A professor named William Whitford and several other Wisconsin Democrats decided that things had gotten out of hand. Their federal court complaint alleged that the gerrymandered electoral map was unconstitutional and "profoundly undemocratic."

There are two ways of framing the constitutional question. One way is to ask whether the state has deprived some of its voters of equal protection under the law, which the Fourteenth Amendment says it may not do. The other is whether the state has abridged their First Amendment rights of free speech (voting) and free association (party membership).

By a 2 to 1 decision, the three-judge court in Wisconsin found that the map was so lopsided that it would take an "unprecedented political earthquake" to dislodge it. The majority was persuaded by social science and statistical evidence, including something called the "Efficiency Gap," which measures the extent to which gerrymandering gives one party an undue advantage over the other. Accordingly, the court ordered the state assembly to redraw the lines, and the State of Wisconsin appealed.

At the October 3 hearing, eight of the nine Supreme Court justices engaged in a lively dialogue with the opposing lawyers. Justice Thomas, following his usual practice, did not speak.[121] Justice Alito called gerrymandering "distasteful," but seemed unwilling to wade into what Justice Felix Frankfurter called a "political thicket," the term he used in 1962 when he dissented from the one person/one vote decision. Justice Gorsuch, the Court's newest Justice at the time of the hearing, asked where the Constitution gives the Supreme Court the right to tell state legislatures how to draw electoral lines. Justice Ginsburg answered his question with a question. "Where did one

---

121  During the 2020–2021 Covid-19 pandemic, the Supreme Court moved from courtroom arguments to online hearings. Chief Justice Roberts called on each justice, and Justice Thomas participated actively.

person/one vote come from?"

I doubt that the justices will agree on this question of "justiciability." Assuming for the sake of this article, however, that at least five justices agree to address the problem on the merits, the issue will be whether the Constitution requires at least an approximation of "partisan symmetry."

Justice Kagan seems to believe that the Court could establish standards that election officials and lower courts would be able to follow and enforce. Her view is that gerrymandering science is not some kind of "hypothetical airy-fairy" guesswork but rather "pretty scientific." Chief Justice Roberts called it "sociological gobbledygook."

Many Supreme Court watchers believe that Justice Kennedy will, once again, cast the deciding vote. He has often sided with the conservative bloc, as he did in such 5 to 4 decisions as *Bush v. Gore*, *Heller v. District of Columbia* (the gun ownership case), and *Citizens United*. On the other hand, he is often a strong advocate for equal protection, having written the Court's 5 to 4 opinion in the gay marriage case.

At the hearing, Justice Ginsburg asked, "What becomes of the precious right to vote?" My guess is that Justice Kennedy will answer that rhetorical question by voting with the "liberal" bloc to do something about this type of extreme "outlier" case.[122] That won't mean the end of political gerrymandering, but it will, at least, impose some limits. Otherwise, in the words of Paul Smith, the lawyer who argued the case, "in 2020 you're going to have a festival of copycat gerrymandering the likes of which this country has never seen."

---

122   I could not have been more wrong. Justice Kennedy joined the majority, holding that Professor Whitford and his co-plaintiffs had failed to show sufficient personal interest ("standing") to bring the case. The result was that the "efficiency gap" in Wisconsin got worse in 2018, when 54 percent of the electorate voted Democratic and Republicans still maintained a sixty-three-seat majority in the legislature. In 2019, the Supreme Court, with Kavanaugh sitting in Kennedy's seat, sounded the death knell for judicial consideration of partisan gerrymandering, holding in Rucho v. Common Cause that while partisan gerrymandering is "incompatible with democratic principles," the solution does not lie in the federal courts because, according to Chief Justice Roberts, "this is not law." In her dissent, Justice Kagan warned that the Court had failed in its duty to defend the foundations of our government.

# The Right to Vote Is Being Wronged (2020)

On April 6, 2020, the Supreme Court decided a case called *Republican National Committee v. Democratic National Committee*. The Court's opinion, with no justice's name attached to it, ruled in favor of the Republican Party and held that absentee ballots for the April 7, 2020, Wisconsin primary had to be postmarked by that day to be counted—this even though many absentee ballots had not yet been delivered to voters and the results were not to be announced until the following Monday, April 13. Justice Ginsburg's dissent predicted that by failing to consider the public health crisis, the decision would "result in massive disenfranchisement."

This decision, combined with a ruling by the majority-Republican Wisconsin Supreme Court, left voters with an unenviable choice. Stay home and be safe or go vote and take a risk. Thousands of Wisconsin voters chose to take the risk, but only a handful of polling places were able to open, so many voters ended up standing in line for hours, some until after midnight.

Despite the Republican victory in court, that party's conservative candidate for a seat on the state Supreme Court lost, and the liberal Democrat won decisively. This outcome offers at least two takeaways. One is that when it comes to our most fundamental American institution, government "of the people," no one should underestimate the American voter. Another is that in a rational world, the "Wisconsin model" is a good example of how not to run an election during a pandemic.

The Supreme Court's decision in the Wisconsin primary case is just one of many cases where the Court has disenfranchised voters by ignoring the inevitable effect of a narrow, literalist approach to voting rights. And these rulings, not just in the Wisconsin case but also in cases from Alabama, Florida, and Texas, have one thing in common: by 5 to 4 votes, the Court's conservatives have sided with the Republican party.

Chief Justice Roberts has taken the lead, as he did in 2013 when he wrote the opinion in *Shelby County v. Holder*. In that case he wrote that the preclearance provisions of the Voting Rights Act of 1965, designed to ensure the right of minorities to vote, were no longer needed, and therefore imposed an unconstitutional burden on state control of elections. According to Roberts and four other justices, discrimination in the 1960s may have justified federal election controls in certain states, but the "flagrant," "widespread," and "rampant" discrimination that justified the law is a thing of the past.[123]

It took no time for Texas, Mississippi, and Florida to revive old ways of making it harder for some citizens to vote. Other states have followed suit, including Alabama, Arkansas, and North Carolina. I don't suppose it's a coincidence that the impact has disproportionately affected citizens of color, and that these are all red states.[124]

We are in the midst of a pandemic. But the Supreme Court seems all but indifferent to that inconvenience. In July, after federal judges in Alabama tried to make it easier to vote absentee, the Court said no.

Later that month, the Court turned to Florida's recent constitutional amendment granting most convicted felons the right to vote after serving their prison terms. Without giving any explanation, the Court ruled that these newly enfranchised voters could be barred from voting if they hadn't paid their court fines. Justice Sotomayor noted that this ruling prevented otherwise eligible voters from participating in the election "simply because they are poor."[125]

Back in the late nineteenth century, many southern states limited access to the ballot by imposing poll taxes and literacy tests. The effect was to disenfranchise African Americans which, of course, was the whole idea. In 1898, in *Williams v. Mississippi*, the Court said that the laws were not discriminatory since they applied to everyone, just like *Plessy v. Ferguson*, decided two years earlier, where the Court upheld "separate but equal" segregated facilities on the basis that they were race-neutral and therefore

---

123  Within days after his inauguration on January 20, 2021, President Biden called on Congress to reinstate and expand the Voting Rights Act. Such an effort failed in 2019 and would likely meet with Republican opposition in the Senate.

124  On March 25, 2021, Georgia, which changed from red to blue in the 2020 national election, passed a law that restricts voting access. According to President Biden, "This makes Jim Crow look like Jim Eagle." Within days, several civil rights groups challenged the law in federal court.

125  In September 2020, former New York City Mayor (and former presidential candidate) Mike Bloomberg donated $16 million to help convicted felons pay their fines. President Trump accused Bloomberg of committing a "criminal act."

did not violate the equal protection clause of the Fourteenth Amendment.

While the school desegregation case, *Brown v. Board of Education* (1954), put an end to that mistaken ruling, nothing seems to have changed when it comes to voting rights. The chief justice and his conservative colleagues did a great disservice to democracy in 2019 when they refused to take up the question of political gerrymandering. This year, they continue to let partisan politicians run roughshod over the most non-partisan right of all, the right to vote.

I have long resisted the notion that the Supreme Court has become a political institution. Even after *Bush v. Gore* I held to that view. It appears that I was mistaken.

# In a Democracy There Is No Place for the Filibuster or Gerrymandering (2021)

The Founding Fathers did not debate either the filibuster or gerrymandering, and the Constitution makes no mention of either anti-majoritarian device. The explanation for these omissions is that Madison and his cohorts believed in majority rule as a "fundamental principle" of democracy. Hamilton wrote in one of the Federalist Papers that to give the minority "a negative upon the majority" would subject the "greater number" to the "sense of the lesser." If a "pernicious minority" can control the outcome, he went on, then government in America would ultimately be subject to "contemptible compromises of the public good."

How did we get from this original understanding of "We the people" to the point where forty-one senators can override the wishes of fifty-nine senators? The filibuster emerged as a serious political weapon in the 1940s, when southern Democratic senators realized they could use it to delay or prevent antidiscrimination legislation. Then, in 1957, Strom Thurmond from South Carolina got up and set a record by filibustering a civil rights bill for more than twenty-four hours. (The bill ultimately passed.)

It got worse in the 1960s, with southern Democrats fighting against the Civil Rights Act of 1964. The only way to stop them was by means of "cloture," meaning a three-fifths (sixty senators) vote. The filibuster, as it then existed, meant that one or more senators monopolized senate business by talking for hours on end.

Today, after trying various ways of both keeping the filibuster and getting Senate work done at the same time, we have a system where its simply takes sixty senators to pass most bills, no need for long-winded senatorial speechifying. That used to include judicial confirmation votes as well, but under the arcane rules of the Senate, it only takes a majority to change the rules.

First came the Democrats, holding a majority in 2013. They eliminated the filibuster for federal judicial appointments except for the Supreme Court. Then came the Republicans, holding a majority in 2017, and they voted to change the rule again, this time so that Supreme Court nominees were also exempt from the filibuster. The so-called "nuclear option" cuts both ways.

There is another way of getting around the filibuster, something called "budget reconciliation." It is too complicated for me to understand, much less explain, but it has to do with certain kinds of appropriations laws. That is how the Biden administration was able to enact the 2021 $1.9 trillion American Rescue Plan with fifty senators voting "aye."

What we have, in the case of the filibuster, is the opposite of majority rule. The same is true of gerrymandering, the whole point of which is for the party in power to arrange voting districts every ten years in such a way as to remain in power. It is a noxious practice, every bit as bad as the current wave of proposed state laws designed to impede qualified voters from voting.

Believers in good government have tried various ways to cure the evils of gerrymandering, with limited success. Although the Supreme Court has adopted a "hands off" approach, not all courts have avoided the issue. Two years ago, the Pennsylvania Supreme Court began an opinion with the words, "It is a core principle of our republican form of government that the voters should choose their representatives, not the other way around." Unlike the Supreme Court, that state court had no problem taking up the question of gerrymandering on the merits, deciding that it violated the Free and Equal Elections Clause of the state constitution, and finding a workable standard that would give the power to decide back to the people.

Both the filibuster and gerrymandering effectively violate the principle of "one person/one vote," announced by the Supreme Court's 1962 *Baker v. Carr* decision. Under that ruling, which dealt with voting districts in Tennessee, one hundred people in one district could no longer get the same number of legislators as one thousand people in another district. But that notable case did not deal with the thornier problem of the *weight* each vote gets.

I won't mention the Electoral College except to say that it is a kind of gerrymandering clothed in constitutional armor. Twice in this century the presidential candidate with the most votes lost. Theoretically, we could amend the Constitution, but even if Congress voted to do so, getting three-fourths (thirty-eight) of the states to agree is somewhere between improbable and out of the question.

According to a recent Pew Research poll, 70 percent of Americans favor the virus relief bill, which passed by a vote of 50 to 49. If it were not for the reconciliation process workaround, which is no solution to most of our pressing national problems, this law would have never made it to a vote. That, I suppose, would have pleased 30 percent of the population.

# THE SUPREME COURT

## Sometimes Judges and Senators Have to Hold Their Noses and Do Their Jobs (2016)

David Souter went from the New Hampshire Supreme Court to the First Circuit Court of Appeals (briefly) to the United States Supreme Court. After President George H. W. Bush appointed him in 1990, and the Senate confirmed him by a vote of 90 to 9, Justice Souter spent nineteen years doing what a judge should do—taking each case as it comes, applying the law to the best of his ability, and always remembering that his job as a member of the Court was to put his personal and political beliefs to one side.

Justice Souter was principled, even-handed, and non-ideological. The same can be said, though perhaps to a somewhat lesser extent, for Anthony Kennedy, appointed by President Reagan late in 1987 and confirmed by the Senate, 97 to 0, in 1988, an election year.

Supreme Court justices do not always have the discretion to vote their personal preferences. Two cases illustrate the point. One is the 1989 flag-burning case, *Texas v. Johnson*, where the Court ruled that the First Amendment protects the act of burning an American flag. The second is *Snyder v. Phelps*, the 2011 funeral demonstration case, in which members of a fringe group called the Westboro Baptist Church carried homophobic and anti-American signs on a public sidewalk near where a soldier's funeral was being held.

In the flag-burning case, Justice Kennedy wrote, "The hard fact is that sometimes we must make decisions we do not like. We make them because they are right." He joined the majority even though he found the act in question "repellant."

In the funeral protest case, Chief Justice Roberts wrote, "If we protect the words 'God Bless America,' we must also protect painful words such as 'God Hates America.'" In other words, the First Amendment does not take sides.

Fortunately, we do not ask the judiciary to serve as arbiters of social mores or good taste. This means that sometimes, as in these and many other cases, judges must hold their noses when they vote.

I have never met Judge Merrick Garland, but his record speaks for itself. Everyone agrees that he is brilliant, and most people, both Democrats and Republicans, consider him fully qualified for the Supreme Court. He does not appear to be burdened with any ideology that would prevent him from putting his personal preferences to one side when it comes to deciding difficult constitutional issues. In that sense, he appears to be cut from the same mold as Justices Souter and Kennedy.

Right now, Senate Republican leaders say that they will not even *consider* him. They say that "the people" should decide at the polls in November 2016 who gets to fill the vacancy on the Court. This is a wrong-headed idea for at least two reasons.

First, the Constitution says the "the President" shall fill any vacancy, with the "advice and consent" of the Senate. Nowhere does it say, "but only if they feel like it," much less that the "next president" should make the appointment.

Second, senators have a job to do. How would it look if they simply refused to vote on anything on the theory that "the people" should first elect a new president, who might use the veto power more to their liking?

Nothing in the Constitution says that the Senate is *required* to consider every nominee, but surely the Founding Fathers intended and expected it to do so. That, plus the fact that virtually every person ever nominated to the Supreme Court has received a Senate vote, should be sufficient to proceed with Judge Garland's nomination. Like judges, some senators may find themselves holding their noses when they cast an "aye" or a "nay," but that's their job. [126]

---

[126] President Obama's March 16, 2016, nomination of Judge Garland to replace Justice Scalia never came up for a vote. Under the leadership of Senate Majority Leader McConnell, he was never even given a hearing, and the nomination expired on January 3, 2017, the end of the 114th Congress. On April 7, 2017, the Senate confirmed President Trump's nominee, Neil Gorsuch. By comparison, eight days after Justice Ruth Bader Ginsburg's death on September 18, 2020, and five weeks before the presidential election, President Trump nominated Amy Coney Barrett as Ginsburg's successor. On October 26, 2020, the Senate confirmed Barrett by a vote of 52 to 48. All Senate Democrats (and Maine Republican Susan Collins, who objected on the grounds of timing) voted against confirmation, the first time since 1870 that no member of the minority party voted in favor of a Supreme Court nominee.

Judge Garland continued to serve as a member of the District of Columbia Court of Appeals. On March 10, 2021, he resigned from the judiciary and the following day was sworn in as Attorney General of the United States.

# Chief Justice John Roberts
## and an Independent Judiciary (2018)

We rarely experience a "war of words" between the president and the chief justice, but that is what happened just before Thanksgiving 2018. A California federal judge ruled that under federal law, migrants can seek asylum anywhere on United States soil, even if they did not enter through an authorized checkpoint. Trump called him an "Obama Judge," adding "it's not going to happen like this anymore."

Chief Justice Roberts reacted quickly and publicly. "We do not have Obama judges or Trump judges, Bush judges or Clinton judges." To which Trump tweeted, "Sorry Chief Justice Roberts, but you do indeed have 'Obama judges.'"

Maybe this is a new form of "checks and balances."

As it happens, a day or two later a Trump-appointed judge ruled against Trump and reinstated the White House press credentials of CNN's Jim Acosta. If the president took note of how that judge got his job, he didn't say so.

But this column is not about the president, it is about John G. Roberts Jr., who in 2005 at age fifty, became our seventeenth chief justice. Since then, he has presided over an increasingly divided and politicized Supreme Court, where Republican and Democratic appointees often vote as separate blocs in cases involving constitutional issues. Roberts has been identified with the "conservative" wing of the Court, regularly siding with Justices Thomas, Alito, Scalia, and Kennedy, the latter two now succeeded by Gorsuch and Kavanaugh. He has often led that group, assigning to himself such opinions as *Trump v. Hawaii*, where the Court upheld the Trump travel ban.

Chief Justice Roberts is widely regarded as an exceptionally smart person who cherishes the institution that he leads. He is no "secret liberal," but his conservatism is less doctrinaire than that of other members of the Court.

Perhaps the most notable example of this was in 2012, when Roberts cast the deciding vote to uphold the Affordable Care Act (Obamacare), albeit on grounds different from the other four members of the majority. That vote told us that he does not march in lockstep with his fellow conservatives, and his judicial positions since then reflect a judge who compares his job to that

Me with Chief Justice John Roberts

of an umpire calling constitutional balls and strikes, as he put it during his confirmation hearings.

If Roberts has shifted somewhat ideologically, he would be following in the footsteps of several previous justices—Chief Justice Earl Warren (appointing him was the "biggest damn fool mistake I ever made," said President Eisenhower), as well as Justices Harry Blackmun, John Paul Stevens, Kennedy, and Souter. All were appointed by Republican presidents; all are now regarded as somewhere between "moderate" (Kennedy) and "liberal" (Stevens).

Not to be misunderstood, Chief Justice Roberts has repeatedly shown that he is a judicial "conservative" true and blue. He was in the majority in the *Citizens United* case, and he wrote the opinion in *Shelby County v. Holder*, which invalidated much of the Voting Rights Act. He dissented in *Obergefell v. Hodges*, the gay marriage case. In *Gill v. Whitford*, he expressed skepticism that social science could provide a means of remedying partisan gerrymandering. *Trump v. Hawaii* is but one of many cases in which he has been highly deferential to the power of the Executive.

Still, this member of the Court understands that not everything is black or white. In the 2017–2018 Supreme Court term, Roberts can be found on both sides of the ideological divide. He was with the conservatives in the *Janus* case, which decided that requiring a non-union public employee to pay a fee in lieu of union dues violates the First Amendment; but he was with the liberals in the *Carpenter* case, which held that the government must obtain a warrant for cell phone site location information. His last words in the recent exchange with the president bear repeating. "The independent judiciary is something we should all be thankful for."

We usually look at what the Court decides, but in December 2018, the Court sided with Planned Parenthood and declined to review lower court decisions dealing with when states can terminate Medicaid contracts. It takes four justices to hear a case, and three—Thomas, Alito, and Gorsuch—wanted to do so. Roberts did not, and neither did the newest member of the Court, Brett Kavanaugh. We don't know how they would vote on the merits, but this decision not to decide shows, once again, that the chief justice goes his own way. That same may be true of Justice Kavanaugh, but it is too soon to tell.[127]

Ours is a "government of laws and not of men." John Adams wrote those words into the Massachusetts Constitution in 1780, and they remain true today as an axiom of democracy. When the chief justice said, "We do not have Obama judges," he was trying to explain that fundamental principle to the president. [128]

---

127   On February 22, 2021, the Supreme Court declined to consider another case, Donald Trump's effort to prevent a New York grand jury from obtaining his personal and corporate tax returns. None of the three justices appointed by Trump noted any disagreement, and the impact of this "non-decision" is to give the New York District Attorney millions of pages, not just Trump's tax returns but all of the underlying business records as well.

128   During Donald Trump's challenges to the outcome of the 2020 election, several Trump-appointed judges rejected his attempts to undermine the electoral system.

# The Sometimes-Shifting Alliances of the Justices (2019)

Supreme Court opinions are sometimes unanimous.[129] But in the important constitutional cases, the Court is almost always divided. These split decisions often break down according to the justices' "liberal" or "conservative" leanings, but not always.

Some members of the Supreme Court are predictable, but others less so, meaning that liberals and conservatives will from time to time find themselves on the same side. Such shifting alliances were a recurring phenomenon during the term that ended in June of 2019.

A striking example is the "Bladensburg Cross" case, *American Legion v. American Humanist Association*, decided on June 20, 2019. As I had expected, the Court decided that a war memorial cross on public land, maintained with public funds, did not run afoul of the First Amendment's separation of church and state (the "Establishment Clause").

The vote was 7 to 2, with liberal Justices Breyer and Kagan joining the conservatives, Chief Justice Roberts and Justices Thomas, Alito, Gorsuch, and Kavanaugh. Justice Alito's majority opinion says that while the cross "has long been a preeminent Christian symbol," this particular cross, when viewed through the lens of history, has special significance as a "central symbol" of World War I cemeteries. It seems that age takes on constitutional importance by creating "a presumption of constitutionality for longstanding monuments, symbols, and practices."

Justices Ginsburg and Sotomayor dissented, arguing that the cross is the "defining symbol" of Christianity and cannot, indeed should not, be secularized.

In *Flowers v. Mississippi*, the Court ruled, also 7 to 2, that Mississippi prosecutors went too far to keep blacks off the jury, a practice forbidden since the 1986 case of *Batson v. Kentucky*. The *Flowers* case was the sixth time this defendant faced trial for murder, and it came to the Court with a prior history of consistent race-based prosecutorial misconduct. Justice

---

129  A notable recent example is the 2020 "Bridgegate Case," *Kelly v. United States,* dealing with political retaliation in the form of a scheme to create a traffic jam headache by realigning the toll lanes leading from Fort Lee, New Jersey, to the George Washington Bridge. Writing for the full Court, Justice Kagan reminds us that "not every corrupt act by state or local officials is a federal crime."

Kavanaugh wrote the majority opinion, stressing that the Court was applying well-settled law rather than breaking new ground. Six times is too much, even for this conservative justice and fellow conservative Justice Alito.

But Justice Thomas, joined by Justice Gorsuch in dissent, says that the seven justices in the majority have their facts wrong, don't understand how trials work, and in any case shouldn't allow Flowers, who is black, to object because the government's race-based motive was not directed at him but rather to the excluded juror.[130]

As if that myopic view were not bad enough, Justice Thomas then accuses the Court of using the Constitution "to remedy a general societal wrong." He would overrule *Batson* and allow race-based jury selection, forgetting it seems that two wrongs don't make a right. The irony is that he succeeded Justice Thurgood Marshall on the Court. One can only wonder whether if, given the chance, Thomas would overrule *Brown v. Board of Education* (1954), which Marshall argued and won, and reinstate the discredited notion of "separate but equal" schools.

The June 24 decision in *Iancu v. Brunetti* deals with the arcane world of trademark registration and the federal law against "immoral or scandalous" trademarks. The mark in question was a clothing brand named "FUCT." Justice Kagan's eleven-page majority opinion treats the statutory words "immoral or scandalous," as a "unified standard," despite the word "or," and concludes that it is "viewpoint discriminatory." That is another way of saying that the First Amendment may not single out offensive ideas. Therefore, the government may not withhold trademark registration for the colorful (or off-color) brand name in question.

The two most senior members of the Court, the conservative Thomas and the liberal Ginsburg, joined Justice Kagan, along with conservatives Alito, Gorsuch, and Kavanaugh. Justice Alito went so far as to add, "Viewpoint discrimination is poison to a free society."

This left the curious alliance of Chief Justice Roberts and Justices Sotomayor and Breyer. Yes, they say, "immoral" is constitutionally overbroad, but "scandalous" is not because it can be limited to "the small group of lewd words or 'swear' words not commonly used around children or in polite company." (Justice Sotomayor notes that she is sparing the reader a list

---

130  This is a flawed view of the right to trial by jury, which belongs to the person charged, not to any individual juror.

of such words but that "the apparent homonym" of the particular mark at issue would "plainly qualify.") Besides, Sotomayor points out, the company could still use the word, but without governmental help in the form of a trademark.

When the chips are down, as in the partisan gerrymandering case, the ideological differences are plainly visible. In *Rucho v. Common Cause*, the chief justice and his four conservative colleagues decided that partisan gerrymandering, undemocratic though it may be, is "political," not "justiciable." Yes, *Marbury v. Madison*, the Court's landmark 1803 decision, dictates that the Court's duty is "to say what the law is," but "we have no commission to allocate political power," says Roberts, and the question of partisan gerrymandering "is not law."

Justice Kagan's dissent says that this is not just any constitutional question. It goes to the very heart of democracy, allowing politicians, in her words, "to entrench themselves in office as against voters' preferences." But, as is so often the case, Chief Justice Roberts had the last word. His opinion looks less like calling balls and strikes than it does like calling the batter out before he gets to the plate.

# The 2019–2020 Supreme Court Term—A Look Ahead (2019)

Every year, the first Monday of October marks the beginning of the Supreme Court term. The 2018–2019 term year saw some momentous decisions and non-decisions, the former including the Court's rebuff to the Trump administration's attempt to add a "citizenship" question to the 2020 census, the latter including the Court's refusal to adjudicate the issue of "partisan gerrymandering."

Since June, the Court has reviewed thousands of applications to decide on its docket for the next nine months beginning in October 2019. Typically, the Court adds cases even after it goes back to work in October, but we now have at least some sense of the coming lineup.

On October 8, 2019, the justices will address the subject of gender equality in three cases, each dealing with employees' claims of sex discrimination under Title VII of the Civil Rights Act of 1964, which forbids firing someone "because of sex."

*R. G. & G. R. Harris Funeral Homes v. Equal Employment Opportunity Commission*, deals with "transgender equality." A Michigan funeral director informed the funeral home's owner that he intended to live and work as female and would later have sex reassignment surgery. The owner fired her because continuing to employ the director in such circumstances would violate his religious beliefs. The other two cases—*Altitude Express v. Zarda* and *Bostock v. Clayton County, Georgia*—present the issue of whether Title VII protects gay people.

In the funeral home case, the Equal Employment Opportunity Commission (EEOC) said that the words "because of sex" include a transgender person, and the federal Court of Appeals agreed. The other cases involve a skydiver and a county employee, both fired on account of being gay. According to the Second Circuit, "sexual orientation discrimination is motivated, at least in part, by sex." In the Georgia case, the Eleventh Circuit, relying on earlier cases, construed Title VII more narrowly, thereby creating a "circuit split" for the Supreme Court to resolve.

What makes these cases especially notable is that they will be decided without Justice Kennedy, a staunch defender of gay rights, whose seat is now occupied by Justice Kavanaugh. The Trump administration is siding with the employers in these cases, without the support of the EEOC, which has refused to sign on to the briefs.

I will be surprised if the Court rules in favor of the employees. More likely, the Court will rule narrowly, based on the words of the statute and not on equal protection grounds. If I am correct, many will see the decision as a change of direction, signaling a slowdown, if not a halt, to the expansion of gay rights.[131]

Another potentially important case is *New York State Rifle & Pistol Association v. City of New York*, which involves a challenge to New York City's ban on transporting a handgun to a home or shooting range outside city limits. In July, the city asked the Court to remove the case from the docket on the grounds that state and local law had changed in favor of the gun owners, making the matter moot. The rifle association, on the other hand, wants the Court to keep the case, no doubt seeing an opportunity to solidify gun owners' Second Amendment rights.

My guess is that the case will go off the docket, allowing the Court to dodge a bullet, so to speak. But if it stays, the Court will face the question of whether, under the 2008 *Heller* decision upholding gun owners' rights, such state and local regulation is constitutional. Justice Scalia's *Heller* opinion leaves the subject of reasonable regulation open, and public opinion seems to have turned in the wake of so many mass shootings. Whatever the Court does, the case is bound to produce extensive publicity and public controversy.[132]

On the first day of the term, the Court will hear two important criminal law cases. One deals with the insanity defense, which has always been

---

131   Fortunately, I was surprised. On June 15, 2020, in a single opinion covering all three cases, Justice Gorsuch, joined by the four liberals (Ginsburg, Breyer, Sotomayor, and Kagan), wrote that Title VII protects gay and transgender employees because "sex plays a necessary and undisguisable role in the decision," which the statute (not the Constitution) prohibits. The Court left for another day such practical questions as sex-segregated bathrooms, locker rooms, dress codes, and the like.

132   This one I got right, or nearly so. The Court did keep and hear the case, but on April 27, 2020, voted 6 to 3 not to decide it on the basis that the changed law made the matter moot. On November 3, 2021, the Court heard another case brought by the same New York gun organization, which has challenged the denial of applications under a New York law that requires "proper cause" before anyone may carry a gun outside the home. Based on comments made during the hearing, it appears that a majority of the justices believe the law is too restrictive and that Americans have a right to carry a handgun outside the home, though the extent of that right will not be known until a decision comes down, sometime before the end of June 2022.

part of American law. Under the M'Naghten Rule, dating back to an 1843 British case, "every man is presumed to be sane," but if the accused did not understand the "nature and quality of the act" and "did not know he was doing what was wrong," then in the eyes of the law he was legally blameless.

Until the 1970s, every state had such an insanity rule, the exact formulation of which varied from state to state. In New Hampshire, for example, the question for the jury to decide is whether the crime was a "product of" or was "caused by" the defendant's illness.

What I had not realized is that five states have abolished the insanity defense. On October 7, 2020, the Court will hear *Kahler v. Kansas*. Kahler, was convicted of killing four family members and sentenced to death. Constitutionally speaking, the question is whether abolishing the insanity defense, as Kansas has done, violates Kahler's rights under the Eighth (prohibiting cruel and unusual punishment) and Fourteenth (requiring due process of law) Amendments.

This case raises deep moral and philosophical questions. The petition filed with the Court cites Christian, Jewish, and Islamic tradition along with the writings of Plato, Saint Augustine, Justinian, and others. Some justices may say that none of that matters, narrowing the question to what was understood at the time of these amendments; but others may note that the Founding Fathers were aware of such teachings, going back thousands of years, as well as the deep-rooted common law tradition.[133]

I'm stumped on how this case will come out. In 2012, the Court refused to hear an Idaho case raising the same issue, with three justices (Breyer, Ginsburg, and Sotomayor) dissenting. It takes four votes to grant an appeal, so at least one more justice, perhaps Justice Kagan, has joined in.[134]

The other criminal case to be heard on the first day presents a challenge to another tradition—the requirement of juror unanimity in criminal cases. It comes from the Louisiana Court of Appeals, which upheld that state's 1898

---

133  During the hearing, Justice Breyer, perhaps the most cerebral member of the Court, came up with a headscratcher of a question. He asked the lawyer for Kansas to imagine two defendants, "both crazy" in his words. One thinks Smith is a dog and kills him; the other kills Jones thinking a dog told him to do it. In Kansas, it seems, one would be guilty of murder while the other would not. How, Breyer repeatedly asked, can that be? He finally threw his hands up in the air and said, "it's quite deep, this question. It's like ethics and Aristotle."

134  It turned out that Justice Kagan wrote the Court's 6 to 3 decision upholding the law, joined by the Court's five conservative justices (Roberts, Thomas, Alito, Gorsuch, and Kavanaugh). She emphasized that the issues raised by the case were matters usually left up to the states. And she pointed out that Kansas still takes mental illness into account during the sentencing process.

Jim Crow-era constitutional amendment that allows less than a unanimous vote in non-capital cases.[135] The offense in *Ramos v. Louisiana* was second degree murder, the penalty life in prison.

Like the Kansas case, this appeal raises historical issues, beginning with the common law unanimity requirement that had existed at common law long before the jury trial clause was included in the Sixth Amendment. It also raises practical issues of fairness: If the Sixth Amendment requires unanimity in federal court, how can it not do so in state court? Further, it raises a fundamental issue of how the judicial system can ensure justice, perhaps best understood if the justices watch *12 Angry Men*, that great 1957 movie where, as in the *Ramos* case, the accused was also Hispanic.[136]

---

135   It was during the 1890s post-Reconstruction period that Louisiana and other states came up with a way to diminish any influence the occasional black juror might have on a verdict. Originally the law allowed a majority of nine jurors (out of twelve) to convict; the number was later changed to ten. Justice Kavanaugh commented at the hearing that one argument against the law is that it is "rooted in racism."

136   The movie depicts twelve men deliberating the fate of a teenager accused of murder. Henry Fonda plays an architect, the sole holdout against eleven "guilty" votes. The movie succeeds on two levels: one the human qualities and prejudices of the jurors, the other the dynamics of group decision-making. As for the Ramos case, the Court had its hands full grappling with precedent in the form of a 1972 decision where four justices said that the Sixth Amendment does not require a unanimous verdict at all; four justices said that it does, in both state and federal courts; and one member of the Court, Justice Lewis Powell, said it does require unanimity, but only in federal court. On April 20, 2020, that 4-4-1 decision became history. The opinion by Justice Gorsuch overturns the earlier case and holds that the Sixth Amendment is fully applicable to the states, meaning that juror unanimity is required in every criminal case.

## The Supreme Court Is Not Protecting Democracy (2021)

Has the Supreme Court become the enemy of democracy? The very question jars the senses. How can someone even make such a suggestion?

My answer is that it's time to face a sad truth about twenty-first-century America. The Court is letting the people of America down.

You may question my use of the word "truth" and say, "That's just your opinion." I concede the point but consider the evidence.

In 2010, in *Citizens United v. Federal Election Commission,* the Court decided that money equals speech and, therefore, the government cannot impose a limit on the size of political contributions by corporations and unions. The ruling took free speech where it didn't have to go, thereby magnifying the political power of the rich. The Court assured us that public disclosure would provide sufficient accountability. More on that subject below.

In 2013, in *Shelby County v. Holder,* the Court killed Section 5 of the Voting Rights Act of 1965, which subjected states having a seriously flawed voting record to federal approval before they could change their election laws. But, according to Chief Justice Roberts, the passage of time had cleared up the problem the law was designed to fix, so preclearance was no longer needed. Based on that questionable premise, which ignored both the contrary evidence and Congress's reaffirmation of the Act, the Court concluded that Section 5 was no longer constitutional.

Then, in 2019, the Court continued its assault on voters' interests, this time by refusing to adjudicate the constitutionality of partisan gerrymandering. According to *Rucho v. Common Cause,* the practice of allowing the party in power to use the redistricting process to stay in power, even if a majority of the state's voters disagree, is "incompatible with democratic principles," but the Court can't do anything about it because the issue is not "justiciable."

How can that be? The Supreme Court has the power to decide what issues it should and should not take up, and a fundamental rule of democracy is that the electoral majority decides. If gerrymandering is beyond the Court's reach—according to the chief justice, it "is not law"—then why wasn't the existence of segregated schools beyond the Court's reach in the 1950s? Would today's Court tell Oliver Brown and his daughter, Linda, who sued the Topeka Board of Education, "that's not law?" The question is not frivolous, since both school segregation and gerrymandering impose disproportionate burdens on members of minority groups.

The *Citizens United, Shelby County,* and *Rucho* cases were all 5 to 4 decisions. But then Justice Ginsburg died in late 2020, and the appointment of Justice Barrett enlarged the "conservative" majority.

In 2021, by a 6 to 3 vote in two cases, the Court continued its march against democracy. *Americans for Prosperity Foundation v. Bonta* overturned a California law requiring disclosure to the state attorney general of the names of large donors to non-profit organizations, including political action committees. The law had a legitimate purpose, but the Court said you can't do that because freedom of association under the First Amendment protects anonymous giving.

Never mind that giving money to a political group isn't "association," much less "assembly" which is the word the First Amendment uses. If it were, then gerrymandering would be "law" because it dilutes the impact of a citizen's vote for the party with which he or she chooses to "associate." Apparently, *Citizens United*'s assurance that disclosure of donors' names provided a safeguard wasn't meant to be taken seriously or maybe, like federal review of election law changes, it has somehow become unnecessary. The Court seems to have forgotten that "sunlight is the best disinfectant" and instead compares donors' secrecy to protecting the right of NAACP members to remain anonymous.[137]

The other 2021 case, *Brnovich v. Democratic National Committee,* rejected a challenge to Arizona laws that invalidate ballots cast in the wrong precinct and limit who can deliver absentee ballots. The fact that these laws have a disparate impact on minority voters, the very evil that Section 2 of the 1965 Voting Rights Law was designed to combat, was not enough to persuade these six justices.

When laws protect the right to vote—there is no better example than the Voting Rights Act of 1965—the Court should bend over backwards to carry out Congress's intent. Instead of seizing the opportunity to cast a lifeline to a drowning democracy, the majority now inhabits a "law-free zone," as Justice Kagan wrote in her *Brnovich* dissent.

These political contribution and voter restriction laws are the suspenders to the partisan gerrymandering belt. Taken together, they are a perfect way

---

137 The words "sunlight is said to be the best disinfectant" appear in an article written by Justice Louis Brandeis and published in Harper's Weekly in 1913.

to defeat the will of the majority. It happens that Republicans are the ones driving the antidemocratic bus, but election fairness and voter equality are not partisan issues. The Supreme Court's refusal to maintain election law guardrails and enforce electoral speed limits is making America a less perfect union.

# It's Not Just About Abortion Rights
# —It's About the Constitution (2022)

The Supreme Court has issued two opinions in *Whole Woman's Health v. Jackson*, the first on September 1 and the second on December 10, 2021. The case deals with the Texas abortion law known as S. B. 8, which prohibits abortion in Texas after six weeks of pregnancy.

By enacting this law, the lawmakers effectively thumbed their noses at *Roe v. Wade*, which sets the abortion barrier at "viability," meaning a gestational age of about twenty-four weeks. Some clever person came up with a private civil-enforcement scheme that takes government out of the process. Instead, the law authorizes anyone from anywhere to bring a civil lawsuit against a physician who violates the six-week limit, as well as anyone who "aids or abets" the doctor.

Such a private "enforcer" doesn't need to show any personal interest in the matter, any connection to Texas, or for that matter any opinion one way or the other regarding a woman's right to choose. Success in court rewards the person with a $10,000 bounty for each violation plus lawyers' fees.

The question on the Court's "Shadow Docket" last September was whether to leave the law in effect while various challenges wend their way through the courts. You don't have to be a lawyer, or pro-choice, to know that when a law is unconstitutional, as this one is so long as *Roe v. Wade* remains the law of the land, then a state can't opt out from Article VI, paragraph 2, of the US Constitution.

That Article says that the Constitution "shall be the supreme Law of the Land." It goes on to say that "the Judges in every State shall be bound thereby," no matter what law the state may enact.

The September 1 ruling, consisting of one very long paragraph, says that the healthcare clinic had not met its preliminary-injunction burden to show that it is likely to succeed on the merits, or that putting a hold on the statute would be consistent with the public interest. In other words, the "Supremacy Clause" is not so supreme.

How would any of us feel if we were hauled into court by a bounty hunter in a state that had passed a law prohibiting the use of birth control devices, even though the Supreme Court decided in 1965, in *Griswold v.*

*Connecticut*, that we have a constitutional right to do so?

The December 10 opinion does not deal with the six-weeks law—the Court is already considering whether to uphold the Mississippi fifteen-week rule and thereby overturn the *Roe v. Wade* viability standard. Instead, the issue this time was whether Texas has outwitted the Constitution by creating a virtually unchallengeable enforcement system.

The clinic prevailed, but just barely. While holding that the sovereign immunity doctrine and the federal "case or controversy" requirement rule out suing judges, court clerks, and the state attorney general as parties, the Court decided that state licensing officials were properly named, so the case can proceed against them. At the same time, the Court held to its earlier ruling, once again leaving the Texas law fully operational.

In his separate opinion, Chief Justice Roberts, no fan of *Roe v. Wade*, acknowledged that the effect of S. B. 8 is to deny a right protected under the federal Constitution. As he pointed out, what's at stake in the case is not the particular federal right but rather the role of the Supreme Court in our constitutional system.

Justice Sotomayor, writing for herself and Justices Breyer and Kagan, dissented from both decisions. As usual, she minced no words, finding the September refusal to enjoin S. B. 8 "stunning" and accusing the Justices in the majority of burying their heads in the sand. "It cannot be the law," she wrote, that a state can evade constitutional scrutiny "by outsourcing the enforcement of unconstitutional laws to its citizenry."

In her December dissent, Sotomayor would keep state court officials and the state attorney general in the case. But her wrath with the Texas legislature and her fellow justices remains unabated. She compares S. B. 8 to the philosophy of slavery supporter John C. Calhoun, who insisted that the states have the right to "nullify" federal law with which they disagree. And she hasn't gotten over the previous ruling which refused to put a stop to "the havoc S. B. 8's unconstitutional scheme has wrought for Texas women."

How disappointing it is that our highest court has allowed the State of Texas to nullify the Supremacy Clause, even for a minute much less months. Allowing abortion providers to pursue their challenge, even though only against state licensing officials, represents a partial victory for the clinic and common sense, and it may be that the Texas enforcement scheme will be held unconstitutional. In the meanwhile, pregnant women whose constitutional rights have been taken away will never get them back.

# Acknowledgements

I am grateful to the publisher of the *Monadnock Ledger-Transcript*, Heather McKernan, and to my editors at *The Keene Sentinel* and the *Concord Monitor*, Wilfred (Bill) Bilodeau and Steve Leone. Without their support, these articles would not have seen the light of day.

Thanks also go to Heather Jasmin, program coordinator of the Cheshire Academy for Lifelong Learning. Teaching constitutional law to "lifelong learners" has given me a wonderful opportunity to interact with my contemporaries and to gain new insights.

I tried out most of these articles on my wife, Virginia Eskin (the "Pianist"), and she provided valuable feedback. My children, Frank, Ken, and Elizabeth offered many useful comments, and in Ken's case, corrections on the law and the facts when I got them wrong.

Credit for the photograph on the cover goes to Frank. I grew up with that grandfather's clock, which is making its second appearance; the first was on the inside cover page of *Claremont Boy*, a photo of my proud father helping me put on my coat on March 1, 1952, the date of my bar mitzvah. The clock now resides in Brookline, Massachusetts, with Frank and my daughter-in-law, Rebecca.

Sarah Bauhan published my previous book, and I am grateful to her, and to her colleagues Mary Ann Faughnan and Henry James, for taking on this one. They exemplify professionalism and have, once again, provided guidance and encouragement.

Even in the age of social media, some people still read newspapers, either in print or online, and over the years I have received many e-mails, and even a few letters, commenting on what I have written. My thanks to the readers, without whose encouragement I would not have kept at it for so long.

Ironically, the State of California may enact copycat legislation permitting private bounty hunters to sue people who are exercising gun ownership rights protected by the Court's Second Amendment ruling. Such a law would suffer the same enforcement infirmities as S. B. 8.

Yale has taken Calhoun's name off the undergraduate residential hall long known as Calhoun College, but he must be smiling from the grave.

## Afterword

As I went back over these essays and tried to organize them in some sort of coherent order, I reflected on what has animated me since I left home and went out into the world. The answer, I think, is curiosity. Even so, I wish I had asked a lot more questions when I was young. Why didn't I ask my grandparents more about their lives in Russia, about their parents and other family members, the ones who stayed behind? My grandparents never seemed to talk about their early years, but that's no excuse for my failure to ask.

My father was born in 1891, in Chelsea, Massachusetts. I know very little about his early years, or about his father, for whom I am named. I don't even know the names of the towns (in Lithuania, I think) where my Steinfield grandparents grew up. Ancestry.com, MyHeritage, or one of the other heritage websites await me.

Having a strong curiosity streak is essential for a trial lawyer and useful in life generally. Over the decades mine has become stronger. For one thing, it causes me to change my mind when I realize that I have been wrong-headed about something. For another, it helps me get to know people better.

One subject I never tire of is learning about other people. I ask questions. "Where are you from?" Whenever I meet a tradesman I ask, "Do you like what you do?" The answer is invariably "yes," especially from people who work with their hands out-of-doors.

One of my favorite stories in this collection is the one about the Muslim cab driver in New York. "We're brothers," he told me at the end of our cross-town journey. Another favorite is the story of how I wandered into the shop of Antonio Natola, Tony the Tailor, and made a friend who was like a brother. I placed that story at the beginning of this book for a reason. Tony enriched my life for so many years, and I miss him greatly. The same is true of many others who are no longer living, several of whom grace the pages of this book.

These connections, some fleeting and others long-lasting, have been my curiosity's rewards. And now, at eighty-three, I still ask questions and intend to keep at it for as long as I can.

## Photo credits

All photos supplied by the author except:

p. 19.   Photo of Antonio (Tony) Natola with his partner Gaetano Cataldi; Courtesy of Anna Bruno

p. 21.   Photo of Bob Abernethy; Photo credit: David Scott Holloway

p. 24.   Photo of Kahlil Gibran; courtesy of Jean Gibran

p. 25.   Photo of Carl Sapers; courtesy of Jonathan Sapers

p. 26.   Photo of Camille Sarrouf; courtesy of Camille Sarrouf Jr.

p. 28.   Photo of David J. Fischer, courtesy Photo.

p. 31.   Photo of Bud Collins; Photo credit: Anita Klaussen

p. 39.   Photo of James Bolle; Photo courtesy of Jocelyn Bolle

p. 47.   Photo of Martin Feldman; courtesy of Alice Feldman

p. 57.   Photo of Henry David Thoreau by Benjamin D. Maxham, 1856, Public Domain (PD)

p. 61.   Photo of Chiune Sugihara, PD

p. 63.   Photo of the main entrance to Auschwitz by Paul Arps, PD

p. 65.   Photo of the Hill of Crosses, by Dezidor (někdy naskenovat), PD

p. 69.   Photo of the Crazy Horse Memorial, by Jim Bowen, PD

p. 71.   Photo of Kremówka papieska by Vetulani, PD

p. 73.   Photo of Lublijana Old Town by Andrew Milligan Sumo, PD

p. 74.   Photo of Danilo Türk, PD

p. 77.   Photo of Rob, Jesse and Patrick; Courtesy of Rob Barber

p. 79.   Photo of Luiz Vaz de Camões sculpture, Lisbon, by Pedro Ribeiro Simões, PD

p. 83.   Photo of Dred Scott circa 1857, PD

p. 90.   Photo of Rabbi Michael Szenes; Courtesy of Gail C. Szenes.

p. 92   Photo of a shofar, PD

p 109.   Photo of Barbara Cook in "No One Is Alone"; Saturday, November 18, 2006, at the Isaac Stern Auditorium, Carnegie Hall, New York City ©2006 Richard Termine

p. 114   Photo of Duncan Watson; courtesy of Duncan Watson

p. 195.   Photo of Justice Benjamin Cardozo, PD.

p. 214.   Photo of Justice William J. Brennan, PD

p. 236.  Joint Resolution proposing an amendment to the Constitution o United States, proposed June 13, 1866 (National Archives Iden 1408913)

p. 240.  Photo of Wong Kim Ark, PD